PENGUIN BOOKS

BIHAR IS IN THE EYE OF THE BEHOLDER

Vijay Nambisan has worked as a journalist in Delhi, Mumbai, Chennai, Bihar and Kerala. A selection of his poems appeared in *Gemini*, a two-poet volume published in Viking in 1992.

He is married to the novelist and surgeon Kavery Nambisan. They live in the Anamalai Hills.

BIHAR
is in the eye of the beholder

Vijay Nambisan

With illustrations by the author

PENGUIN BOOKS

Penguin Books India (P) Ltd., 11 Community Centre, Panchsheel Park, New Delhi 110 017, India
Penguin Books Ltd., 27 Wrights Lane, London W8 5TZ, UK
Penguin Putnam Inc., 375 Hudson Street, New York, NY 10014, USA
Penguin Books Australia Ltd., Ringwood, Victoria, Australia
Penguin Books Canada Ltd., 10 Alcorn Avenue, Suite 300, Toronto, Ontario, M4V 3B2, Canada
Penguin Books (NZ) Ltd., Cnr Rosedale & Airborne Roads, Albany, Auckland, New Zealand

First published in Viking by Penguin Books India 2000
Published in Penguin Books 2001

10 9 8 7 6 5 4 3 2 1

Grateful acknowledgement is made to the following for permission to use copyright material: William Dalrymple for the extract from 'Caste Wars', first published in *Granta 57: India! The Golden Jubilee* (1997); and Ian Jack for the extract from the 'Introduction' to *Granta 57: India! The Golden Jubilee* (1997).

While every effort has been made to trace copyright holders and seek permission, this has not been possible in every case. Any omissions brought to our notice will be rectified in future editions.

Typeset in New Baskerville by Digital Technologies and Printing Solutions, New Delhi
Printed at Chaman Offset Printers, New Delhi

This book is for my editors
Probir Dasgupta
Adil Jussawalla
Nirmala Lakshman

but it is dedicated to
the people of M____

Quidquid delirant reges plectuntur Achivi.

(For any madness of their kings, it is the Greeks who take the beating.)

—Horace, *Epistles*

Contents

Acknowledgements

This book had its genesis in six essays on Bihar which were published in *The Hindu* Sunday Magazine between June 1997 and March 1998. I am grateful to N. Ravi, Editor and Nirmala Lakshman, Joint Editor, *The Hindu* for permission to use or adapt those essays, and another which appeared in December 1998; also for encouragement and support in excess of my deserts.

I thank Granta Magazine and *The Times of India*, Patna for permission to reproduce published material.

I am deeply grateful to the old Patna hand I have referred to as the Journalist; also to Ravi Singh for ruining my sleep two nights running.

My thanks to David, first for asking the question: 'Why don't you write a book about Bihar?' the obvious answer to which then eluded me; and second and never last, for friendship and belief.

Kavery knows why and how much I need or need not thank her, but this book would not have been thought of if she hadn't taken a job in Bihar, so she shares the blame.

Finally I want to thank myself, for only I know how distasteful I find working.

Acknowledgements

Author's Note

THIS BOOK IS AN account of the sixteen months I lived in Bihar from September 1996 to January 1998, and of what I witnessed when I went back to report on the elections in February. It is not regular newspaper journalism because I did not go there at first as a journalist. My wife Kavery is a surgeon who prefers to practise in rural India; so when having grown sick of Madras where, she said, 'There are fifty doctors who can do the same thing,' she pined for the villages again, I resigned my job on a newspaper and we fled north.

Kavery had had an offer from some nuns she knew, who ran a hospital in a small town on the Ganga's bank some 100 km east of Patna. I will not distinguish the town beyond calling it M____; nor will I specify the Order the nuns belong to, though anyone so desiring can easily discover both.

No one in M____, I confidently assert, will read this book; except perhaps some of the Sisters, who will do so for the wrong reasons. If I cloak certain identities, however speciously, it is not out of a wish to avoid retribution. But knowledge must be earned, and it is none of my business to impart it.

A cousin who read a draft of the first chapter said it lacks insights. It's not my business to provide insights either. As a journalist I am out of place among people who quote statistics and interview politicians. I am an essayist and a literary journalist, and facts are not so important to me as attitudes, opinions and impressions. Also, I never was and never will be other than an outsider in Bihar. I might have picked up a fact here or an interview there, but I do not delight in them as I do in the apt quotation.

This book is impressionistic journalism, but not impressionist in the same sense as the school of art whose aim was 'to paint the momentary or transitory appearance of things, and especially the effects of light and atmosphere, rather than form or structure'. On the contrary, I seek to portray form and structure by means of impressions, and will back my impressions against any six journalists' facts. A fact which has crept into this book while my back was turned may occasionally be wrong; an impression I have laboured to understand and detail and fit into its place, never.

Let the reader beware.

Prologue

IT WAS A BLEAK morning in one of the chilliest Januaries in recent memory, and if the clocks were not striking thirteen, I felt, it was only because there were no clocks to strike. I stood outside the Hospital's main gate, waiting to capture a passing rickshaw. At about 8.30, usually, the first patients would begin to arrive from the railway station, but possibly the cold had put them off today.

The fruit seller who squatted just outside the gate was already at his post, however. 'Rickshaw?' he said. 'I'll get you one.' He rose and walked up the rutted road that led to the railway tracks and across them to the market a kilometre away. The road had once been pukka, but like much else in Bihar it had not been kept in repair for years.

I walked alongside, and just to be friendly I said I'd hoped to get a rickshaw bringing a patient from the station. Wasn't this the time they generally began coming to the OPD?

The fruit seller yelled into a shack outside which there stood a vehicle. 'O rickshaw! The doctor saab has to go to the 'tation,' but the rickshaw-wala either wasn't in or had other things to do. The fruit seller resumed his walk up the road, then turned to me. 'Patients?' he said. 'If all the good doctors go away, why will patients come to this hospital?'

As I walked beside him, the bleakness settling on my spirit, I tried to remember—I could not recapture—the euphoria that had accompanied us to Bihar only sixteen months ago.

Laloo Prasad and the secret of democracy

WE REACHED M____ just after the rains, when the Ganga plain is painted its loveliest, richest green. In all the Tal—the flat expanse between the river and the southern horizon—there was no arid spot, and water sparkled in the low-lying areas which flanked the road. It was my first visit to Bihar (discounting the preliminary trip Kavery and I had made in May, when the Sisters at the Hospital had turned on the charm and the skies had turned on the fire) and I thought we could live quite happily here, if we didn't try anything foolish.

I'd not thought of doing anything in the journalistic line, except an occasional review or essay and the monthly literary crossword which I'd been composing for a couple of years and am especially proud of. No English paper needs a features writer in rural Bihar.

But everything about Bihar fascinated me, it was so different from anything I'd ever experienced: The culture, the politics, what people took for granted and what provoked them to rebellion. I was always an outsider, of course: Sixteen months don't make a native of you unless you're Lawrence of Arabia. However, there are events occurring daily in Bihar which in my innocence I thought never happen in the South, and I felt impelled after a time to write about them. As I began to write I began to inquire, and

I read and listened, and learned.

It was around the time that then Union Home Minister Indrajit Gupta termed Uttar Pradesh as being in a state of 'chaos, anarchy and destruction' that Bihar seemed to float into focus for me. Why was he saying this about Uttar Pradesh? Worse things by far were happening in Bihar. Politics aside—Laloo Prasad Yadav was Chief Minister then and Gupta's ally in the United Front—was no one in Delhi concerned?

Everyone said, of course, that Bihar is India's most backward state; some estimates worked out its backwardness relative to the Indian average as fifty years. The implication was somehow that nothing could be done about it.

Bihar is actually one of India's richest states. It has agricultural and mineral wealth in abundance (I have no need to quote figures, and anyway I have promised not to do so). But it is the political backwardness of Bihar that sets all right-thinking newspaper readers to shaking their heads. The state is, in this sense, so backward that educated Biharis speak in admiring tones of neighbouring Uttar Pradesh. If UP is foundering in 'chaos, anarchy and destruction', the men in New Delhi have given up describing Bihar even in such terms. Any report of a caste-based massacre in Bihar, or a spate of train robberies, or a political assassination, or especially another instance of corruption, is rarely more than instant news in the national dailies: That is, it is not treated on a day-to-day basis. One would suppose that the wise men in the capital merely mutter '*Bihar*!' and leave it at that.

For quite some time in 1997 and '98 Bihar got a lot of attention in the media. But that was attributable more to Laloo Prasad's antics than to any genuine concern. His striking appearance, his confident attempts to speak

English, his absolute indifference to what his interlocutors thought of him, the flunky with the spittoon . . . He was quite possibly the most charismatic Indian politician since Rajiv Gandhi copped it, and Rajiv's charisma lay mostly in his genes. Laloo Prasad was, for months, to every TV watcher, the Face of Bihar. (A friend of mine in Hyderabad said his two favourite TV characters were Laloo and film actor Govinda.) And nothing could be more grotesque than that—or more irredeemably stupid on the part of the media.

Laloo is not an aberration. Nor is Bihar. What is happening in Bihar is happening all over India. But Bihar is a microcosm of the whole; a laboratory specimen, as it were, most easily brought under the microscope of analysis. For there is something going on in Bihar which is of great relevance to India's polity, and perhaps not to India's alone. A study of Bihar as an organism, and not merely of Patna as a stage, might provide a really radical yet thoroughly practical critique of our thusness—of premises we understand as fundamental to our existence as a nation, particularly as a democratic nation.

This has little to do with fodder scams and the role of Laloo Prasad Yadav as arbiter of destinies in the state, but has everything to do with his years in office. I began this book about a month after Atal Behari Vajpayee was sworn in as Prime Minister for the second time, in early 1998, and am about to complete it almost two years later, as Bihar prepares to elect a new Assembly. The last ten years have been indisputably Laloo's era, and now (as throughout the last three years) there is much speculation about Laloo's fate.

The last ten years have been Laloo's era: But that is not the same thing as Laloo being representative of Bihar. It is of course cheaper and easier for the media to work on that premise, instead of focussing on the policies he sought in vain to implement, or the forces with which in vain he contended, and why these battles of his were in vain. The impression the media convey is that Laloo has brought Bihar to its knees. That is not quite true. And if Laloo has defeated Bihar, equally Bihar has defeated Laloo.

I wrote for my paper in '98 that it seemed likely (at least to me) that Sonia Gandhi would find the withdrawal of Congress (I) support from Rabri Devi's government a handy brush to use in her repainting job. That did happen—or, at any rate, the Congress (I) went to the Assembly polls two years later with savage anti-Laloo war-cries, and their subsequent flip-flops have done much to bring laughter into our lives. A lot of other things have happened which I might or might not go into . . . No doubt affairs will be clearer (or more clearly murkier) by the time this book goes to press. But it will in any event be out of date when it is published—even though I've had time to see what happened in the Assembly elections—and so I talk of what I see as permanencies, using topical cases only for illumination. The game of looting Bihar will go on. It is what Laloo represents that is relevant.

It was my chance receipt in April 1997 of a review copy of the literary journal *Granta* (the celebration or whatever of fifty years of India's freedom) and my chance presence at a local mela which Laloo Prasad Yadav makes a point of attending, that made me think of Bihar not merely as *what-I-am-living-in-now* but as a paradigm of the not-so-distant future: *what-I-may-well-be-living-in-ten-years-from-now,* wherever in India I am. Bihar is developing into one of the political possibilities open to democracy which increasingly looks like coming to fruition.

The two relevant passages in *Granta 57: India* (1997) I quote below:

> More than ever, [those below the poverty line] and the people just above them seek political action to meet their demands: more subsidized food, more government jobs. They vote for the people who are most like them. In this sense, India has never had such *representative* politicians. Patrician, English-speaking leaders have almost disappeared, though English is the language of the new commercial vitality and many of the people who have benefited from it. The forces of economics and democracy are opposed.
>
> —Ian Jack, 'Introduction'

> When Delhi newspapers publish articles on Bihar's disorders and atrocities, they tend to make a point of emphasizing the state's 'backwardness'. What is needed . . . they say, is development . . . But it seems equally likely that Bihar could be not so much backward as forward: a trendsetter for the rest of India. The first ballot-rigging recorded in India took place in Bihar [in 1962] . . . the first example of major criminals being awarded parliamentary seats took place in Bihar [in 1980] . . .
> So infectious is the Bihar disease that it throws into question the whole notion of an Indian economic miracle . . .
>
> —William Dalrymple, 'Caste Wars'
> also in *At the Court of the Fish-eyed Goddess*

That the forces of economics and democracy are opposed is no secret. The high incidence of corruption in our daily life—not speaking of politicians or 'public services'—bears this out. Open a new box of matches, the 'carborized' 50s that are sold at anything from fifty paise to a buck, and count the sticks. I'd be very surprised if you found more than forty-five. And this is just a box of matches. A consumer movement, and consumer laws, are surely on the side of democracy; but where does it start when there is corruption involved in the sale of *a box of matches*?

And when economics and democracy are opposed, it is no secret either which side the politicians are on. Bihar, one of the richest states of India, is also perhaps the poorest. In May 1998 there were news reports that the state government had used only about one-third of Eighth Plan allocations. Why? Because after the spate of scandals, those who run the state have become frightened of being caught with their hands in the till even for purposes which are legitimate. Development be damned, and democracy too: Those who need the money, who need development, don't have the money and are not 'developed' enough to ask for it.

Ian Jack is right up to a certain point; where he is wrong is in thinking the forces of economics are linked to 'patrician' politicians because both speak English. The forces of economics in India have nothing to do with whether you can speak English; your success depends on how well you can use existing conditions and shape developments to your advantage. Both politics and economics speak the language of money, democracy has nothing to with either.

Dalrymple, who is at best a superficial kind of travel writer, has stated a superficial truth which is nonetheless a truth. Bihar *is* a trendsetter for the rest of us. I can see young politicians from all over the country being sent there as to a finishing school (an alternative career for Laloo Prasad if ever he dares to quit politics: a new Dotheboys Hall) and coming back wide-eyed from a prospect of heaven, having learned

- how to keep the electorate ignorant
- how to bully them if they persist in educating themselves

• advanced populist finance

and no doubt other titles in the curriculum will suggest themselves to you.

These ideas are lying around everywhere to be picked up, and not only in India. But to me, they were nakedly and brutally manifest in Bihar.

*

No one who has seen the Ganga plain after the monsoon and the annual flood, who has seen what it produces despite more than two thousand years of intensive cultivation, can think that the state of Bihar is a poor one. The soil is incredibly fertile: Poke in a seed and it sprouts. The first winter we were there, potatoes and onions sold for a rupee a kilo. I've seen roses and dahlias the size of cauliflowers and cauliflowers the size of footballs.

Yet the irrigation system is positively medieval. There are no canals in the Tal to drain away the vast quantities of water which stand in the fields to places where they might be more useful. (In medieval times, before barrages and the enormous pressure of modern populations, canals were presumably unnecessary.) Neither are there many tubewells in operation in the dry months.

A former Union Secretary of Agriculture whom I happened to meet in Hyderabad told me, 'Irrigation is a State subject. Money is sanctioned from the Centre and in Plan outlays for these schemes; but the Centre is not in charge of implementation, and all the funds are eaten up by the engineers.' I don't suppose the Centre worries itself sick about this in any case.

Neither do the big landlords. It is in their interest to keep the landless classes in their place—where their fathers and grandfathers kept them. At harvest-time crowds of the village poor flock early every morning to fields often ten or twenty kilometres away, there to slave in the sun until well into the afternoon and bring home, as their wages, a small fraction of what they picked: Maybe a kilo or two of daal or mustard seeds or a small bag of grain. Not a paisa in cash; no food. In Kerala, now, not even an unskilled labourer will spill his sweat for less than a hundred and fifty rupees a day, two meals and tea . . . (There are other things to be said about Kerala, and I will say them later; at least no one can deny that land reform and unionization have resulted in a high degree of social justice by the standards of other states.)

Tractors, like tubewells, are a rare sight in these fields. Why waste money on such luxuries when labour is so plentiful and so cheap? Even the old-fashioned wells, from which you drag buckets of water up by hand, are not equipped with the elementary pulley wheel or drum windlass. But the landlords have to be sure it will remain so, that the poor will have no opportunity to move on to better things; and whatever the party in power, since Jayaprakash Narayan's death the poor have been denied even the opportunity for envy, because they do not know anything about the rest of the world.

And not only the poor. Most natives of Bihar—excepting the millions of migrant labourers in Bombay, Calcutta, Delhi and Nepal—have never travelled further west than Varanasi, not far from the Uttar Pradesh border, and it is a rare man of the world who has even been to Calcutta, ten hours east of Patna by train. I knew a doctor at M____ whose brother found a job somewhere on the Andhra-Maharashtra border, and has since refused to return to his roots. 'Why should I come back to Bihar?' he asked on one of his rare visits home. 'There is no crime where I live, I can get a seat on the bus, and my children can learn English in school.' Those who know the Andhra-Maharashtra border will vouch for the fact that it is no land of milk and honey.

Despite railroads, industries like the thermal power station and the Indian Oil refinery in the Barauni area (where most trained workers are from outside Bihar), and a semblance of educational facilities, little has changed in the dynamics of Bihar society. (I must say I never visited Jamshedpur or the more industrialized south of Bihar.) Another doctor I knew took a week off from work at harvest-time to help his family in a nearby village bring in the crop. Local criminals attempted to extort a share from them; when they refused, the doctor's brother was abducted and held for ransom. A few days after he was released came the news that two of the gangsters had been killed—'. . . by tribals armed with bows and arrows,' said the newspaper report.

The Patna Medical College Hospital, Bihar's most prestigious (if the word can mean anything), according to a news report in early 1997 lacked essential facilities. Few of the ambulances ran, the lone X-ray machine hadn't worked for a year or two, and the doctors were mostly occupied with private practice. But, I later heard, there was a Janata Dal office on the ground floor—probably a Rashtriya Janata Dal office now. I was also told that citizens who dwelt in the vicinity could sometimes be seen jumping over the walls and making away with mattresses and cots. So what if the mortality rate is high? Dead men don't vote.

Yet, while health care for the very poor is practically non-existent, there are fancy clinics in Patna and even in smaller towns with all the latest fancy equipment.

You can do anything you like in Bihar—and avoid doing anything you don't want to do—if you have the right connections. The throwing around of political weight in all directions is a common, almost an everyday feature of life. You can't sack any 'Class IV' employee in Patna, you can't even take action against an orderly in a government department, because you are likely to discover his cousin's uncle's brother-in-law is an MLA, and the disciplinary action will be taken against you.

Before any political rally, gangs roam Patna city and block the highways, appropriating buses and private cars all over the state. Ram Vilas Paswan is the patron saint of Bihar Dalits, and when he was Union Minister for Railways, any time there was a big Dalit gathering the trains were virtually hijacked by his constituents. But the entourage (meaning goons with guns) of any MLA or MP can do that at any time without an excuse.

There appears to be nothing *illegal* about such appropriation of private vehicles. The police do it too. The Pulse Polio programme is a major public relations exercise in Bihar, and the state government makes a big media effort. To make sure enough resources are mobilized, private cars and jeeps in Patna are commandeered in the public interest.

When the police do it, of course, there is almost no way of resisting such oppression. There is no public resistance because those who travel in reserved railway berths and who have cars that can be commandeered are not the public. The public travel without tickets in and on trains, even perched on the gangways around the engine. They walk where they have to, or travel (in the city) eight or ten to an auto-rickshaw and (on the highways) fifteen or twenty to a jeep.

*

Laloo Prasad Yadav came to power on a one-line platform:

Bash the upper castes. This is nothing new in Bihar, but no one had ever been so direct before. As I learned more about the man I learned also who his enemies were. In all his election speeches in 1990 and '95 he had said: 'We will destroy the *Bhu-ra-ba-l.*' (This is an acronym for Bhumihar-Rajput-Brahmin-Lala, the land-owning castes.) I was to hear him say it again in 1998.

Laloo Prasad *said* many other things—that people from the Scheduled Castes would be made temple priests, for instance . . . I don't know if anyone actually got to be one. Laloo Prasad is a powerful orator, and this kind of directness has a powerful appeal to the mass of downtrodden, for all practical purposes disenfranchised voters. For two generations Bihar politicians had treated them like dirt. In a sense, Laloo was true to this tradition; in another, he was reaping the benefits of disenchantment with the upper-caste politicians who had preceded him in power.

It is naturally easier to destroy than to create, and once the Laloo Revolution in '90 had succeeded it found itself at a loss for further action. Laloo had been all his life an opposition politician, and perhaps he had no interest in 'development' anyway. The fruits of power were tempting, and Laloo took the obvious course of consolidating his bases and letting everything else go hang. His constituents were unused to the good life, and possibly unaware that it was attainable: They didn't mind. What they enjoyed was the sight of the Bhu-ra-ba-l being smashed.

But in the process of consolidating his power, Laloo had to treat with power-brokers; and this eroded his own vote-banks. A classic little story, and it has been told before, notably by American writer Robert Penn Warren in *All the King's Men,* the sad and cautionary tale of Willie Stark.

American democracy, before it got sanitized between Franklin Roosevelt's time and Martin Luther King's, was a good deal like Indian democracy today. No politician needs to keep it a secret that he is after the fruits of power. In Raymond Chandler's *The Lady in the Lake* a police captain compares the 'police business' to politics: 'It asks for the highest type of men, and there's nothing in it to attract the highest type of men. So we have to work with what we get.'

What we get is by and large a gang of rogues, but it is difficult even for one who comes to democratic office with the best of intentions to remain untainted by power. This is especially so if the politician concerned is not linked to any time-tested ideology such as the Communists have, or had. Gandhi had the right idea when he suggested that the Viceroy's Palace in New Delhi be converted into a hospital and that the first President of India be a Harijan girl. But Nehru and the Congress were seduced by the appurtenances of the Raj: They felt they had earned them with all their tribulations and years in prison.

So we adopted it all; all the paraphernalia and rituals that a conquering nation had used to glorify its superiority; and we thereby assured that the attitude of the people to the leaders would continue to be an upward-looking one. The flunkeys in archaic costumes, the chairs of State, the elaborate panoply of Empire. (And no doubt it appears more ridiculous when we see, in the Chair of State, not a 'patrician' politician like Nehru but Laloo Prasad, and behind him a flunkey with a spittoon. Are we deluding ourselves or is he deluding us?) Why do our newspapers still use the word 'rule' when speaking of elected officers? Why do we never behave to public servants as their masters?

Democracy is not a matter of statistics. Down in Kerala

everyone is supposed to be able to read and write. Many of the 'neoliterates', of course, know just enough to be able to sign for their pensions. But there's no denying that at least seventy-five per cent of the population is genuinely literate. Yet their *attitude* is not everywhere a democratic one: Many still fawn upon those economically above them in a more or less feudal manner. There is a certain broad-mindedness which is, to me, inseparable from the democratic instinct, which is lacking in much of Kerala: The *awareness* which is the wellspring of civilization, democratic or otherwise, is absent. That awareness must be of both rights and duties, of course. And if that is lacking in Kerala—which even Mr Clinton's speechwriters have told him is a model state—judge how much it is in evidence in Bihar.

That people are literate does not mean they are educated. In countries which have evolved their democratic systems, not adopted them, there is a stabilizing force, the good old Status Quo which keeps the Ship of State on an Even Keel. This is what in the UK helps secretaries prevent their ministers, of whatever party, from making asses of themselves. In the US the stabilizing force is business: Whichever party the cosmetic face before the cameras on the White House lawns belongs to, the power is with the faceless industrial, weapons and information consortia run by people who can use politicians like toilet paper.

In India all the democratic apparatus tends to stress the 'aboveness' of the elected representatives vis-a-vis their constituents. Where is the answerability, the responsibility to the voters that democracy at its highest calls for, outside the all too brief five-yearly episode when the voter is made to feel like a god? What does Laloo Prasad see when he looks down from the *manch*? People, or voters? . . . When your constituents appear to you only in the indistinguishable

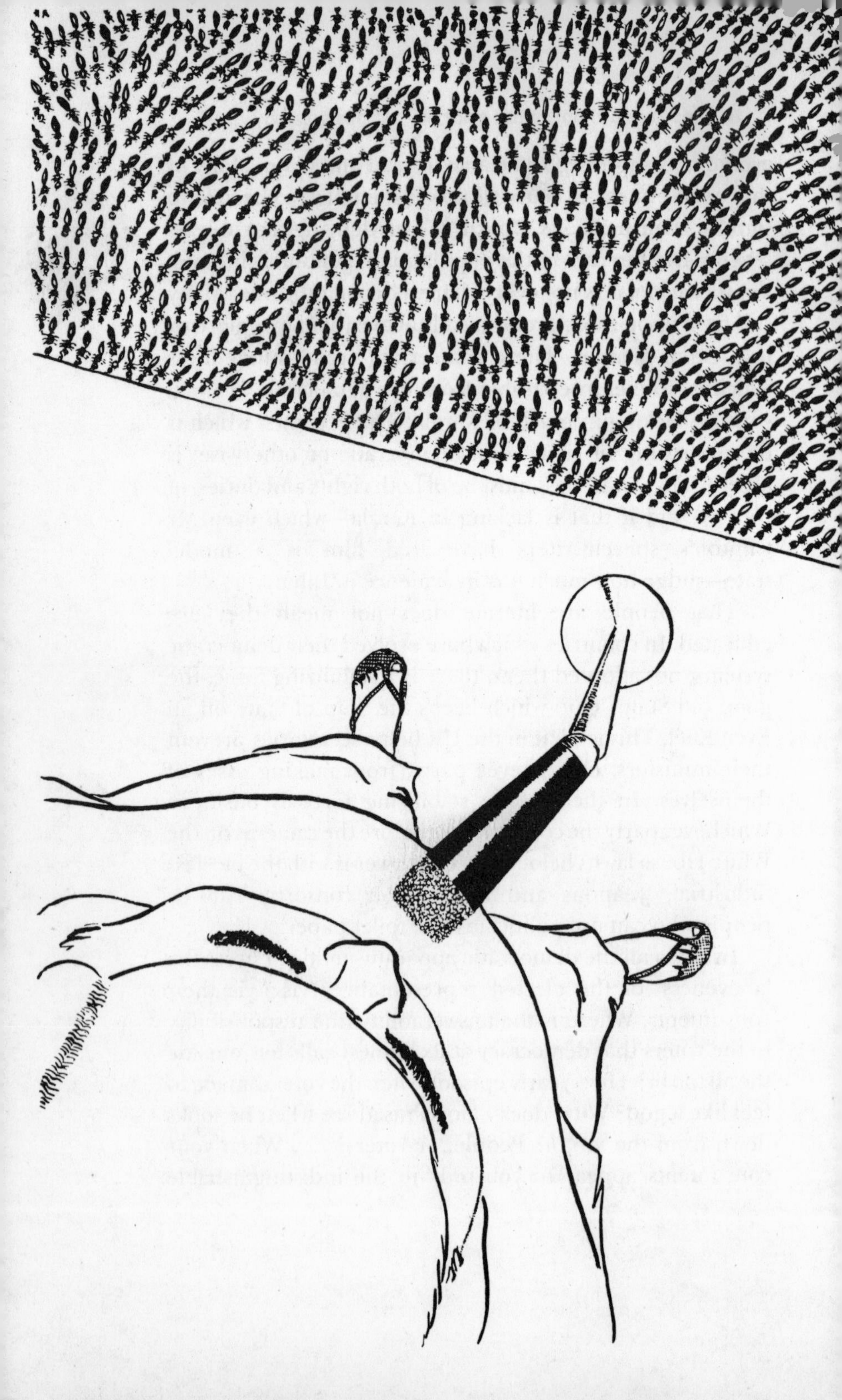

mass standing below the platform from where you are delivering the same speech you've already made five times that day; when the only constituents you meet face to face are the businessmen and party lords; then democracy has ceased to exist, and you are a demagogue.

The secret of keeping power in the kind of system we have lies in an abandonment of vision. *Yatha raja, tatha praja*—As the king, so the people, says a Sanskrit proverb, and a ruler with blinkers on succeeds in keeping the benefits of 'development' from his subjects, because he himself, quite honestly, cannot see them. Unlike Nelson at the Battle of Copenhagen, who knew the signal for disengagement had been hoisted but wilfully put the telescope to his blind eye, and perhaps unlike predecessors such as the canny Jagannath Mishra, Laloo Prasad does not differentiate between the uses of power and its abuses. Just as he is not immoral but only amoral, he is not illiberal but only aliberal.

The mela at which I first saw, or rather heard him, is held every year in the Hindi month of Chaith, that is Chaitra, in March-April. It is held at a desolate and arid spot (in summer; at flood-time it is waist-deep in water) about 110 km east of Patna, in celebration of a local Dalit saint who vanquished his Bhumihar adversaries in love and war about a century ago. (Singing the traditional song in his praise will still earn you a beating in a Bhumihar area, for the hero not only ran away with a Bhumihar girl but also soundly thrashed her relations.) Laloo Prasad's energetic participation in the fair in the 1990s made it a rallying point for Dalits, and probably won him at least a lakh of votes at state expense.

The mela itself is like any other in the hot months in rural India: the temple (a crude plastered building with an extension providing both shelter to the pilgrims and a platform to speak from); dusty lanes lined with rows of shacks selling food, dubious coloured drinks and toys; and a giant wheel or merry-go-round or some such special attraction. That year the attraction was a Well of Death, with Marutis and not just motorbikes: The troupe had come all the way from Delhi, it was said in tones of wonder.

As there were politicians attending, there was a lot of protective muscle, not all of it provided by the police. Besides, every hospital in the area was expected to send a team, so there were half a dozen white jeeps parked around the square where the command post and the first-aid tent were located. I had volunteered to accompany the Sister, two nurses and some of the young men from the community health department who comprised our Hospital team; so all through one long, hot, dusty afternoon we took it in turns to sit gossiping in the jeep and wander through the fair, sampling some of the eatables and buying souvenirs. I came away with some sealed glass tubes, each about eighteen inches long, almost filled with coloured water in which bits of tinsel were suspended; also a booklet in the local dialect containing the *gatha* in praise of the Dalit saint, with a commentary.

A helipad had been cleared for Laloo Prasad, who was expected to arrive by air. This, too, provoked intense excitement, and every half-hour or so, moved by a whisper that he was arriving, the crowds would flock to the enclosed half-acre of land. But he arrived, tamely enough, by road. He had just that morning returned from Delhi where he had been helping to anoint I.K. Gujral (after all his attempts to make a Bihari Prime Minister had failed) and he drove from Patna in a twelve- or fifteen-car cavalcade which included several Gypsy-loads of armed police, an ambulance from the Indira Gandhi Heart institute in Patna and another, inexplicably, from the Maternity Hospital ('Just to make up the numbers,' I was told).

He watched the local Chaith dances, of which he is said to be very fond, and distributed cash prizes to the dancers. Then he made a twenty-minute speech from the platform which extended from the saint's temple. He was some 200 metres away, and we could not make out his face or gestures. But his figure in white was conspicuous enough, and his voice was borne strongly by dozens of loudspeakers to a crowd of about a lakh.

'Just as peddlers visit your villages saying, "Choose what you like for four annas,"' he thundered, 'the officers of my government will come to you with whatever you want. Free saris, free dhotis . . . [A free clothes scheme was on then, but petered out; after Laloo abdicated in favour of his wife it was discovered there had been corruption in the handlooms department too, and the scheme was hurriedly abandoned. But it got a good deal of publicity while it was on, and no doubt a good number of votes.] 'They will camp in your village . . . they are your servants . . . take what you want.'

This is of course a thrilling prospect to the oppressed—those powerful *sarkari babus,* high-caste and citified, doing their bidding. Laloo had probably said the same thing the previous year and the year before. But the promise was still there, as genuine as the reality.

Perhaps deep down these voters knew that they were being had. But they were not used to having promises fulfilled, anyway; and Laloo had certainly kept part of his promise: He had smashed the upper castes. Not completely, of course, for there was nothing to fill the void which that would have created in the power structure, but enough to let them know he could have finished the job had he chosen to.

Democracy has often been warped, perverted and

defiled; indeed almost the whole history of the USA and Great Britain throughout the nineteenth century is a discourse on its abuses. But rarely in recent years has it been *wielded* as it is in Bihar, where everybody does have the vote and there is a free press.

Unwittingly or no, Laloo Prasad has arrived at the very secret heart of democracy, he has succeeded in refining it to its fundamentals as no one before him has. He was, I think, the first really humble peasant to battle his way to the top without a populist movement or a (Congress) party structure. But the fact that he is a son of the soil does not mean that he knows what is good for his land, or that he will ensure its welfare. Hemingway writes in *A Farewell to Arms:* '. . . the peasant has wisdom, because he is defeated from the start. Put him in power and you will see how wise he is.'

Hemingway might not have known much about peasants either; but there's no doubt Laloo Prasad could have been better prepared for his term in office. But then, is there any possible preparation, any safeguard against the temptations of office? He overcame enormous odds to become Chief Minister, and he had a chance to make a difference, much like Rajiv Gandhi in 1984. Had he not become Chief Minister of Bihar, Deve Gowda could never have become Prime Minister. He has 'empowered' the 'downtrodden' in a way no one else could, though it is perhaps not quite what Gandhi had in mind. And this craft of the mastery of the democratic process he will bequeath freely to his successors.

For democracy at its rawest does not require vision; it does not insist on the betterment of the human condition, it does not need the rule of order, it does not distinguish between the law-abiding and the criminal. It does not require the granting of opportunity. It does not ask for transformation: Indeed it is the status quo which contents it best. All democracy implies is that some large fraction of the populace has the right to choose one of themselves—to do what? To represent them? No. To enact laws? *No*. Only to do this—to wield power. In its starkest form democracy is the rule of the mob, and it is only the decency and the foresight of a truly good leader which can resist the temptation to abuse it.

Laloo Prasad Yadav is a very obviously powerful man. He tolerates no rivals; he kowtows to no one. He is widely perceived as a man who has kept his honour, in that peculiar male way in which a man can rob and kill and keep his honour. And in a still largely feudal society, *izzat*—honour—and *mardaangi*—manhood—are often valued higher than the nebulous temptations of 'development'. Laloo harnessed the might of the masses (while retaining the influence of the classes) . . . but to do only one thing: retain power. That is the essential secret of democracy; every other ideal is a wraith in the effulgence of that reality.

The fodder scam and other instances of corruption tarnished Laloo's image, even with the poor of Bihar. But he had done enough for large sections of them to ensure that, whatever happens, he has a massive electoral base and proportionate clout. He has enough money and muscle power on his side to make his followers' boast come true, that there will be a bloodbath if anything happens to Laloo Prasad. Yet he still has a dream, of being a statesman, of bestriding the national stage. He does not want to be forgotten. And he cannot be forgotten. His legacy will remain untarnished and will undoubtedly be a shining beacon for popular politicians. One of the promises of democracy, out of all its many possibilities, is coming here to fruition.

'As the king, so the people.' Alternatively, as the people, so the king. And Laloo is truly representative, as Ian Jack has noted in *Granta*. William Dalrymple's interview with Laloo is punctuated with remarks like 'Laloo scratches his groin.' But few Indians are embarrassed by such behaviour, and even fewer Biharis. They scratch where they like, they spit where they like . . . After Laloo's speech at the mela, the Hospital driver with some clever manoeuvres managed to get our jeep right behind his party, so we wouldn't be stuck in the exodus. We jolted behind the convoy, eating their dust. Halfway along the eight-kilometre dirt track to the highway, all the state vehicles came to a halt. So, perforce, did we. A furlong or so ahead, half a dozen khadi-clad figures disembarked from their air-conditioned cars, made their way into the stubble of the just-cropped fields and squatted there.

Of course, this is good for the land. Perhaps, then, though Ian Jack thinks otherwise, the forces of economics and democracy are not inevitably opposed. Besides, this was thoroughly representative behaviour. It was a triumph of democracy.

Sisters under the skin

BECAUSE I DID NOT go to Bihar as a journalist, and resided there as a citizen for almost a year and a half, these essays will be more valuable—or less meretricious—if I simply record my observations of life as she is lived in Bihar and carry on from there.

M____ was once a fairly important town, a node in the network of Empire. Before bridges spanned the Ganga it was the only ferry crossing in a thousand miles or so where large cargoes could be taken from one bank to the other, and also a major railway junction. Even now that the water traffic has been abandoned—the Ganga being a temperamental river—the road-and-rail bridge some twelve kilometres from M____ is the only one across the river between Patna and Bengal.

M____ is celebrated in literature, too: Jim Corbett lived and worked here for twenty-odd years as a coaling contractor for the railways before he made his name as an exterminator of vermin. He has written about it in *My India* . . . and anyone who has read it knows what M____ stands for.

Alas, the days of its glory are gone and M____ is a small, mean place now. It could have been a wealthy town, for it is excellently placed to serve the long-distance truck traffic on the Grand Trunk Road, and it is still a junction for east-west and north-south railway lines; but a lack of vision and a reputation for violence have driven away all capital. It has a bad name in a state which has a bad name in a country which has . . . and now the only local industry is muscle. The gangsters of M____ are much in demand in other districts at election time, and their services have been exported to Uttar Pradesh as well. There's lots of money in the business, but you can't say it has trickled down.

The Howrah-Delhi line must be the busiest long railway route in the country, and one of the busiest in the world, and the section from M____ for a few stations eastward is notorious for train dacoities. But these are the small pickings. There are—or were when we left—two big gangs in the town, who are at outs with each other and occasionally fight gun battles in the streets.

I've since been told that the leaders of both gangs are in jail, but it's still business as usual for their henchmen; when a state can be run from within prison, what's so difficult about running a few thugs, most of whom are related to you by blood in one way or the other? The same blood is either in your veins or on your hands . . . In the Assembly elections in 2000, one of the two *capos* in jail was elected as an independent supported by the National Democratic Alliance.

Residents of M____ can furnish the eager inquirer with a history of crime in the town and the present ganglords' spiritual descent from the First Criminal: a tale not unlike that of the genealogy of the Kurus which you find in *Adiparva*. But it hardly matters to newcomers. The big rackets used to be extortion and kidnapping, which fetched enough money to buy more sophisticated weaponry; now the gangsters are guns for hire (albeit with political connections and caste loyalties), willing to go in for anything which has money in it. Around the big shots flourish the small-timers, some of whom are freelances and the rest ambitious types who broke off from the *dadas* to operate on their own and occasionally get wiped out when they think too big.

But big shots or little, they all left the Hospital strictly alone. For one thing, they needed it when they were sick or wounded; for another, in fifty years the Sisters had done a lot of good work and made friends with anybody who was somebody in the area. Their convent, the Hospital, and the ten acres or so of fertile land where both stood—which constituted a haven of peace in that troubled region—had in fact been practically a gift from one of the biggest and most powerful Bhumihar landlords of the area. The ganglords, by the way, are also Bhumihar; in that part of the Ganga plain, theirs is the dominant community.

We had a decently-sized flat in the doctors' quarters in one corner of the campus, conveniently situated so that we could look out of our eastern windows on to the road which led into town and to the Ganga, along which often passed threadbare funeral processions with the monotonous chant of *Ram nam satya hai.* More common even than that was the keening of professional mourners from the Hospital's main door, only a hundred metres away, or from the door of the morgue which was even closer.

The Ganga plain is packed tight with villages within a gunshot of each other, and M____ for all its perils is the local market town. It was always crowded with townspeople and villagers. The traffic below our windows did not trouble us much, as it consisted largely of cycle-rickshaws. But there were always the familiar sounds of people and cattle near by.

Most irritating was the incessant bleating from the movie house in town. The owner had only a couple of cassettes of music and didn't want to tie up his capital in a search for variety. Scarcely a day passed without us being subjected to *Jai jagdish hare* and *Maalik tere bande hum* some half a dozen times each. When national holidays came around the mood became sterner, and I sometimes found myself marching around the flat to the strains of *Ae mere watan ke logon* and *Chhodo kal ki baatein*.

As for night life, it would have taken a brave heart or a couple of bodyguards to enjoy one. Everything slept by nine, except the jackals in the countryside—the campus was at the southern edge of town. I remember, though, that a couple of times some 'pop group' from the big city played in M____, rendering the latest hits—*Pardesi pardesi jaana nahin* was very big then—no doubt with the requisite gyrations and special effects in all colours of the rainbow.

It was a life circumscribed in many ways. It was unsafe to go out after dark; even in the day there was no saying when the town might erupt. (I went out about once a week, sometimes just into town, occasionally to Patna by train or Begusarai by bus, but I don't think Kavery went into town more than half a dozen times.) It was unsafe, we were told, to own a vehicle and drive around in a place where we were obviously foreigners; it was unsafe to go to the cinema hall; it was unsafe and uncomfortable to go out together for a cup of tea, and there was no way we could drop by a restaurant for a Sunday-morning masala dosa as had been our habit in Madras, even had there been any restaurants or masala dosas.

So I got on with my reading and writing, and Kavery was busy at the Hospital. It was very well equipped and staffed (for a rural hospital) and the operating theatre, according to Kavery, was a joy to work in. Only the narrow-mindedness and lack of vision of the Sisters—mostly Malayalis—made the job less than desirable. Kerala is not very different from

Bihar in some ways.

We had a maid who came in twice a day for a total of about four hours and whom we paid Rs 250 a month; high wages, we were told, which would lead to ill-feeling among other householders on campus. She was quiet and honest and suited us very well. A local boy came twice a week to take a grocery list and do our shopping in the market. It was a peaceful life—in retrospect, at least; only summer made it unbearable, but in 1997 we had a prolonged winter and the real heat did not set in until the end of April. Then we came south for six weeks and so escaped the worst of the summer.

Winter, which is enjoyable even in Delhi and gives Madras its two months of the year which can be borne, was a blessing in Bihar. For one, coming so soon after the rains and the flood, it preserved the lush greens of the land which so soothe the eye; then it was deliciously chill under the *razai* and the sunlight came as a benison. I would spend every winter of my life in north India under those conditions.

*

Living in a well-made flat on a self-sufficient campus attached to a place of sanctuary, provided with the necessities of life and insulated from its dangers, cannot perhaps be said to be 'living in Bihar', although technically that was accurate. We had running water all the time and electricity most of the time; as importantly, we had money and a support system. Our life was real enough to us and to our neighbours: I don't want to echo those who attack Indians writing in English, saying that what they describe is not 'the real India'. Yet we saw events around us as if through a glass, not necessarily darkly. I should say 'I saw', for Kavery was in daily contact with local people and local happenings. *She* should be writing this book, but has more important things to do.

In many ways, though, I had the advantage, for I had the time and leisure to ask questions and in a sense—with no object in view—interview people, while she was too occupied with her work to get interested or curious in the details of people's lives except as they were vouchsafed to her as symptoms. I went out a few times with the 'boys' of the community health department of the Hospital, which conducted weekly clinics at a nearby village; I volunteered for the Pulse Polio programme; and I travelled many times to Patna by train. I also attended the big local festival, Chhatth (the second consonant is an aspirated retroflex), which comes six days after Divali. And then, just because I am a journalist, and my time was my own, and my wife was an influential member of the community, my ear was used as a receptacle for confidences of all kinds.

One of the locals we knew best was the younger son of a family which owned a chemist's shop and a pharmaceuticals trading agency. The family had come from Marwar over a century ago—soon after 1857, I gathered—and in the catholic fashion of Marwaris had adopted the local customs as their own. Theirs was not the only family which came: There was a whole street called the Marwari *mohalla*.

The Marwaris' inevitable success in business had led to their being chosen as the first victims of extortion at the beginning of the reign of terror in M____; and of the nineteen houses in the mohalla, only six were now tenanted. Those remaining, too, were seeking alternatives. It was tragic that this community, one of India's most inoffensive and industrious, which brings prosperity wherever it is settled, should have been hounded out of the town. The Marwari exodus had much to do with the decline of M____ as the economic capital of the area.

Kishan, as I shall call him, was short and dark and full of a boundless energy. He reminded me of one of those 'excited electrons' of Rutherford's time. He was invaluable to us: He helped Kavery's work by stocking items like tantalum mesh for hernia repair, and cancer chemotherapy drugs, which the Hospital Sisters wouldn't out of ignorance and a refusal to be enlightened. (The success of Marwari businessmen, I think, is attributable to the fact that they will go to any lengths to satisfy the customer.)

Besides, Kishan would mail our letters in Patna, and send off articles and reviews by courier, and buy for us miscellaneous items unavailable in M____. The mail was most important. Shortly after our arrival in M____, we had discovered that the local Railway Mail Service was most unreliable. At festival time—chiefly Holi and Chhatth—the sorter, or the postman, or both, would take a month or so off to visit his village. Upon returning, if the number of letters to be sorted or delivered was inconveniently large, he would simply burn them. I'm not joking; we were told this by several people, both locals and Sisters, and I know we lost a couple of dozen letters both coming and going. Registered letters were more reliable but it is inconvenient and expensive to send all your letters thus.

Banking was a major trial. Cheques from the south took between three and six months to clear, and I finally had to ask the journals from whom my infrequent payments came to stop sending them altogether until, on our visit home in the summer of 1997, I could open an account in Madras. Banking is not, strictly speaking, a *service* in India; it is more of an ordeal (and this goes for the much-touted multinationals as well); but in relation to what we had to go through in M____, any previous misadventure was tinged with a roseate hue in retrospect.

The difficulty of staying in touch was one of our greatest quotidian sorrows in M____. The telecommunications service there is a joke. It was almost impossible to get any telephone number south of the Vindhyas, and quite often the meter would begin racing while we were being told in soothing accents, '*All* lines . . . on *this* route . . . are *bu*sy.' This also often happens when you dial a Bihar number outside Patna from the south: So it's not that the telephone booth operator in M____ was feathering his nest. Some little scam, unnoticed among all the hundred-crore-rupee scams, but fetching somebody a tidy little sum all the same . . .

Not, either, that the telephone booth's owner was above feathering his nest. He was a Bhumihar named Shyam Nandan Singh, an old-timer with dhoti tucked up behind him and typical north Indian courtesy. Also a *chamcha* of the Sisters. He was, besides, an office-bearer of the local branch of one of the Eastern Railway unions. I once asked him what post he'd held in the Railways, and he answered with the air of one inspecting a dead rat that of course he'd never *worked* for the Railways. The customs of Indian unions are passing strange . . .

Shyam Babu came from a rich family but had been defrauded by his brothers of his share in the proceeds from his father's death. So he was reduced to running the telephone booth on campus and fiddling with the meter—pastimes, it was generally agreed, beneath a Bhumihar. He did all right though, for after 7.30 p.m. there were always five or six nurses in the cramped little room with the telephone, calling or being called by Kerala. But I never had much luck with Madras or Bangalore.

A few months after we'd left I sent off a long telegram to M____ from Kerala. It cost me nineteen rupees, ordinary class. It must have got to the town, but it didn't get to the person it was meant for: It was never delivered. Just too much of a hassle for the local P&T. And whom do you complain to?

I had always been an indifferent letter writer, but in M____ I realized, too late, the value of keeping in touch, and wrote letters as if I was making up for the wasted years. They were sometimes six or ten pages long, and I felt aggrieved when I got no reply or a page-long scrawl three months later. Almost all my friends are in computers and gossip by e-mail; my relations live in civilized places and talk on the phone. My reformation was delayed too long; my spiritual progress had not kept pace with the world's technological progress.

So Kishan helped us immensely. He would also drop in sometimes, tired from arguing with the Sister in the hospital pharmacy (who was somewhat impaired mathematically) and tell me what was happening in town. I got to know his family quite well too, especially his mother, a loud-voiced matriarch; it was at their invitation that I participated in the Chhatth puja on the Ganga's southern bank, and I also attended Kishan's elder brother's wedding in Patna and danced in the *baaraat*.

Kishan's mother bullied all her family, and everyone she met, without mercy. The only way of getting on terms with her—if you were someone she did not have to particularly respect, such as a shiftless journalist who wrote in a foreign language and drank too much—was to shout back at her. I discovered this the first time I visited Kishan's house for tea and *paav-bhaaji*. It was a Sunday, but Kavery had been called for an emergency laparotomy. 'Why didn't you bring Doctor?' the matriarch yelled at me, and I surprised myself and her by yelling back, 'What can I do if she has an operation?' She was quite mellow whenever we met after that and I was respectful. But that evening I had to go back home anyway and fetch Kavery in a rickshaw, the only mode of public transport in town.

It's always impressive—at least, I'm impressed—to meet a dominant female in a traditional setting. In much of India it is not a comfortable thing to be born female. This is borne in upon most Indian women especially poignantly when they are married and go to live in their husbands' houses; particularly in the Ganga plain, where most men no matter how affluent or professional live on in their ancestral homes all their lives.

It is strange that older women do not remember their own situation of twenty-five years earlier and take pity upon their daughters-in-law. Or maybe it is not so strange; as a species in the raw we have not much heart-room for pity. I have often thought that it takes a strong-minded, determined wife to make a success of being a daughter-in-law; for even where the husband's family is not malicious or hard-hearted, they have to be seen to be treating the bride in a proper manner.

We saw this for ourselves at Kishan's house, a month or two after his brother's wedding. The new daughter-in-law was a sweet, pliant young thing, but Kishan's mother, and even Kishan himself, would shout at her: '*Bahu*! do this!' 'Get that!' in a fashion which would have driven me to tears or revolt. But then I was not reared to such behaviour, and I'm not a woman. The girl took it meekly enough, and of course her new in-laws were not in any way cruel. It was the usual thing: 'You haven't put enough ghee in the sweets!' 'The tea is too strong!' 'Can't you bring water, don't you know water is to be brought for guests?' She looked like Lucy Gray in an acre of seaweed.

But that was only her housebreaking, so to speak, and the manners were to some extent assumed for the benefit of the company, who squirmed. I thought of Kishan's mother and what she must have been like thirty or thirty-five years ago when she entered this same house. Her mother-in-law was long dead, but there was a 'marriage photograph' on the wall, and she looked rather grim. Kishan's father was meek enough (and long-suffering, I thought) and perhaps his father had been too; yet Kishan's mother must have changed: and how and where did she summon up the spirit within her to adapt, resist, and be herself?

And in a queer way, this led me to think of Rabri Devi; and even more queerly, of Sonia Gandhi.

*

I don't know much more about Laloo Prasad Yadav's early life than the official version reveals. It's easy enough to find out, but I'm afraid that would detract from the fun I have in writing all this. I don't know much about his personal life, either, and I don't want to know any more than I do: What I have heard is mostly unflattering and in some measure unprintable.

The public biography is this—that Laloo grew up in a very poor family, in miserable surroundings, and by sheer force and determination clawed his way through school and college. He graduated with honours in political science from Patna University in 1969, and took his LL.B. in 1975. He was one of Jayaprakash Narayan's young firebrands (jailed during the Emergency), and president of the students' union from 1973 (having been general secretary from 1967 to '69 and then an assistant in the Patna Veterinary College from 1970 to '72); his victorious running mate for general secretary in '73 was Sushil Kumar Modi, now state BJP chief.

There are Yadavs and Yadavs in the Ganga plain, and not all of them herd cows. The Yadavs of north Bihar—Madhepura, for example, where two foreign Yadavs, Laloo and Sharad, contested the 1998 and '99 Lok Sabha elections—are landed and at the right end of the feudal stick. (The Yadavs of course claim to be descended from Lord Krishna's clan, but that is a myth, as Iravati Karve says in *Yuganta*. Those Yadavas were a warrior race, and were eliminated and supplanted by a nomadic people who were cattle-herders—I think this is found in the *Svargaarohanaparva*—possibly the Ahirs, who, as so many peoples did before written records were kept, adopted the name and caste, the condition and gods, of the vanquished tribe.)

But it is true that the Yadavs of central Bihar are by and large miserably poor, and much of their lifestyle has to do with cows and buffaloes. Laloo Prasad herded cattle when he was a boy, and has spoken of his resentment at the treatment of his people by the higher castes. He has never forgotten that (and what he seems to have forgiven is only out of political expediency), and it has played a formative role in making him the kind of politician he is.

Laloo rose out of this wretchedness, becoming a man of the world, but it cannot be assumed that his wife and family rose with him. Much laughter has been occasioned by the names of his children: Kursi (chair) and Misa, for instance. But it is actually quite sensible to name a child for the circumstances of its birth, or for some everyday object—it probably has some mnemonic value as well when you have twelve or sixteen children—and it is a common practice among the 'backward' Yadavs. Name a child 'Apratiratha' or 'Swargasundari' and see how it bears the burden of expectation. I was told by a doctor at the Hospital in M____, 'In my village I know a Yadav family with children named Chaurasiya (Eighty-four) and Athasiya (Eighty-eight) for the years of their birth.' These are *names,* not nicknames. Misa is named for the Maintenance of Internal Security Act, under which draconian piece of legislation Laloo was in prison when the child was born.

Laloo's wife's name, Rabri, of course, means the milk-based cooling drink which may briefly make you thankful for the ferocity of the Delhi summer. It's a sweet name, yet many sophisticates laugh at it who call their spouses 'Honey' or 'Kissums'. (The name 'Jalebi' is also found among the Yadavs, and for all I know 'Laddoo' . . . But then, one of the meanings of 'Misra' is sugar. And if you suggest that Rabri is misnamed, so is Madeleine Albright: She is small and rich, but she's no piece of cake.)

One of the cruellest things Laloo Prasad ever did—in a career not marked by ruth—was to pitchfork his wife into the Chief Minister's chair. It was a bad time for mentors, who were then being betrayed at the rate of about one a week by their protégés and protégées in Gujarat, Uttar Pradesh, Karnataka and Delhi; and Laloo was taking no chances. Rabri Devi had no option but to be a puppet, given her circumstances and rearing.

But consider the feelings of a quiet, not very educated middle-aged Indian woman who has all her life quietly accepted the mores of an extremely hidebound society, whose duty has lain in looking after father and brothers, husband and in-laws, running the house, providing meals on time, bearing children, being faithful and patient and uncomplaining no matter what the provocation—consider her feelings when she has to sit in a plush chair in an air-conditioned office, meet and listen to strange men

without her husband's or brothers' familiar (if not protective) presence, address vast crowds of people whom she would be much more comfortable among than above; and all this after seeing her husband taken off to jail, pilloried in the press and insulted in the Assembly. Would you be able to take it? I dare say only one with her training could have; for her training as daughter, wife and daughter-in-law was to accept, accept, accept and obey, obey, obey. And she did it all with a certain quiet dignity, so that in the end you could not laugh at her, or if you did it was as you laughed at Falstaff or Don Quixote, not Malvolio or Johnny Lever.

What did she think about it all? Her own pronouncements in public were for a few months limited to a couple of lines written for her which she read out like a schoolgirl. Later she blossomed somewhat, even cracking a joke about *presswalen*, and picking up some of the nuances of political oratory when she defended her husband, which she rather often had to do. But what did she think about her sudden, starring role in Democracy?

My own guess is that she didn't think much about it. Her duty was to her husband, not to the people of Bihar.

That is our singular feature as a democratic nation, the discrepancy between our constitution and our Constitution: We do not think or act as if we have any duty to the nation. We do what we do, first, for ourselves and our families; then for our caste community; then for our state, defined in linguistic terms. In fifty years we have not been able to change this way of thinking, perhaps because we perpetuated fifty years ago a system of governance which had found in this way of thinking a handy tool to govern with. Besides, in the ancient Hindu framework, since monarchies supplanted republics, there is no such thing as

Nation (and this reduces the BJP's attempts to invent it and at the same time proclaim it to be an ancient Hindu concept, to farce).

When a politician gets into power, he is called a fool if he does not first ensure that his family will not have to do any honest work for at least three generations; then he does something or the other for the members of his caste-fraternity; then for his constituency or his state. He does not lose honour, according to this way of thought, if he is caught and has to go to court or to jail: His wife does not refuse him her bed, his sisters and his cousins and his aunts do not avoid all mention of his name. His neighbours do not turn their backs on him, his fellow-partymen are moved more to emulation than contempt.

So criminals are picked as candidates again, and returned to power, what's more. One reason why they are not drummed out of their constituencies is demagoguery, which we see in the person of Jayalalitha in Tamil Nadu; another is that they have not actually defrauded their constituents, which explains Sukh Ram in Himachal Pradesh; and the third and simplest reason, evident in Bihar and increasingly elsewhere, is simply lots of muscle and an overwhelming willingness to use it. And the clever ones are careful to take only a percentage of their earnings for themselves, giving the rest to the Party, which thereupon renominates them.

After all, in a democracy you only have to keep half the people happy; and in a multi-party tamasha such as ours a mere third will do.

(It's no different anywhere else in the world. Bill Clinton—whose middle name is taken from the man who wrote the US Constitution—is perhaps just as amoral as Laloo Prasad Yadav. There have been reports that he had no qualms about accepting money from the Chinese government to get re-elected, even if the required quid pro quo harmed US interests. And since a lot of the moolah was also used to elect Democratic senators and representatives, they fade off into corners when he's caught with his pants down. This amorality is what voters in any democracy have come to expect from their leaders; at the time when Clinton was being caught with his pants down every other Saturday, he had one of the highest approval ratings of any second-term US President, even though a majority of those polled also said they did not believe him.)

I think Rabri Devi also sees her husband as any other housewife sees her husband: A man going out to work every morning to keep the family going. He makes a little more than most husbands, true; but then he works longer hours, and holds a much more distasteful job, which entails being insulted in public places and drawn and quartered in print.

So if Rabri has to hold the fort while her husband spends a few months in a luxuriously appointed state guest house rather than his own mansion, well then, she'll do it, for the kiddies' sake. And she'll repulse all attacks on his name and position to the best of her ability, for the sake of family honour. And the strange thing is that, as an Indian with a sense of bloodline, I can actually almost see the point in all this. Rabri Devi is not very different from Rani Lakshmibai or Shivaji's mother, who also did what they did for their dynasty and not for some mythical national honour, and were yet remarkable women.

*

For the Colonel's Lady an' Judy O'Grady
Are sisters under their skins!

—Kipling, 'The Ladies'

There were few sympathetic voices in the media when Laloo abdicated in favour of his wife. Almost without exception commentators and editors clad themselves in stainless steel and trumpeted their indignation at this 'Travesty of the democratic process'. One of the few who actually defended the transfer of power was—I did a double-take when I saw the name—Mani Shankar Aiyar.

Laloo was perfectly within his rights, wrote Aiyar, to nominate a successor so long as that successor was a Member of the Legislature (or was elected within six months) and had the confidence of the House. That's what is written in the Constitution. Well, yes. True enough. The *spirit* of the Constitution is somewhat different, but things spiritual had been on the decline since Aiyar's master Rajiv Gandhi's time, and even before that in the time of Rajiv's mother. But when had Mani Shankar Aiyar become such a literalist?

Literal or not, he is seldom subtle, and his drift was clear upon cogitation: He was making out a case for Sonia Gandhi becoming Congress (I) president and thereafter, hopefully, Prime Minister. One dynast's right to the throne is just as good as another's, and so is one queen-dowager's. Sonia Gandhi had inherited a legacy just as untarnished as had Rabri Devi.

There's another remarkable woman for you: Sonia Gandhi. Born into a wealthy Italian family (and Italy is much like India in one respect, that if you're rich you can do pretty much as you please and ignore the world . . . I suppose most countries are like that, really), she has done all that she has done for love. But for love of Rajiv and the dynasty, not of India. She didn't even become an Indian citizen until she had to, and who can blame her? Oh yes, she's from a very different background to Rabri Devi's, and left to herself she would prefer to stay in her Janpath ivory tower with a fat government pension. But she, too, is doing it for the kiddies. And if Rabri sets a precedent for her, well and good—especially for chamchas like Mani Shankar Aiyar.

But the propaganda exercise building up Sonia Gandhi is on a vastly larger scale, and far more skilfully managed, than anything Laloo Prasad can drum up. A lot of people fall for the 'Oh, she's such a nice lady, so sweet' line; others remember how fair-complexioned and fine of feature her husband was. Why do people who should know better find it so hard to accept even the possibility that Rajiv Gandhi might have been corrupt while heaping execration upon Laloo? Just because Rajiv had a better profile and could wisecrack in English? After all, they are products, even shapers, of the same system.

Sonia Gandhi's attitude to Indian democracy reminds me [this was written before the series of setbacks which followed the 2000 assembly polls] of an adult indulging a gang of unruly adolescents. Like Sweet Alice with Ben Bolt, Congressmen 'weep with delight when she gives them a smile, and tremble with fear at her frown', and for as flimsy a reason. She's the only person who can make you feel sorry for Sitaram Kesri . . . and those in the media who espouse her cause have a good reason for doing it. But whatever our political and press kings may say or do, what do the voters think?

In Bihar, in February '98, Sonia Gandhi got a lot of attention. Here, too, the media effort was an exercise in exaggeration. A college lecturer and news agency stringer told me and fellow journalists in Begusarai (where we had stopped on our way to Madhepura) that the rally Sonia Gandhi addressed in nearby Lakhisarai had attracted 'two lakhs of people'. But the veteran Patna journalist I was tagging along behind told me later, cynically, 'There is no place in Lakhisarai to hold such a crowd, unless the Ganga dries up.'

I got the impression that people went to 'see Sonia', all over India, not as they would go to check out a bride for the son of the house, but as they might go to the circus. It was a satisfying experience, but the number of sightseers perhaps misled the experts. Some of the biggest crowds were in Uttar Pradesh, where the Congress (I) did not win a single seat.

Say what we will about it, there is something sound and strong at the core of our democracy. I could not live here if I did not believe that it is only the top of the tree which is rotten, and I live on in hope of a tree surgeon coming along some day who is both well-qualified and honest, *integer vitae scelerisque purus*.

Bihar was, I thought, among the worst affected by the rot, until the returns from Tamil Nadu (in '98) came in. This is a cycle that has gone on too long: Misgoverning for five years, getting booted out in elections, then waiting five years for the other gang to get kicked out so you can misgovern again. Something has to snap, and I devoutly hope it's the top of the tree that will.

Corruption in Bihar is nakedly open to the eye, and smells of sweat and earth. More expensively perfumed people rob us with an air, as if they're doing us a favour. As I wrote in the first chapter, Kesri's Congress supported Laloo Prasad for old times' sake, and when Sonia Gandhi began whitewashing her party, refusal of support in Bihar was an obvious, simple, and potentially richly-paying step (until the Assembly election results were declared for 2000 and the Rashtriya Janata Dal did better than anybody except I had expected).

Democracy is often a matter of theft, particularly at election time, when votes have to be stolen from the electorate with soft blandishments (in Delhi) or by twisting their arms (in Bihar). Someone's pinching your wallet leaves you the poorer, even if she's cooing soft words into your ear at the same time. There's no such thing as a stainless steal.

'Biharis need to be kicked'

ONE EVENING IN EARLY June, towards the end of our first year in Bihar, Kavery and I were walking up and down the wide cemented path which leads from the Hospital to the doctors' quarters when there was an urgent call for her. It was still hot though the sun had set half an hour ago, but near the gate the tubelight which all the doctors had been demanding for months had not yet been installed, so at least we were spared the swarms of summer insects.

The gate cut the path in two, separating some hundred feet on our side (on sunny winter mornings I used to incessantly pace there, and it was forty of my paces long) which was the doctors' preserve, from the Hospital and the rabble. The gate was for our protection, and there was always supposed to be a 'security' there to prevent members of the public from troubling the doctors at home; but as the members of the public were often armed or drunk or both and the security was some puny cast-off from the police, without a gun, he used to let them through. We had a lot of trouble at one time or another over this.

Anyway, the message said a police officer had an abdominal bullet injury and would Kavery come at once. She'd had a hard day as usual, and we were due to leave next week on our first trip home in a year—so she wouldn't be around to attend to post-operative complications after a few days—and she was tempted to refer the case to Patna. But the victim was a) a policeman and b) gutshot, which meant he might not survive the three-hour road journey to the city; so she said she'd come in ten minutes. The operating theatre staff, having had plenty of experience, needed no instructions about getting ready for an emergency operation and would already have started the process. On impulse I said, 'Can I come and watch?'

I went back and changed, got to the operating theatre, and was shown how to scrub. Kavery and her assistants were already at the table and there was some banter about my fainting and which way to fall if I did. The operation was fascinating, and I realized for the first time (at first hand) why an operating room is called a theatre. Under the sharp white lights, with the head theatre Sister sternly but unobtrusively marshalling the nurses, and three gowned and masked figures at the centre of things, the scene was drama.

The cop was about five-eight but very well-muscled, and Kavery peeled back layers of fat and muscle which I thought remarkably thick. An entry and an exit wound were obvious, one on either side of the abdomen. But they had to go a good way down to find the colon, the large intestine, which was literally cut into three pieces. It took a while to sew it up, or resect it as they say. Then another wound had to be attended to in the neck, where the bullet had somehow missed any vital body part.

Kavery works extremely fast but it was still long past dinner time when they had finished. I stood or walked up and down, staying out of the Sisters' way, occasionally climbing on to a stool to see better, being summoned to the table to see some gory organ or witness some tricky procedure, taking part in the banter when the difficult bit was done. Two hours and fifty minutes. Without a cigarette.

Why? I had never asked to see one of Kavery's operations before, and I would have if I had been curious—never having been invaded myself either, because I've always enjoyed rude good health, rude being the operative word: rude enough to know I wouldn't turn squeamish at the sight of blood or bowel.

But I'd just recently begun to see Bihar in a journalistic way, having a few days earlier sent off to Madras a 3,000-word piece. In Bihar as nowhere else I had seen, in a few months, how close death is to life, how weak and easily extinguished a life is and how domitable the thought of imminent death. So I wanted to see for myself that brown-and-white-and-red thing on the table, under the pitiless lights. I wanted, if you like, to get closer to my theme.

*

Picture yourself a *daroga*—something like a head-constable—young, ambitious, and fearless too, for whatever that's worth. You've just been posted to a town known in the area for its violent crime. It doesn't faze you: All the more opportunities for promotion. You are, yourself, from down in the south of the state, from a tribal community which has distinguished itself in military service and in sport. You take leave of your aged parents, promising to come back with sweets 'at Divali or my next promotion, whichever is earlier'.

Soon after joining at M____ (you have already scornfully noted that the *thana* is understaffed and under-armed for a town with such a high degree of criminal activity, that the man who gives you orders and dresses like a cross between Shatrughan Sinha and Clint Eastwood is taking handouts from the local bosses, and that the rank and file are demoralized and willing not to trouble trouble)—soon after joining, you're told off one evening to patrol the market. You march briskly from the thana, with the constables, lugging their old-fashioned and unwieldy rifles, following you rather less briskly, and enter the market street.

It's a northern small-town market street much like any other: dusty, with clouds of insects around the streetlamps and tubelights, a few cows still to be herded home . . . Many of the shopkeepers greet you. 'Namaskar saab.' You nod briskly and walk on, looking to right and left and with the corners of your eyes open as you were taught to do, alert for any hint of lawlessness.

Is there a smile on the faces of the shopkeepers behind you? Either you don't notice or you don't care. Everyone knows who you are, of course; there are few secrets in a town like this one. You march on—briskly. Night has fallen.

Suddenly there is a confused murmur behind you. You turn: Your men are excited. 'Saab, Sanjay Singh is there.' 'In the *chowk* next to the Pipalwadi *basti*.' 'He is alone in the open.'

Sanjay Singh! You've never seen him but you know his features well enough from the mug sheets of wanted criminals. And he's unguarded—but is he?

Suspicion: 'Where are his men then?'

'They say he's sent them to the Marwari mohalla again.'

Extortion? And so early in the evening? But why not, even jackals are fearless when the watchman's drunk. And in M____ the watchman's in the jackals' pay. But never mind. Sanjay Singh is sure not to be *totally* unprotected, but you have four men and even these spineless wretches seem enthused. Quickly you give orders; send one man back to the thana, and take the shortest route to the Pipalwadi basti with the rest.

You leave the shop lights behind; the houses along the

narrow lanes are feebly lit with yellow as if from deep within a well. There are no women, no children in the streets, hardly any men. You know the geography of the town, though you've been here so short a time: The importance of such knowledge was impressed upon you in the special short-term course you took. Your legs move along the *galis*, take the correct turns, step over broken bricks and ruts in the path, as if of their own volition.

The next right turn, and there's the chowk, suddenly lit by a tubelight from above; and there in the middle of the thirty-foot square, surrounded by dark doorways, sitting all by himself on a steel chair, alone, casually handling an automatic weapon, is Sanjay Singh. You've never seen him but you know his face by heart.

You pull out your revolver. At the back of your mind is the sick envy that these sons of dogs have better guns than you. You intensify the thought into an iron hate. 'Surrender!'

'Piss off.'

As you half-turn to your men the thought strikes you that you've heard no footfalls behind you since you took that last right turn. Therefore your men have not made that last right turn into the chowk, therefore you're . . .

Sanjay Singh fires first, and your shot follows just as a searing sharpness cuts through you. Out of the dark doorways all around, gunfire sounds, with an enormous and frightening thunder which must be worse than actually being hit. You feel a blow on the neck which half twists your head off. You don't feel the pain at once, then suddenly you do and know it's worse than the sound of gunfire. But even sharper is the thought that you've been suckered.

*

That's more or less the story as I pieced it together from occasional laughing remarks and sly hints. The inspector came rushing from across the river, the SHO (station house officer, a sub-inspector) had already got all his men on a war-footing, all the cops were frantic with rage and fear. If you've read enough American stories of big-city crime you know the one thing cops don't forgive is an assault on one of their own. Even in M____ it was thought that this time the criminals would be wiped out. A contingent of armed police arrived from Begusarai.

In Patna a minister—or it might even have been the local MLA—was given the message by a furious IPS man.

'*Kyaa*?' the man drawled. 'Shot a policeman?'

'*Hanji*. Condition is very serious. Shall I order action?'

Those silly cowboy heroes, the MLA thought. Always wanting glory, the young fools. When would they understand that Sanjay Singh and his gang, the 'criminals', were worth more to him for three months every five years than *they* would be in their whole careers?

'No, no,' he told the IPS man. 'No action.'

So for three days the armed policemen sat in the thana, looking very grim and efficient, and after that they softly and silently vanished away. Once more it had been demonstrated where political power comes from, and the people of M____ knew who their masters were.

The daroga *lived;* his youth and fitness and excellent musculature helped to get him out of hospital without any permanent harm—to his body. Kavery didn't even have to postpone our trip south, he was doing so well a week later. But I guess he would not have marched so briskly out of the thana on evening patrol ever again, at least not in M____. He, too, had been shown who his masters were.

The citizens of course had to turn it into a story against

the cops. They laughed behind their hands for days. It was more than their self-respect was worth to think how they had been suckered too, and at what little cost to the ones who did the suckering.

I have always had a great sympathy for Indian policemen since I spent a day in a thana in Old Delhi when I was much younger. I was writing a 'Day in the Life' kind of piece, but what the cops told me out of the corners of their mouths has influenced me, ever since, to stretch a point when it comes to a minor bit of propaganda or just unofficial help—like stopping to give a policeman off duty a lift home. They are underpaid and overworked; in the cities they stay for months without a sight of wife and children.

They are also undertrained. After all, they come from the same class as do the criminals: Are they taught to love those they guard? Are they taught to be humane, apart from the occasional PR exercises put on by the top brass? Is any effort made to soften them or put a gloss on their appearance and actions?

Most hurtful is the political control of police work. It's worse in Bihar than anywhere else that I've seen, though I suppose it's pretty bad in UP and the militant-affected states; and in Bombay the politician-gangster-police game is in a different league altogether. In Bihar, the only reason for the proliferation of such well-armed, organized criminal gangs is political patronage. They are there because they have become necessary to the winning of elections.

And the gangs of Bihar do not operate only in Bihar. Sri Prakash Shukla, who was killed by a police party in Ghaziabad near Delhi in October 1998, and was said to be plotting to kill then UP Chief Minister Kalyan Singh, was trained in Bihar—by Sanjay Singh or his arch rival, I don't remember which. Singh himself, or maybe, again, it was the rival gang, murdered an Uttar Pradesh MLA in Lucknow a couple of years back. The 'criminals' have become valuable mercenaries in the north Indian political arena.

The gangs of M____, when they can be spared from election duties, are often called to other districts of Bihar where the musclemen are too moral to kill easily, or too effete, or just not as easy with a gun. And now those they trained are more and more visible in the other districts of Bihar at election time, and are proving to be worthy disciples.

In M____ the gangs have made a lot of money from extortion and contracts, and own the town in one sense or another. And speaking of contracts, they are legally contractors too, mostly for railway projects. Indian Railways is a major source of income and employment for the region; but these modern contractors have unorthodox methods of getting the job. All they do is ensure that no tenders are handed in but theirs. Other, legitimate contractors have almost been put out of business, because any punk with a couple of automatic weapons can stop them from making a bid for the work. And the punk doesn't even have to do the work, as long as some of the money he makes finds its way to the appropriate minister, MP or MLA. The higher incidence of accidents and unpunctuality in the Railways has not *entirely* to do with obsolete technology and an increasing ratio of passengers and freight to rolling stock and line length.

*

Travelling south ten days after the daroga was shot, on one of India's most tedious trains—the Patna-Cochin Passenger, euphemistically called an Express in the official handouts—we heard a middle-aged fellow-sufferer talking to his wife and a friend about the work culture in Patna. He was obviously a Tamil, and I gathered that he worked in the Income-Tax department. He had been in Patna eight months and was already seeking a transfer to Bombay, no matter that Patna was miles cheaper a city to live in.

'You have seen the walls in the Secretariat building?' he asked. 'To a height of four feet they are covered with paan-juice. Why Secretariat, even Chief Minister's office is like that. And work culture, what work culture? Class IV fellow will come at eleven, go home at two after lunch. You cannot do anything to him or he will tell some MLA and you are in trouble.

'Yes, yes, I admit it is very cheap. But where is the safety? And if you cannot do any work what is the point in saving money? At least in Bombay work culture is there.'

Perfectly true. And the paan-chewing is one of the Bihari's least endearing habits. (The addiction cuts a wide swathe across society. Laloo Prasad made a resolution to give it up on New Year's Day 1996, but the stresses of the last few years appear to have broken his will.) As a matter of fact, the men lower down the social scale rarely chew paan; what they are constantly masticating and expectorating is *khaini,* tobacco. Wherever you go in Bihar you will not escape it.

It's prepared for consumption in much the same way that we used to process grass in college, and it forms a social bonding in much the same way that tobacco chewing in America did as Mark Twain describes it in *Huckleberry Finn.* The man powders it between his palms for many minutes and with great application, peering at it every now and then to see if it's fine enough. When it is, there's a great slapping of the palms—a tremendous sound which jerks your head up on its stalk the first few times you hear it—and a great puffing at the precious stuff to get rid of the dust and waste. He then passes it around to his cronies or any social equals with whom he may happen to be conversing, who each takes a pinch and tucks it into one cheek, and they're all set for an hour or so.

Khaini has a decidedly intoxicating effect, and as you can get a day's supply for a rupee or two (much cheaper than paan or *zarda)* it no doubt takes the place of food and drink for a while, which is important to the poor Bihari. The married women of course chew paan, and it's a pity to see so many pretty young matrons with discoloured teeth. The poorer Biharis spit where they like; in the houses of those with pretensions to gentility, you find pink washbasins. The women of some castes, and the men of all, smoke beedis.

As to work culture too, the gentleman from Income-Tax was perfectly justified in sounding off as he did. In Patna city almost the only people who seem active are the thousands of rickshaw-pullers; and even their body language as they push the pedals suggests that they don't have to do this and would rather be sitting in the shade chewing khaini. The other energetic class is made up of the railway station touts and people of that persuasion.

Even in the fields there is no great suggestion of activity. As I said, there are practically no tractors or tubewells, so everything is done in the lazy unhurried motions of what Nirad Chaudhuri called 'timeless India'. My enduring image of the rural Bihari in the mass is men and women squatting, idly talking, doing nothing. Except in Orissa, where the addiction to bhang produces an even greater state of natural indolence, I've not had a more deep-felt need to kick people's butts and say, '*Do* something!'

But what is there to do? If they do not earn a desultory living in the villages or go to Patna to starve, where do the poorer Biharis find work?

One of the most amazing sights I ever saw in Bihar was at Patna Junction early one November. The Kurla Express was about to pull in on its way to Howrah, and when the announcement of its arrival was made my companion pulled me away to the back of the platform. 'Watch out,' he said.

And when the train came in hardly any of it was visible. Roofs, couplings, windows were all one struggling, writhing mass of people. I had seen enough of train travel in Bihar by then, the ticketless perched in great droves atop and the frantic day-of-judgement maelstrom at each carriage door. This was on a larger scale, but there was something else to it, I thought as the train trembled to rest and great streamers of people flung themselves off and tangled with the rush of Patna-dwellers going further east.

Then it struck me: All these people had luggage. Suitcases, nylon holdalls, denim bags. They were better-dressed, too, than the general condition of the roof-travelling railway passenger permits: jeans, sneakers; polyester saris inside the compartments.

All was made clear. These were Biharis paying their annual visit home for Chhatth, which comes six days after Divali and is the one festival no native would care to spend away from home. Bengalis under the pressure of work will not come home for Puja, expatriate Malayalis feel less and less the call of Onam, to Punjabis it hardly matters any more where they are on Gurupurab or Divali; but nothing will excuse the Bihari who is not on his native soil at Chhatth. They were coming from Bombay, from Pune and Nagpur and Bhopal—but mainly from Bombay, and some from even further afield, from the Gulf. They were the lucky ones, who had got jobs in a city which was not Patna.

But what jobs? There are, I'm sure, relatively few

Bombay executives who return to Bihar for Chhatth and have to travel on the roof of the Kurla Express. These were Bombay's lower classes: the third division clerks, the peons, the restaurant waiters, the hairdresser's assistants. And no doubt the sweepers, the construction workers. And yet they were the lucky ones, and on every railway platform in Bihar they stood out in their aura of affluence.

Bihar exports millions of these menials. You find them in Bombay, Delhi and Calcutta, where they form a majority of the rickshaw-pullers. You find them breaking stone and carrying bricks all over the roads and towns of north India. Of course, construction workers in the north come in their hundreds of thousands from Andhra Pradesh, Orissa and Tamil Nadu as well. But to none of these states do they return as the better-off.

In Nepal there are thousands of Biharis from the northern districts, illegal entrants, stateless citizens. Even in Nepal—not a rich country—they are looked down upon and exploited, often ill-treated by the police. The Indian Consul does not rush to their defence; in fact the High Commission pretends they do not exist. They're wanted by nobody—until they come home for Chhatth.

*

It is always possible to find *some* work, wherever you are in the world. It only matters how desperate you are. What follows is not a story about Bihar, but it seems appropriate. Ten years ago, the Bombay magazine I was then working for carried a lead story on gigolos in the city, carrying interviews with many of them. It was written by Mohan Deep, who has recently produced a biography of Meena Kumari. Mohan was our expert on sleaze—which is easy to find in Bombay but slips from your fingers when you try to dig for it—and especially good on anything relating to films and the gangs. Mohan was a tough, sensitive, reliable man with his head screwed on very straight.

Mohan's gigolo story evoked a number of responses, many callers wanting to know how they could get into that line of work. We had expected that, and brushed them off. But then quite early one morning, about ten-thirty or eleven, there wandered into the office a thin, sad-looking youth carrying a cheap briefcase and dressed in long-sleeved shirt tucked into his trousers, and black shoes: I thought, a clerk in some office.

I was alone that day, as I always came in early when sober. I sat the visitor down and asked what I could do for him. 'Sir,' he said mournfully, taking a copy of the magazine out of his briefcase, 'please tell me how I can become a gigolo.'

I asked what his problem was. He said he had come up from somewhere in the Andhra backwoods for an interview, his pocket had been picked and he had no money for a ticket back. And no one he knew in Bombay. So I called Mohan and had him read my guest a stern lecture, gave the chap a hundred bucks for a ticket and sent him on his grateful way. I didn't know whether to laugh or cry. But I got back my hundred, by money order.

There are always ways to make money, to get enough for what needs to be done. If my visitor hadn't been too much of a small-town boy, he might have turned to crime. That he asked about the flesh trade only shows how much of a small-town boy he was.

There is no doubt that much of the blame for the Bihari's poverty can be laid upon his own unwillingness to work. Surely two generations of incompetent administration, lack of land reform, a decaying and corrupt educational system and a political regime based on manipulation and terror have had something to do with it; but ask the professionals, the educated and well-employed Biharis, and they usually have nothing but contempt for the less privileged. For the professionals you meet, almost without exception, come from the upper castes, and they have in a sense been freeloaders on the system all their lives.

I did not notice much of a work culture among them, for that matter. The Bihari born and bred and employed in Bihar has a curious reluctance to work to achieve something when it can be done without work—through connections, or with a bribe, or with a dharna. Professional professionals are few; and of these you will find a large number have been educated in Delhi or Bombay or, of course, Jamshedpur or Ranchi.

The newly-returned FRCS will set up a clinic at once; then he will meet the minister for health, a couple of MLAs, all the druggists and scanner operators in the area and sit back, assured of a steady supply of patients no matter what he does to them. The fresh graduate will get a hundred of his ilk and stage a demonstration in front of the Chief Minister's house, asking for job quotas or reservations. The hack will send her manuscript to Khushwant Singh, hoping for a mention in his next column which she can peddle to a publisher . . .

Of course this happens everywhere in India, and I'm not for a moment insisting that no one works in Bihar: After all, someone must be doing it, or all of them must be working some of the time. What I find absurd, amazing, about Bihar is the prevalent attitude of cynicism towards one's profession, and of contempt for the impoverished citizen who cannot or does not work.

In October 1997 I spent a week in Muzaffarpur district in

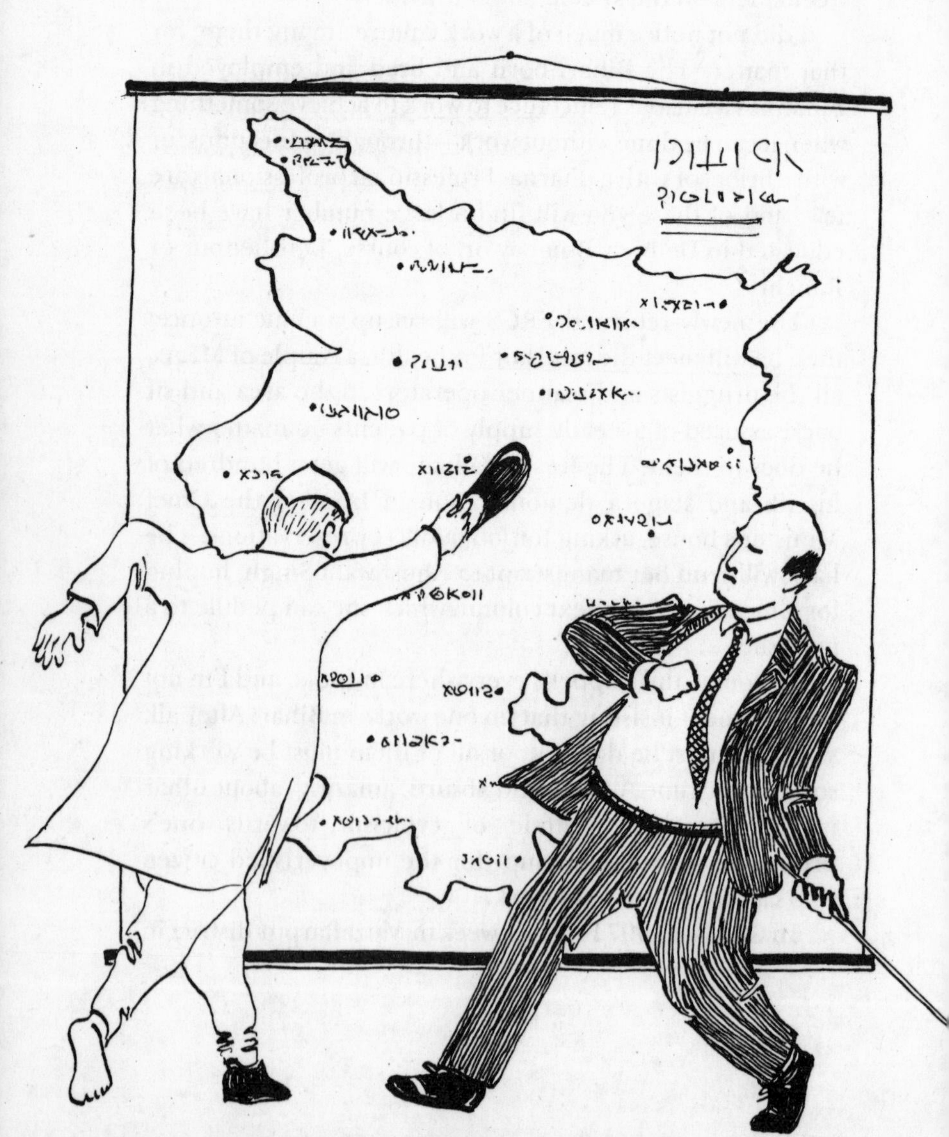

north-central Bihar, reporting on a teacher-training programme for UNICEF, who were partly funding a visionary educational project—but that will come later in this book. It was an exercise in social integration as well, and one of the trainees was an ambitious 31-year-old Brahmin who was teaching in a school where almost all the children were Musahars, the lowest of the low.

Mrityunjay Kumar Sharma wore city clothes, close-cropped hair and an incongruous tuft. He was very much a Brahmin, but fiercely proud of his students—the bright ones, that is (the point of the programme was not to discriminate against less intelligent students, but he thought that didn't make sense. Perhaps it doesn't. Anyway, it was his first experience with a new teaching system).

'Give me two more teachers and I'll educate the whole village!' he said like a latter-day Archimedes. 'How will you do that,' I asked him, 'when people don't see the advantages of education?' 'By punishing people,' he answered at once. 'Tell them they won't get their rations if they can't sign their names. In two months they'll all have learned to read and write. Some fear is necessary to spread these movements. Biharis need to be kicked to get somewhere.'

Again and again I heard this: 'Biharis need to be kicked.' From both trainees and tutors in this same programme—who all realized they were being left behind and were desperate for the state to move forward; from doctors sitting safe in their living rooms on the Hospital campus in M____ while gangsters took over the town; in casual conversations on the train. Those who said it were, of course, the ones supposed to do the kicking. I never heard any of the kickees volunteer: 'Kick me, I want to get on in life.'

This is, essentially, an NRI attitude. 'I'm not part of this society; I'm looking down from above; I'm doing all right, Jack. But just watch those lazy bastards down there.'

I remember sitting in a Birmingham suburb ten years ago, sipping Scotch and listening in horror as two Indian doctors settled in the Midlands agreed upon how to revitalize India. 'Sanjay Gandhi had the right idea,' said my host, who'd left his—and my—native village in Kerala thirty years previously and now had a flourishing practice. 'Compulsory sterilization, that's the only thing. Catch everyone who has two or more children and tie their tubes.' The other doctor nodded sagely. This was too much for me. 'Why didn't he have it done to himself then?' I asked. They looked at me, surprised. 'But he had only one child,' they said in unison.

(Imagine it: At a checkpost on the UP-Delhi border, a luxury bus is stopped. State officials with scarves around their faces swarm aboard and drag out a tall, lean, clean-shaven man with long sideburns and black-rimmed glasses, dressed in kurta-pyjama and shawl. They tear off his clothes and bring out the gelding knives, glistening in the moonlight. 'But I have only one child,' he cries, mouth wide in anguish, as the men prepare to do what they must do for the good of the State. 'I have only one child! You can't do this to *me* . . . !' Ah, sweet dreams . . .

Such expert opinion is practically unanimous in holding that Indian—or Bihari—society cannot be awakened from within. (Even the parties of Hindutva, for all their talk of swadeshi, of atom bombs in the *Mahabharata* and autogyros in the *Ramayana*, must go to Enron for a power project.) Laloo Prasad Yadav went on a brief NRI shopping binge himself, after he'd won his second term with a comfortable majority and before he got embroiled with things like cattlefeed.

This was in October 1995, and he made the same old

US-UK tour that every Chief Minister makes, selling agro-based industry, power projects, mining operations . . . Then in December the NRIs came to Patna for a 'Meet' in which Laloo indulged his addiction to rhetoric, promising them uninterrupted power, cheap labour . . . The only memorable part of the show was that Laloo attended the formal dinner dressed in sola topi and dressing gown: He'd been supervising the demolition of unauthorized constructions in the Patna city centre, for which this was his preferred garb, and had come straight off the streets to the dinner. A photograph of him dressed thus, royally enthroned among suit-and-tie-clad NRIs who're obviously uneasy, is among my prized possessions.

With Bihar politics and society being what they are, no major investment from abroad seems likely to be made; but late 1995, with the Janata Dal still united and possessed of a majority in the Bihar Assembly, was a more hopeful time.

Yet, what could the NRIs have done for Bihar? Look at the big industrial complexes that do exist in the state. Along the Ganga, in the power stations and refineries, little of the top management and skilled workforce is composed of native Biharis. I should think much the same is true of the Tata plants and the mines in the south. As I said in the first chapter, Bihar's mineral wealth does not enrich Bihar; Laloo Prasad has a genuine grouse in this regard. But bringing in NRI investment is not going to motivate Biharis to honestly enrich themselves either.

*

Use every man after his desert, and who should 'scape whipping?

—Shakespeare, *Hamlet*, II, ii, 561

There is a limit to how much government- and UNICEF-sponsored programmes can enthuse the people. A spirit of free enterprise can prosper even in a nationalized economy; but the only wildly successful kind of private enterprise I have observed in Bihar is criminal activity. And in a way even that is government-sponsored.

The main Bihar roads are unsafe after dark, but before any important Hindu festival they are unsafe in the daytime as well. Gangs of young men and boys not yet sixteen will halt your car on the highway every few kilometres and ask for a donation. (This forced subscription, or *chanda,* was first heard of in Bombay many years ago, but it is in Bihar that it really provides an alternative to employment.) Saraswati Puja, Ganesh Chaturthi, Ramnavami, Janmashtami—no matter what, they will take at least ten bucks (the minimum may be more by now) or else not allow your vehicle to proceed. The amount accepted is higher for trucks and buses, naturally.

This happened a couple of times when I was travelling with the Sisters in one of the Hospital vehicles, and I was impressed by their polite but adamant refusal to contribute. But why is this kind of extortion tolerated at all by the public? The government allows it, of course, purely because unemployment levels are so high. The answer is surely to create more gainful jobs, not permit hooliganism.

An interesting parallel to this custom is found in the old English tradition of 'hocking'. According to Brewer's classic *Dictionary of Phrase and Fable,* Hock Tuesday—the second Tuesday after Easter—for long commemorated an English victory over the Danes in 1012. (There is a description of Hocktide festivities at Elizabeth's court in *Kenilworth.*) Brewer quotes Brand's *Antiquities*:

'Hoke Monday was for the men, and Hock Tuesday for

the women. On both days the men and women alternately, with great merryment, obstructed the public road with ropes, and pulled passengers to them, from whom they exacted money to be laid out in pious uses.'

Pious uses indeed . . . How much of the tolls exacted on Bihar roads (at festival time) is spent on pujas? Brewer adds that landlords received an annual tribute called Hock-money for permitting their tenants and serfs to celebrate the day—which is to say the local dons get their cut.

Idle minds in Bihar and everywhere can be downright destructive. From not being gainfully employed, to *taking pride* in not being gainfully employed is a short step for mardangi to take—and it's not much further to interfering with those who *are* going about their lawful business.

One winter morning, stationed as a volunteer in the Pulse Polio programme at some little village, I was approached by a couple of young men. 'Who is funding this programme?' they asked me. 'Is any money coming from *videsh?*' 'No,' I lied, 'it's all Bharat *sarkar*.' 'All right,' they said. 'If it had been foreign money we wouldn't have supported it'—which means they'd have prevented any children from being brought to our team for immunization.

Just look at the attitude of these people. Immunization is necessary, that they accept. They won't arrange for it to be done themselves, but they'd rather it wasn't done at all if foreigners are paying. The attitude to Deepa Mehta's *Water* has something of the same schizophrenia: Widows may be leading miserable lives in Varanasi or Vrindaban, but it's not for a 'foreign' film-maker to depict it, whether in a striving for change or not doesn't matter.

So who needs to be kicked? And who decides who does the kicking? Go to the root of it: Who decides who's privileged and who's not?

I have seen one man whip another in Patna, and in M____ I heard of one famous kicking at least; but these are properly methods of social interaction, not of encouragement, and as such belong in the next chapter. 'Kicking' as a metaphor is a reference to the feudal attitudes which still rule Bihar society.

The entire dependence of the people is on the 'mai-baap sarkar': Whether benevolent or tyrannical, what the Guy on Top says is The Law with which there's no arguing. Not only is it The Law, nothing can be achieved without His setting things in motion. The gangsters of Laloo's rule were the mercenaries and police spies of Chandragupta Maurya's. Under the feudal system, there's nothing you can do if these guys kick you.

(Is this true only of Bihar? After the stunning Congress-I victories in Rajasthan and Madhya Pradesh in the Assembly elections of November '98, Ashok Gehlot and Digvijay Singh—who had striven tirelessly, often in the teeth of opposition from their own party rivals, to ensure success—both gave all the credit to 'Soniaji'. Digvijay Singh even said, 'If the Congress loses, the blame is mine. If it wins, the credit goes to Soniaji.' He was willing to be kicked, or at least he was willing to say he was.)

Why do the people of M____ let the 'criminals' rule their town? It is difficult to argue with AK-47s, but why did they let it all begin? They all thought someone else high up would stop it. But they *knew* Bihar politics; they *knew* the value of the gangs to the politicians. Now all they can do is hope to be useful to the gangs, or hope to be left in peace. They were willing to be kicked, and they are being kicked.

In Muzaffarpur when some of the teacher-trainees and I were talking about how to initiate change, they were unanimous in saying that the motivation has to come from above. I said, 'Why do we call ourselves a *janatantra,* then?' They nodded, struck by the cleverness of the argument. But they were not convinced.

A feudal set-up, with power percolating from above, has great stability in a society whose members have no idea of bettering themselves: It gives them security. This might sound strange to outsiders, but most native Biharis are *homesick* when they leave Bihar. They do not willingly leave the state even if the move promises a chance of betterment. So do Punjabis and Malayalis—to name two of our farthest-faring races—feel homesick; but they go to another city, or to another country, make their pile and then often come back, to enjoy in luxury what their native lands afford.

In M____, a local named Durga Paswan (his elder brother worked in the kitchen and was named Ram Vilas) did all our shopping for groceries. Twice a week he'd come home, take a list and sufficient money from me, and return an hour or two later. He was honest and willing, and literate; not only literate, but—rare for a Paswan—a matriculate.

Kavery's sister and brother-in-law in Coorg just then needed someone trustworthy to work in their house, and we thought Durga would fit the bill. We had come south by then but by means of registered letters and telephone calls (put through with great difficulty) we managed to get across detailed instructions on how he should make the long and arduous journey to Madras, then Bangalore and finally Mercara, where he would be met at the bus stand. He made it, and we were relieved; on his behalf too, for if he proved hardworking he could get a more responsible position on the estate itself, and . . . Coorg is full of outsiders who have bettered themselves and ended up with estates of their own.

Imagine our surprise and shock then to be told two weeks

later that Durga wanted to go home. I spoke to him on the phone and he would give me no reason, just kept repeating, '*Mujhe gaon jaana hai*'—I want to go to my village. They had to let him go; they gave him some money and instructions on how to get home and sent him off.

I was furious and wrote to the friend in M____ who'd passed on our instructions, 'He could easily have made a life for himself down south, and he'd have made enough money to support his mother in comfort too. But what can you do with people who won't take advantage of their opportunities?'

That was one Bihari I'd willingly have kicked.

'I was kicking someone'

A BHUMIHAR CAME ONE Monday to Kavery's out-patient clinic at the Hospital with a sprained knee. She asked him how it had happened. 'Oh,' he replied matter-of-factly, '*Main kisi ko maar raha tha.*' I was kicking someone.

The Bhumihars are the richest and most influential caste along the Ganga plain. They own most of the land (as their name seems to imply) and where they rule they have practically absolute power. It is said that their ancestors, 2,500 years ago, were early Brahmin converts to the *sangha.* When the temporal power of Buddhism began to wane a thousand years later they sought readmission into the (for want of a better word) Hindu fold, but were not given back their original status in the caste hierarchy. How true this story is there is no saying. They conduct themselves more as warrior-chieftains—but that could be because they are landlords—and invariably bear names ending in 'Singh'.

I have written in chapter one that Laloo Prasad's campaign platform in 1990 (though he later denied he had said it in so many words) had been that he would smash the Bhu-ra-ba-l—that is, the coalition of Bhumihars, Rajputs, Brahmins and Lalas (or Kayasths): the upper-caste landowners and businessmen, and traditional Congress supporters. Once he had come to power, of course, Laloo realized he could not quite *smash* them. At least, not without a redistribution of land and authority on a massive scale, and he was not yet ready for that: He did not have the numbers in the Assembly.

It is doubtful if Laloo ever really meant to reform the zamindari system, but it's possible he might have begun to do it in his second term when he had consolidated political power in his hands. Just then, however, the fodder scam, the first in a long list of corruption scandals, came to light, and Laloo had to think of his survival. He's still having to think of it and will have to do so for a long time to come. Meanwhile the pattern of land ownership remains what it has been for generations, except where leftist armies and Dalit *senas* are making their own justice.

Another problem Laloo had was that not all of the Bhu-ra-ba-l were his enemies. The popular alliance he mustered on his side, radical though it was, was not the result of a complete polarization of society. Some of his trusted lieutenants were Bhumihars; there were many he could not afford to displease. Dilip Singh, the Rashtriya Janata Dal MLA for M____ in our time, is himself a Bhumihar. So are Sanjay Singh and Suraj Bhan Singh, then the two top gangsters in M____. And so are many businessmen and old-time politicians all over Bihar whose support Laloo still needs or covets.

When the first American Sisters came to M____ fifty years ago, there was nothing there but a railway station and a ferry crossing. Also a shrine to the Virgin built by a railway owner who'd had a dream, and a Jesuit priest who had done such good work in the area that at his request the Bhumihar landowners willingly donated some thirty acres for a mission. Bhim Singh, who gave most of the land, is still around: Hale and erect, though he must be at least seventy-five, he walks through M____ every day to his fields, which are beyond the Hospital and convent. He and the one or two other Bhumihars who continue to own the greater part of the land in and around M____ are not disturbed by the 'criminals' who are probably related to them anyway by blood or marriage, if not by the ties of power.

The Sisters have left the social structure practically undisturbed. In Bihar as elsewhere in India where the Church has a hold, it is the Fathers—who do not have the security of the cloister, and most often have to work alone in uncharted areas a hundred kilometres away from the headquarters of the diocese—who get caught up in land reform or social movements and end up being slaughtered; sometimes by Naxalites, sometimes by the landlords.

The American nuns, however, knew nothing about castes and hierarchies, and treated all manner of men in the same way. It is still remembered how the last American administrator of the Hospital, Sister Mary Jude, would travel second class on the train to Patna every week to do the Hospital's shopping, would offer a chair to anyone, landlord or sweeper, who came to her office for whatever reason, and was so loved by all that when she died the rickshaw pullers and railway porters of M____ crowded her funeral.

The Hospital, and all the Order's other operations in India, are now run by Indian nuns, mostly Malayalis. They have degrees in management and hospital administration, and go to Patna by car more often than by train and to Bombay and Delhi and the USA by air. Born and bred here, they are keenly alive to social distinctions: You won't catch them offering a chair to a sweeper or calling him anything but '*tum*'; to Bhim Singh and his fellows they are all respect and attention.

The Christian missions have struck an easy and profitable balance in their mission work. They offer medical care to all sections of society, which is a very necessary service and not always performed for money; but they strive to convert only the Dalits, whom established Hinduism does not have much use for. The missions don't have much use for the converted Dalit themselves; but they have taught him English and he can hold down a post in the office; also he swells the head count, which is always of use back in the States or in Germany and Holland, where rich Catholics give generously but want positive statistics in return.

This kind of social commentary is not going to make me popular, I know. The most innocent and well-founded observation on the Church's activities now brings forth shouts of 'Hindu bigot!' and 'anti-minority!' In November '98 the Malayalam scholar Dr Sukumaran Azheekode got into trouble when he observed that some Christian priests drink more than is healthy for themselves and for their following—a perfectly legitimate and well-meant observation, because he was advocating total Prohibition. (Some time earlier he had got into trouble with the RSS for criticizing the leisure activities of a certain order of sanyasis.)

And those who *are* Hindu bigots are equally stupid. They protest against conversions. But the conversions are taking place among the very classes of society whom they or their fathers reviled and cast out. They could prevent the conversions by accepting the Dalits and assimilating them; if they're not prepared to do that why shouldn't the Dalit convert to Christianity or Islam? He is not assimilated by mainstream Christian society either, but at least he gets an education, a fair chance of a job, and the shelter of the Church . . . but more of this in a later chapter.

The shelter of the Church is not to be scorned, not in M____. We could live comparatively safe lives amidst all the violence because we were attached to a hospital, which was attached to a mission. Everybody needs medical care, and the nuns had a certain nimbus—it cannot be denied—of good works about them. In almost twenty years there had not been an instance of the criminals violating the sanctuary, not since 1979 when the parish Father, an American Jesuit named Martinsek, was shot dead because he'd asked for the return of a power generating set which had been pinched.

*

Bhim Singh came to see us one day. Sturdy—of that broadness you get at the *akhara*—with a rugged face, grey hair combed back from a profile as good as Gregory Peck's, and an iron moustache, you wouldn't have thought him a day over fifty-five. He wore a simple collared kurta and a dhoti girded up at the back, both of which had once been white. I wouldn't have known who it was if our maid hadn't seen him out of the kitchen window and urgently whispered a moment earlier, 'Bhim Babu, Bhim Babu's here.'

It was about 7.30 in the morning and Kavery had finished her breakfast. I said 'Namaskar' to the old gentleman and invited him in.

'So,' he said, 'how do you like this place?'

I said we liked it very well and would like it even better if we could leave the campus occasionally and see more of Bihar with any assurance of safety.

He nodded his head sorrowfully. 'There are such bad people about,' he said. 'M____ is not what it used to be.'

Having by now heard enough stories of what M____ had used to be like, I could discuss the subject intelligently.

When Kavery came in, of course he didn't get up. They said 'namaskar' to each other—or rather, she ducked her head at him and he joined his palms and said 'pranaam', which is the preferred mode of greeting in Bihar, only they pronounce it 'parnaam'. He then lifted from near him—he had brought it in and put it on the floor at his side but I had pretended not to notice it—a string bag with a few cucumbers and other local vegetables in it. (I don't know the words for some of those vegetables in Hindi or any other language. And to my uninstructed ear, they all seemed to be called the same thing in Bihari: *ga-* something.)

Kavery adores fresh vegetables, and could not keep the delight off her face. 'You like them?' Bhim Babu asked, grinning broadly. '*Hanji*,' Kavery assented. 'Good. Then I will bring more,' said Bhim Babu. 'And fish? You like fish?' We said we liked fish, knowing we wouldn't have to clean it. 'And ghee? I eat one *gilaas* of ghee daily, that's why I am still healthy.' He expanded a wrestler's chest. 'My wife makes it, from the milk of our own cows. Good. I will bring you some.' And he departed, evidently pleased that, though not Bihari by birth, we could yet love the highest when we saw it.

He came a couple more times, bringing a few vegetables and I think on one occasion freshwater fish. Kavery would have gone to work by then—it would be mid-morning—and I would chat courteously with the old man, give him a glass of water and then one of tea. He never stayed long.

Then he wanted a favour.

There is a Central Reserve Police Force centre some ten or twelve kilometres east of M____, and their sick were always referred to the Hospital. One day the sons of two CRPF jawans had an altercation, and one stabbed the other. These were boys fifteen or sixteen years old. The victim had been lucky: He had to stay in hospital some days, but the knife, which was short-bladed, had glanced off a rib and only torn a lung. A case was registered against the other boy, naturally.

The parents of the culprit tried to mobilize influence on his behalf, and now Bhim Singh—who was recognized as someone with clout at the Hospital, of which he was in a sense the protector—wanted Kavery to change her police report. The case was medico-legal, and charges and sentence all depended upon whether the surgeon called it 'grievous harm' or 'simple injury'. Of course, with a rib scratched and a lung punctured, Kavery couldn't call it 'simple injury', and she said so. 'The judge will laugh at me,' she told Bhim Babu. He went away without further attempts at persuasion, and he was just as affable if I met him on the road, but we got no more vegetables.

It was a month or so later, when Kishan (our friend, the medical representative) had dropped in for a smoke after exchanging insults with the pharmacy Sister, that an unexpected side to Bhim Singh's affability was revealed. 'You know all those vegetables he brought you?' said Kishan, the paan juice clogging his speech. 'Well, he'd just walk along the market road with a bag and say, "Give me some of that," and the man would put in his choicest cucumbers or whatever. That's where you got all those vegetables and fish.'

Apparently everybody knew this, and no one was surprised; but Kishan, with his fine cosmopolitan Marwari's intuition, had divined that we might not know the true state of affairs. It had never crossed our minds that Bhim Singh was not giving us produce from his own land.

*

What do you do if you are selling vegetables off a pushcart in the marketplace and the richest and most powerful landlord in the area walks up with an empty string bag and says, 'Give

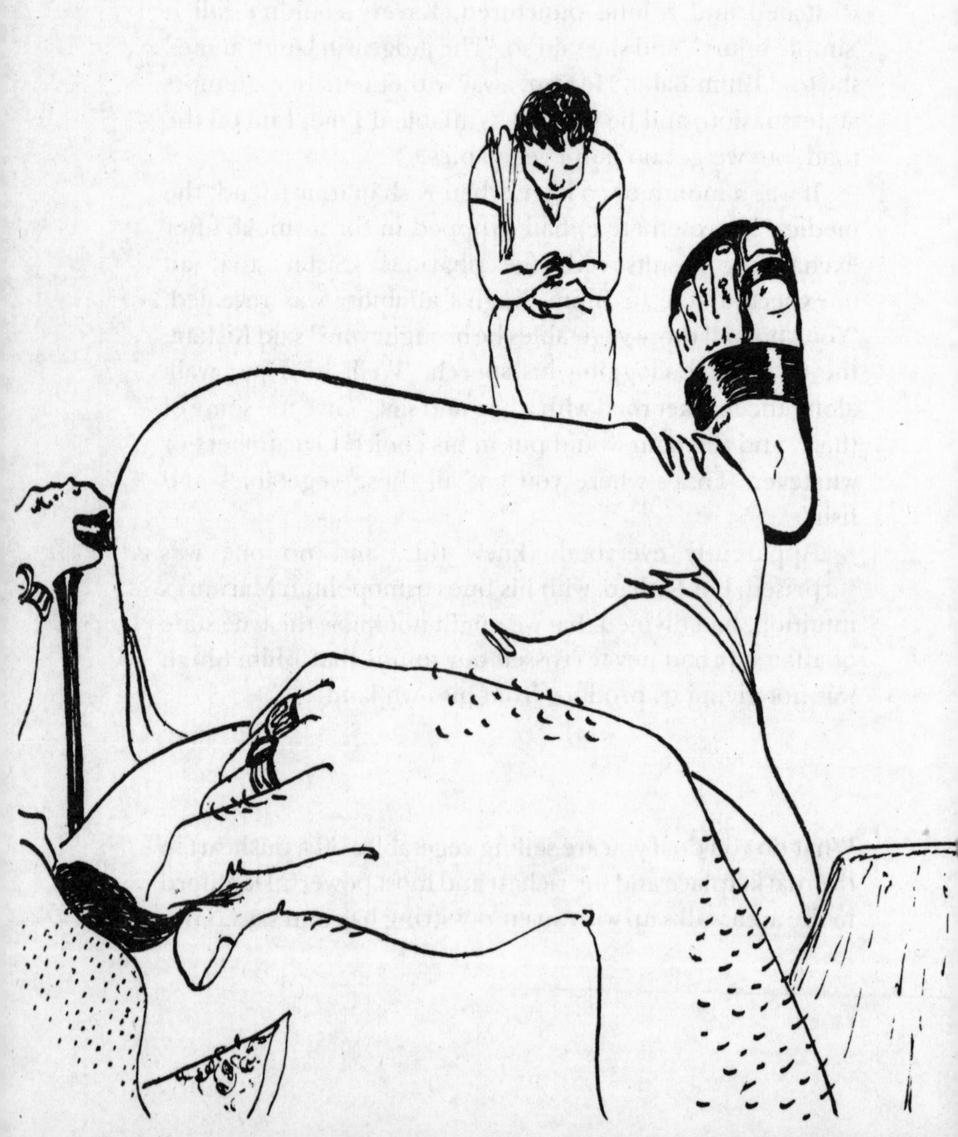

me some of that'? You're probably growing the stuff on land rented from him anyway; or else he arranged for a loan for your daughter's wedding, or got you out of trouble with the police. That's the way feudalism works: it cuts both ways.

So also, if you're a landless peasant working on a Bhumihar's fields, you don't retaliate—perish the thought! —when he kicks you. You cower and maybe smile to show you're pleased at the honour. After all, it could be worse than kicking; he could have killed you, and fixed it so your brother was arrested.

Paul Zacharia's story *Bhaskara Pattelarum Ente Jeevitavum,* on which Adoor Gopalakrishnan's film *Vidheyan* was based, portrayed just such a feudal set-up which is now happily extinct in the south (or do I speak too soon? There are still big landlords in Andhra, and other big people elsewhere, and absolute power always co-exists with a recognition of inequality). But Adoor could have gone to Bihar and filmed it from real life any day of the week. I don't know about *jus primae noctis,* but all the other trappings of sovereignty are there if you look. One reason the 'criminals' rule the area without opposition is that they are Bhumihars; other castes are used to taking it from them. The only people who are powerful enough to stand against them are also Bhumihars, like Bhim Singh, who tacitly condone the gangsters' activities so long as their own interests are not hurt.

Behind the doctors' quarters and outside the Hospital campus was an old ruined building. Its roof had fallen in, and only the old rusty red brick walls stood, twined around by green, on an abandoned plot whose ownership was probably disputed. One morning there were curious people hanging around on the road which ran past the Hospital and the ruin: town loafers from the tea-shop, passing villagers, a few rickshaw pullers. I asked what the matter was and was told a girl had been brought there at night by one of the gangs, raped and murdered. At first there was some attempt at arousing public indignation, but it was put about pretty soon that the girl was not even from M____ but from a neighbouring village, and was besides a Majhi, from a caste pretty close to the bottom of the scale. Interest waned. Though plenty of people went in to take a look, I didn't see any cops. They took the body away after a few hours. I doubt if any investigation was made, whether a case was even filed. To those who told me the story, it was just another of those things.

*

> Thrice is he armed that hath his quarrel just,
> But four times he who gets his blow in fust.
>
> —Josh Billings

The Naxalites had no presence in the area around M____, east of Patna. But their various 'armies' had begun to make trouble for the landlords in peripheral districts in the early '80s, and they soon virtually controlled large areas of Bihar. As it has turned out, their rule has not been any more beneficial to rural Biharis than zamindari has. They rule by terror, too, and kill and kiss just as arbitrarily.

The original Naxalite movement in Bihar, a spillover from Bengal, split up into factions early on, and there are now more splinter groups than one can easily recall. The major ones are the CPI(M-L) and the CPI(M-L)-Party Unity. While both of these believe in land reform, the Party Unity is opposed to elections. The only major non-Naxalite Leftist group is the Maoist Communist Centre (MCC), which believes in total annihilation of the ruling class.

(*Postscript*: I've lost touch in the last couple of years with the dynamics of the Leftist underground. But there have been reports of more dissension about the form action should take, and of tie-ups with the People's War Group in Andhra Pradesh, which is bad news. Already the Naxalite terror is manifesting itself in Madhya Pradesh, and a large swath of east-central India could pass out of the hands of political control at not too distant a date. It must also be mentioned here that the CPI(M-L) won six seats in this year's elections and has a lot of clout in a hung Assembly.)

Their power is not to be laughed away by those in the south who remember Naxalism as a movement that failed. The two main Naxalite groups (not their front organizations, but the fighting arms) have more than 6,000 'soldiers' and some influence in two-thirds of Bihar's fifty-five districts. The MCC has at least a thousand fighting men. And all the armies have modern weapons, including AK-47s and -57s.

To counter these militants of the left, the upper-caste landlords have in the last ten years formed armies of their own, the best known of which is the Ranvir Sena. The Sunlight Sena, which gained a reputation for cruelty in the early '90s, has only local influence now. In many districts, it is open war between the landlords' armies and those of the Naxalites and MCC. The police come on to the scene after the battle is fought, count the dead and clean up. They are often victims, too, of the Naxalites and MCC. In as many as forty-one districts there is extremist activity; eighteen are more or less out of the government's hands (these are statistics quoted by *The Times of India*). Not all the districts where the state is powerless are ruled by the armies; a few have a high proportion of freelances. One of these, West Champaran, is even referred to in some circles as West

'Apaharan', or abduction.

The fight is no longer ideological: Extremism is big business. The MCC and Party Unity are both commercial outfits now, and they make crores from their 'levies' on timber, tobacco and illegal mine operations. In the areas they control, they use extortion and kidnapping to keep the people terrorized in much the same way as the gangsters do in M____. Indeed, the Leftists are worse because from time to time they may rub out somebody for no reason except vaguely stated ideologies; while the gangsters only kill the innocent by accident. It is, of course, mostly the poor who suffer on either count.

In the last year or two, the Leftist armies have been concentrating on wiping each other out: They have actually made a truce with the Ranvir Sena while they battle each other. The Ranvir Sena is also making hay: While the Naxalites and MCC are otherwise occupied, they have offered their services, for payment, to backward-caste landlords who need protection. Ideology be damned; and even caste is not as powerful as lucre.

All this sounds unreal to journalists who were trained or conditioned to have at least a sneaking sympathy for the Naxalite heroes of the '70s. When I went to Bihar I had no idea that Naxalism was viable anywhere, and—perhaps because of that—I, too, shared the sympathy. I didn't actually visit any Naxalite-controlled areas, or meet any confessed Naxalites. But I heard enough to conclude that the Leftists in Bihar are no more morally armed than any other terrorists, people who like violence but like to have an apology for it. The Jehanabad killings of 1 December 1997, when sixty-two backward-caste villagers were butchered one night, were initially blamed on the obvious culprits, the Ranvir Sena; but it has since become at least a possibility that one of the Naxalite groups was responsible.

What is amazing is the openness with which terrorist activities are conducted, without any concerted retaliatory or preventive effort to rid the state of these vermin. All the 'armies' have front organizations, many of which contest elections. The others may not take part in legitimate political activity, but their party headquarters are perfectly visible. Their connections with recognized political parties, too, are not hidden. It is an open secret that the RJD has a special relationship with the murderous MCC. During the 1995 Assembly polls, the MCC's 'overground' leader Vinay Kumar Arya was seen accompanying then Chief Minister Laloo Prasad on the campaign trail, travelling in the same vehicle.

How much of Bihar is actually under the control of the government? I'd say the Legislative Assembly building and the Secretariat and most of Patna city all the time; and the rest of Bihar for varying periods leading up to election time.

Until Laloo Prasad came to power—or let's go further back, until JP's movement took off in 1974—Bihar society was fairly stable. It was built on a basis of gross inequality, but it was more or less undisturbed, static if you will. Laloo Prasad's victory in 1995 marked the culmination of the populist movement of two decades earlier. But it did not eliminate the inequality; Laloo just institutionalized it. On new, heterodox terms, that's all; now Yadav can terrorize Brahmin instead of it being all one-way.

Bihar is a stew, a *khichdi,* a goulash of casteist and economic tensions, stirred hard every now and then when elections are due. It is never given time to settle. And whatever floats to the top is scum.

*

So it's not possible to say any more that the Bhumihars and

the other landowners are on top of the heap everywhere. They are in M____, but in other parts of Bihar they do not necessarily dominate so much. In the north-eastern districts, it's actually Yadavs who have the land and influence; and they look down their noses at the rabble of Yadavs from the south and west, such as Laloo Prasad.

But in M____, as I say, they have a pretty cushy time. One Bhumihar who came to Kavery's out-patient clinic was insulted when Kavery asked him what he did for a living. '*Hum khaate hain, peete hain, sote hain, aur kya?*' he said—I eat, drink, sleep, what else?

Many of the younger Bhumihar men go to college, and some actually find jobs which do not wholly consist of kicking people. In M____ we got to know a young Bhumihar who was a medical representative (and thus in a sense Kishan's competitor). Bipan was lean and poker-faced. He seemed a bit unbalanced, perhaps because he had to reconcile his status as a Bhumihar who could kick people with impunity, to his job as someone who had to win friends and influence people. We were told he indulged in sudden fits of temper sometimes, as when he went to the Hospital's accounts department to get a bill cleared and when shown there was a discrepancy in it began to rant and rave about fixing the accounts man. He had strange silences and sudden smiles and a jerky way of biting off his words, and it was generally rumoured that he was on something more invidious than Pan Parag.

I remember when the company he represented hosted a conference for the local doctors. It was to be held in the guest house of one of the local public sector giants—Bharat Wagon perhaps. All the doctors were ready and all the ladies dolled up and we got transport to the venue. A banner hung outside the guest house announcing the conference and the sponsor's name; and that was the last reminder of any medical meeting.

Inside we were all seated on sofas and chairs both sides of a central aisle; there was a lectern in front and a roving video team. There was Fanta and Coke for the ladies and whisky with a choice of Fanta or Coke for the gentlemen. By and by first Bipan and then his Patna boss made speeches in laboured English, and a presentation in the typical style of the medical rep in a doctor's office—holding up a folder whose pages were turned one at a time to each of the various sovereign specifics manufactured by the company while its virtues were extolled in a medical-rep tone of voice. That was the end of the conference; we were given dinner and a plastic file and a plastic water-bottle each and bussed home.

No one thought there was anything strange about this. After all, the only difference from the 'hospitality' provided by pharma companies in the cities is that it's usually more subtle. Besides, there had been a video camera, and everyone was looking forward to seeing themselves immortalized on magnetic tape.

Some days later—it was a Sunday—our neighbour in the doctors' quarters aroused Kavery and me from our afternoon siesta and insisted we come watch the videotape. We went across grouchily and watched an hour or so of eating and drinking and selling. Luckily there was no soundtrack. When we ventured to suggest that the money would have been better spent on a day's free clinic in the town or something like that nobody actually responded but there was an air in the room of 'Where did these plebs come from?' All the doctors and their wives were intent on the film. I came away only with a dreary recognition of how awful I looked clean-shaven and a resolve to at once begin growing as much beard as was compatible with being able to see and eat.

Forgive the digression, I wanted to put this down before I forgot and it does give a glimpse into the professional way of life in Bihar. Perhaps it should have been in the previous chapter . . . I was talking about Bipan. He once called all the doctors home for dinner. I forget exactly what the cause for celebration was: something like a child's *mundan,* or a wing added to the ancestral house. Bipan lived in town, and Kavery and I went early so as to escape dinner; I had an article to finish. He sent a car for us, a battered Maruti 800 but in M____ that was safer than a brand-new one. We had to go through the market and down a couple of narrow, dusty galis to reach his house, an old-fashioned two-storeyed building which extended a good way from the road.

One thing about these northern small-town and village houses, you can't tell anything about the house and who lives in it from the façade, or how rich or aesthetically attuned the inhabitants are. In Bihar especially, the surest way to have 'demands' (that is, extortion) made on you is to go in for ostentation: Better to pretend there is a wolf at the door than have a gangster there in actuality, complete with automatic rifle.

We went in through the door and across a small unpaved yard where dinner was cooking: tandoori chicken, daal, puris . . . Bipan met us, pranaaming from his waist, and led us into the house proper, into his room.

The way these joint families live is invariant and—to me—stifling. It seems to be common to all communities and castes: I've seen it in the Marwari mohalla, in Patna and in the villages. Each married man gets a room, usually not more than twelve or fifteen feet square. Most of this is taken up by a double bed, built to last. Then there might be a chair or two, a steel almirah, a couple of icons holding up the wall, and among the more affluent a two-in-one. (Bipan also had a TV, and a sofa set.) Here they spend their days; the communal life of the home is in the kitchen, but this is where they rest, sleep, quarrel, procreate and bring up their young.

Other guests were brought in and seated, on the bed, on steel folding chairs. Female members of the family stood. Bipan's wife, an anaemically pretty thing, displayed her baby; other children of the family clustered around. We made polite noises about being unable to stay for dinner, and were given tea and 'snakes'. Kavery had to listen to a list of ailments on the distaff side. I asked Bipan about the house.

'Ah,' he said proudly, with the air of one who had ancestors and was not ashamed of them. 'My great-grandfather built this house ninety years ago. He had four sons, you've met the youngest'—a toothless old man who was squatting on the floor. 'They had sixteen children between them and in my own generation there are sixty-four. Most of us have children . . .' I worked out, with the help of a fascinated look and a couple of careful questions (but no one in M____ minded my questions any more—I was a journalist; besides, it's always good manners to show interest) that the house, not more than twenty-five metres along each side, presently housed one hundred and sixty-four people of all ages from eight months to eighty years.

It had become dark by the time we left, driven by Bipan in the Maruti. We had had to be introduced to a couple of local doctors and agency stringers who were drinking in a pandal outside. I was a little worried, because the 'criminals' had been active of late; a corpse had been picked up that morning near the railway crossing. But the streets were deserted. The other doctors and their families, the wives heavily silk-saried, powdered and bejewelled, were just getting ready to go to Bipan's party. An hour later our dinner of puris, tandoori chicken and its appurtenances was couriered to us. You might have insulted Bipan by disparaging his status, but you would have insulted him more by impugning his hospitality. And it is so everywhere in Bihar.

The postscript was, as usual, provided by Kishan on one of his visits. 'Bipan told the criminals that he was giving a party and nothing should go wrong,' he said. 'In fact there were armed men posted at the street corners. You didn't see them?' He laughed at my bewilderment. Bipan, it seemed, was well-connected to the gangsters, and he had an alternative method of making his way in the world should the pharmaceuticals business at any time fail him.

*

Some weeks later, Bipan threatened Kishan. There was a lot of extortion going on at the time, and Kishan had been asked for a lakh and a half—not by Bipan, of course, but by one of the freelances. As I have mentioned, Kishan's was one of six Marwari families that had not yet fled M____: The Marwari mohalla was almost deserted. The medical wholesale and retail business run by Kishan's uncle, father, brother and himself still made money.

Kishan could not (or more likely would not) pay, and had to run around town trying to find influence to bring to bear on the 'criminal' who had demanded money (the extortion rackets always made 'demands')—a small-timer named Dom who lived just outside the Hospital. (Because of the way it was pronounced, I don't know if 'Dom' was the man's

Christian name or a derogatory reference to his caste.) With the help of a couple of doctors Kishan succeeded in scaling down the demand to a few thousands, but he was under a cloud for many days.

Bipan and Kishan had been friends—indeed, it was Kishan who had introduced Bipan to us. But there seemed to be some problem now, when they met by accident they would hardly speak to each other. Bipan would be stony-faced and Kishan's lip would be curled. Kishan endorsed the view that Bipan was under some kind of *nasha*—addiction. One day Bipan met Kishan in the market and told him he'd set the criminals on him if Kishan didn't get out of town. Kishan must have lost all patience with the gangsters and their demand; he just said, '*Arre jaa, jaa,* I've seen lots of people like you.' He must have known he could get away with it, but it seemed to me a foolhardy thing to do. Anyway, there were no dire consequences.

After that Kishan made up his mind to get out of M____. By then Kavery had given notice of her leaving, and he asked us to find some opening for him in the pharmaceuticals business in a southern town with opportunities. If not drugs, anything would do: steel, furniture, cloth. I felt saddened at the way M____ got rid of its brightest; but I had no apprehensions for Kishan's success once he got out of M____ alive. He had tremendous energy, he was a real go-getter. And he'd never do anything really crooked.

That incident threw into sharp relief for me the difference between Bipan and Kishan, Marwari and Bhumihar, cosmopolitan and Bihari. The whole world was Kishan's oyster, he would discharge his family responsibilities and still be confident of doing well on his own, in a strange country whose language and customs he was ignorant of, even in a new trade. While Bipan, though college-educated and in a professional field, would in a crunch fall back on family, would assert his status, threaten instead of compete. Could he do so outside Bihar? No. That was really why these so-called upper-caste professionals were homesick away from their state: They lost the sense of caste and status which identified and defined them.

*

> I shall be an autocrat: That's my trade. And the good Lord will forgive me: That's his.
>
> —Catherine the Great

Kishan could not get away from M____ at once. There was his elder brother's wedding to be conducted. Gopal was no live-wire like Kishan, he was rather dull and stolid, with an eldest-son aura about him which seemed too weighty for words. Kishan had to do everything himself and Gopal let him. Kishan was incredibly speeded up in those days: He consumed Pan Parag and cigarettes at a frantic pace, speech spewed out of his mouth as if there was never enough time to be intelligible. I found it difficult enough to understand him when he was normal.

I'll describe the wedding and all that later, but there is just one incident from our Patna trip which belongs here. I was walking beside Gopal, astride his white mare, in the baraat, when an altercation across the street caught my eye. A distinguished, elderly gent in spotless kurta-pyjama and shawl was lashing away with a horsewhip at a tonga driver. The old chap had a grim, furious expression; his lips were pressed together into a straight line. The tonga driver was sitting in his place looking back, making no attempt to defend himself. He was trying to keep from laughing.

It appeared that the tonga had splashed through a puddle close to the patrician, and a little dirt thrown up by the wheel had soiled the bottom of his stainless pyjamas. He had seized the driver's whip and was flogging him—not very scientifically, for they weren't cutting strokes. The people on the road laughed at this scene, as did the baraatis, and the tableau soon dissolved.

Tell me, where else in India could this have happened?

Hindus are supposed to . . . well, Hindus are not really *supposed* to do or not do anything, in the sense that there is no really binding commandment. But the general understanding is that Hinduism considers all life as equally sacred. In practice today this only seems to work out to mean that killing a man is no worse than killing a fly; that you can own a man as you own a cow and whip him as you whip a bullock. Individual, family, caste: Thus run the circles of sympathy, of belonging.

I don't know . . . We had a good chance fifty years ago to make a new start, to wipe out our centuries of degradation. I don't mean what was done to us; I mean what India did to itself. The more I let my mind dwell upon what I saw in Bihar, the less hopeful I feel that we can amount to any condition which deserves the name of humanity.

'I will be dead by forty'

THEY ARE A SOURCE of constant delight to me, the clippings I have saved from the Patna edition of *The Times of India.* They conjure up, when I peruse them—two years and two thousand kilometres removed—all the oddities and peculiar stresses which are a state of mind: the state of living in Bihar.

The other day I found one from the paper of 16 April 1996. Headlined 'A bizarre case of in-laws burning youth', it dealt, in a way, with what we have come to call a dowry-death. According to the report, Manjur (*sic*) Alam was married to Shahnaj (*sic*) Begum of East Champaran district in 1995, but, said his father (who 'rolls bidis in Nepal for a living'), 'The relation with the bride's family was not very congenial since the very beginning because they had insulted the *baraatis*. So we decided not to send back Shahnaj to her parents' house.'

In course of time, the report continues, Manjur found a job near his wife's village and banked his savings with his father-in-law. But when his father came to hear of this he ordered the young man to bring back the money. On 12 March, his wife's family took him to their home saying they would pay him in full, and 'tried to burn him to death'—how, the report does not say. When last heard of, he was 'struggling for his life' in a private nursing home in

Motihari. As with most such 'human-interest' stories in our papers, there was no follow-up the next day, nor any attempt to find out what had happened to Shahnaj, who was 'not sent back to her parents' house'.

Fascinating though this story is, it's not likely to set a trend. Bihar has set many political trends—such as booth-capturing and the election of known criminals—but something tells me nothing in the way of equal opportunities, with regard to either bridegroom-burning or the reservation of seats for women in Parliament, is going to be given the great leap forward in Bihar. Agreed, Rabri Devi has emerged as a politician and mass leader; but she has not done so in her own right. She was booted out of the kitchen and on to the stage by her husband, and he did it only because he couldn't trust anyone else. Could you call Rabri Devi emancipated?

Talking of women in politics, another bit of reading matter from which I have got a lot of pleasure recently is a wonderful book called *Laloo Prasad Yadav: A Charismatic Leader* (Har-Anand, 1996), which purports to be a biography of the man. It has been written by one Neelam Neelkamal, who is (or was in '96) a professor of English at Babasaheb Bhimrao Ambedkar Bihar University, Muzaffarpur and also District President of the (then) Janata Dal Women's Cell in Muzaffarpur.

She tells with endearing frankness what high connections she has, why despite being a Kayasth she threw in her lot with Laloo (who calls her 'deviji', as he reportedly addresses all women), and how her husband reacted to her going into politics.

I shall have occasion to quote from Dr Neelkamal's biography repeatedly, it's too remarkable and revealing a document to keep away from for long. (Oops, quotes from this book are out. For some reason Har-Anand have refused permission to carry extracts from the book. It surprises me; I didn't think they'd object to a little free publicity. My guess is that Neelkamal's unhitched her wagon from Laloo's star and joined the Samata.) But it does appear that she is, by Indian standards, an emancipated woman. She wouldn't be out of place in most of our larger cities; but in Bihar she stands out like a pillar of salt.

The women we saw most of in M____ were the Sisters, of course, and the nurses and nursing students. More than half of both groups came from Kerala, and this is not the proper place for a discussion of the status of women in Malayali society. Kavery naturally saw dozens of local women every week, but she rarely had time to go into issues other than medical. Then there were the doctors' wives (Kavery was the only female employed as a doctor in either medicine or surgery and the two senior gynaecologists were nuns).

The doctors' wives were all well-educated but unemployed. They usually produced a child every two years—Bihari men who get into professional courses tend to get married in their first or second year, so that the dowry will cover the fees and also the initial expenses on beginning to practise. But this fecundity was not the reason for the women not working. One had an M.Sc. in Zoology, at least two of the others were graduates. But it wouldn't have looked right if they had taken jobs—it would have brought dishonour to the husband's family. No Bihari, unless he is orphaned, is cut off from his village and his roots, and every Bihari professional invariably makes a visit home at least twice a year. These are important occasions, and any rumour that his wife is working would provoke comment:

'She's working? In a job?'

'My cousin's brother-in-law had gone to Khagaria last

month and he saw her teaching in a school.'

'But he is doing *daktari*, no?'

'Maybe he's not making enough.'

'Maybe some people never have enough. But what about the children?'

'Maybe her family didn't give the full dowry.'

'*Hai, hai*. The poor children. Who will marry the older one? So pretty she is too, but somewhat dark. Must be getting it from the mother.'

'What would his father have said if he'd been alive? To have a bahu working in a job! Tch-tch!'

This is serious business (if you will excuse my Indo-Anglicisms: I've been reading a lot of R.K. Narayan recently). A married woman working may well find her daughter's chances of a good marriage imperilled. It is not quite so bad in the cities—but Patna is only an inspissated sample of rural Bihar—and 'lady doctors' are respected, especially when they marry doctors and set up a private nursing home in Patna. (One such couple had their business raided when we were in M____ and fifty-eight lakhs in cash was found in the house.)

Our medical-rep friend Kishan's brother, Gopal, married a graduate in commerce, who was of course not allowed to take up a job even had she wanted to. As I described in chapter two, the whole family was getting down to the business of breaking her in very soon after the wedding—why, *immediately* after the wedding. I remember the sight of the couple in their chairs of state in the pandal constructed on the terrace of her family's house in Patna: He as if preparing to be autocrat of the breakfast-table and she with her eyes fixed on her toes and her head draped, as we all filed past to offer our *badhais*. Later I saw a couple of his friends hanging around the pair, one actually leaning over her where she sat, and teasing her. Gopal looked ahead with the air of a Solomon who is putting Sheba through some age-old test of purity—or a comparison with Rama and Sita on their return to Ayodhya would be more apt. I didn't like the sight. I hadn't fallen for her or anything like that, I just didn't like the sight . . . Gopal was not a graduate, she was taller than he and much more sightly, but he was clearly conferring upon her the honour of becoming his wife. There's no chance she'll ever go to work, certainly not in a job, even if the family find themselves in straitened circumstances.

Dr Kishore, who lived in the flat across from ours, was the seniormost male doctor at the Hospital, with the exception of the Medical Director, who had been there since 1958 and was called Papa by even the Sisters. Kishore's wife, Ratna, was a lively, warm-hearted lady who had her hands full with her husband and two boisterous young sons; but she would find the time to chat with whoever passed by, and to bring us occasional sweets or meat curries she had made. I thought she was not in fear of anyone or anything, until Kishore's mother paid a visit.

After more than ten years of marriage, Ratna was still the bahu. She withdrew into the background, spent most of her time in the kitchen, smiled little and was generally subdued of tone and countenance. Kishore's mother—her husband had been a big-time politico, a well-connected Rajput, and she knew how to handle people—complained about Ratna, loudly, to anyone who would listen, including Kavery. She said that the children were given too much or too little freedom, that Kishore was eating too little or too much, that he should set up private practice back home in Gopalganj. Everything was Ratna's fault. We all defended Ratna, but it was not much use. I still haven't figured out if this daughter-in-law antipathy is put on: whether it is part of the training, or whether it is genuine. But after ten years either you've trained her or you haven't.

Ratna complained about her mother-in-law to Kavery, but only a little. There was nothing Kavery could have done, after all. There's nothing anybody can do.

*

The Bihari woman we knew best was the one who worked in our apartment, doing the floors and dishes, and washing the clothes. She was sent by the Sisters a couple of days after we'd moved in, and we never had occasion to complain or want her changed.

Her name, she told Kavery when she first came, was Pushpa, and that's what we called her. But some months later I heard Ratna, across the landing, call her 'Anjali', and I became aware there were others who referred to her by that name. I asked her one day, 'What is this "Anjali"? Is your name Pushpanjali or something?' but she only giggled and went on into the kitchen. I never got the thing sorted out. But we continued to call her Pushpa and she responded.

Pushpa didn't live in, of course; that was unnecessary and anyway we were too cramped. Pushpa lived somewhere in town, in a one-room shack as she described it to us. There are slums not only in the big cities of India; there are slums in the villages, there are slums even in the slums.

Pushpa would come to work about eight, just before Kavery left for the Hospital; she'd sweep the floors, do the dishes, wash the clothes and leave by eleven. She'd be back at three for an hour or so of chopping vegetables, making chappatis, washing dishes. She did her work well and efficiently, once we'd shown her the way we liked things. I didn't bother her and she didn't bother me. She got used pretty soon to the strange phenomenon of the husband lounging around the house while the wife went out to work. Or else she was used to it already, because that's what *her* husband was like.

A worthless fellow, from what she said, who had gone off to Calcutta to do casual labour some years ago and visited M____ a couple of times a year to scrounge money off her and perhaps try and father another kid. She had a son, about six years old, and a daughter aged about four, when she came to work for us.

Though illiterate and uneducated, Pushpa was not at all unintelligent—except when she bugged us by not considering important the way *we* wanted things. Once a week or so she'd buy fresh vegetables for us in the market: I'd give her money and a bag and a list (committed to memory) in the evening and she'd come a little late to work next morning, bringing her purchases. No matter how many times we told her to put the tomatoes *on top* of the other stuff, she'd come back with them halfway down the heap. They're going to end up cooked and squashed anyway, seemed to be her argument; why take all the trouble?

She did not seem to get the best bargains either, and we thought that surprising in a native until it struck us that perhaps she was not permitted to pick through the heaps of vegetables for the best specimens. She was probably of a lower caste than the shopmen and with gentlemen like Bhim Singh running the show there were probably heaps of differing qualities for different castes. But we never fell sick, and we had no inclination towards doing our own shopping on a regular basis.

Pushpa was thin, dark and short-statured: Women

working as she does age quickly, but she must have been in her mid-twenties. She always, in the street or when men were by, wore her *pallu* draped over her head. She had a sense of her own dignity, and—what is more rare—of others'. And she was above all a realist. She knew there was injustice all around her, and she was its victim in more ways than one, but she also recognized there was nothing she could do about it.

She was very much a realist about the *mores* of society. In the flat she would talk straight to me, not averting her eyes nor draping her head, answering my questions and sometimes volunteering remarks of her own, though naturally she was much easier of manner with Kavery. But if she happened to leave the flat after work when I was pacing the cemented walk downstairs, waiting for Kavery's return, her head would be draped and her eyes low and she would answer monosyllabically if I asked her (for instance) if she'd remembered to put *sattu* in the rotis. I realized why after a few such colloquia and stopped embarrassing her. It wouldn't be an embarrassment in rural Tamil Nadu or Kerala.

Pushpa had once worked in the Hospital itself, as an ayah, but had been let go of. The Sisters said there was nothing against her but implied, darkly, that there was something. Pushpa herself told us, when she'd got to know us fairly well, that there had been an incident with some young men. They had 'teased' her, probably knowing her husband was away and she defenceless; the Sisters had got to hear a distorted version of the episode, and they, whited sepulchres, had sacked her. But they recognized she was a rare worker and recommended her to us. Pushpa did not say all this in a tone of complaint; she said it baldly, without any self-justification.

There was of course a vast gulf between her perception of society and ours. She saw this and attempted at times to explain things to us, but was usually not successful. It was partly her Bihari: We talked to each other in Hindi, but we could manage only the simpler sorts of conversation. When the discussion became complex she would fall back on her native dialect, and we weren't terribly good either at getting metaphysical concepts across in Hindi.

I remember once, after Kavery and I had established one night that there were mice in the house, I tried to convey the fact to Pushpa next morning, desiring her to procure some poison. Very strangely, I thought, she did not seem to understand my reiterated '*chooha*', which I had thought is standard Hindi for 'mouse'. Much air-painting of the size and shape and characteristics of a mouse did not accomplish anything either. I attempted a murine squeak which died away in embarrassment. Finally I summoned up my Sanskrit and said '*mushika*'. 'Oh, *moosa,*' she said, her eyes lighting up. I wondered what Marshall MacLuhan would have thought.

When Kavery discovered that Pushpa's son was not attending school, in fact had not been registered, she tried to convince her to enrol him. (It was no use talking of both children; we thought we would make a start with the son and then get to work on the daughter. She had reported quite openly to us, without any sense of its injustice, that she gave more food, and what better clothes she could, to her son than to her daughter.) By then it was November, and Pushpa said school would be closed soon. Kavery renewed her efforts in January. The parish ran an inexpensive school near by, and we offered to pay the fees and other school costs. Pushpa would not listen, she just smiled vaguely and waved it away. Some months later, the subject came up again when Kavery was with her in the kitchen.

'*Dekhiye,*' Kavery said, 'if he has an education he'll get a better job than just cheap labour.'

'He won't get any job,' said Pushpa, the realist. I realized later, when I'd gone deeper into the subject, that this was true. He would be the wrong caste, or something; in any case, the only jobs worth getting were sarkari appointments, which necessitate a down payment far more than anything Pushpa could have afforded. He would end up among the educated unemployed, like Durga Paswan, which is more miserable than being among the illiterate and occasionally employed.

'But see,' Kavery insisted, 'when you grow old he can look after you better if he has a regular job. And he can't do that without an education.'

'Why should I worry about that?' asked Pushpa, laughing. 'I will be dead by forty.'

Kavery was so horror-stricken she couldn't say anything more, and when she reported the conversation to me, so was I. It seemed incredible that a woman in her mid-twenties, in the year of grace one thousand nine hundred ninety-seven, in a democratic republic which purports to guarantee the welfare of all its citizens, could make such a statement. The most horrible thing about it, of course, was that it was true.

*

Pushpa however got on well with her mother-in-law, who lived a few kilometres out of M____ along the road to Begusarai. She visited her every now and then, and never failed to go to her husband's house for Chhatth and Holi. I suppose the old lady (whom we never met) appreciated her son's worthlessness and Pushpa's realism.

We paid Pushpa Rs 250 a month, ridiculously low by city

standards but, as I have said before, it was high for the area, and the doctors' wives admonished Kavery not to pay more or their maids would be resentful. We gave her gifts at Holi and Chhatth, of course, and odd things now and then such as sweets for her children.

When the harvest season drew near Pushpa asked if she could come to our flat just once a day, at three in the afternoon or so. We asked why and she said she would go to work in the fields. With my memories of hired labour in Kerala, I thought this must be a rewarding few weeks for her, and we had no objection. After the first few days her face was burned almost black with the sun and she was clearly weary. Only then did I think to ask about the conditions of her work on the land.

I have gone into this briefly in chapter one: Pushpa and her neighbours would rise before dawn and walk to fields sometimes as many as six or seven kilometres away. These were probably not Bhim Babu's lands, but maybe she worked on them as well. There was certainly no transport laid on for them. They worked in the sun—and the sun of the Ganga plain scorches—until well past noon, when they set out on the walk home. I suppose they were given water to drink, but certainly no food; and for pay they got no money, but a fraction of their pickings, never more than a kilogramme or two of mustard or daal.

We tried to make it easier for Pushpa: I did the washing-up in the mornings, Kavery gave her some food to take home daily for the children and suggested that she rest for a while at home before coming to the flat. But she was too conscientious to accept that suggestion. Some afternoons she was almost faint from exhaustion and would sink onto the living-room floor as soon as she came in, and I would attempt to revive her with cold water or a cup of tea.

Pushpa's brand of realism needs some thinking about, at least from my point of view it does. She took all that she had to undergo as just part of life, her life; she accepted it all as consistent with her understanding of life. She knew there are rich and idle people; she knew there were injustices being perpetrated all around her on a daily basis; and she knew they were part of her existence. But that did not affect her actions: She did what she had to do, she does what she has to do.

I would not have, I have not had the strength to do that. My instinct is to get out of an unpleasant situation, and my advantages of birth and whatever else goes with it have made it possible for me to contrive that the change of scene works to my benefit. Education is, I suspect, the determining factor, even ahead of will-power . . . no, that's not so. Laloo Prasad Yadav had the power of will to leave a setting where the best he could have hoped for was a job as a peon in a government department, to work through school and not only to work through a political science degree but through another in law, fighting in JP's movement all the while. That took some strength, it took a sense of hurt which was transformed into strength. He may not be a *better* man than I, but he certainly is a better *man* than I am.

Does Pushpa feel no sense of hurt? It's worse for her: She is a woman. She has been conditioned, I suppose, and also her kind of realism has its strength in knowing she will suffer much worse if she fights what carries her along. Much of what activates Laloo and gives him his power is mardangi, manhood and pride of gender. 'This cannot be done to *me,*' he declares, and does something about it. Pushpa is denied access to that strength. So am I, for that matter, but never have I had to feel its lack except in situations of stress and in Bihar, and the life I have fashioned for myself permits me to get along without it, or with a reasonable and temporary simulation of it.

What imitation can console Pushpa or armour her? Damned by being born into her caste, damned by being a woman, damned by her circumstances (not least damning of which is the fact of being a citizen of Bihar and of India)—who can help her but herself, or the gods? And neither she nor I places much reliance upon any probability of a gilded papier-mâché chariot zooming down through the clouds and Nitish Bharadwaj or some Amar Chitra Katha hero beaming his silly smile upon her.

The English phrase 'a place in the sun' means a situation of comfort or prominence. There are many Indian writers who parrot the phrase like fools, when 'a place in the shade' would mean more to us. Well, Pushpa had her place in the sun all right, she would be burned black by it and she fully expected it would kill her by the age of forty.

Hers is a life whose grimness I flinch from, whose realities I am still too much of a coward to confront. I suppose it's an appreciation of reality which drives idealists to Naxalism and pragmatists to social work, or vice versa. I'm only writing about it.

*

Another Bihari woman we knew pretty well was the lady who brought us milk every morning or—her cows were erratic producers—evening. Girija Devi was a cynical old lady, with a broad, hard, flat face and a gap-toothed smile which could set into harshness very easily. She was probably not really old; like Pushpa and all her tribe she led a life which had aged her quickly. If she was not actually buxom, her many tattered draperies at least lent her that appearance; and her grey hair was always covered. She had an easy-going contempt for our ignorance and took advantage of it whenever it offered.

She would come, in the mornings, a little before Pushpa (whom she did not seem to have much use for, perhaps because Pushpa never took advantage of us) and squat just inside the door with her can of milk while I got a vessel—Kavery was usually getting ready to leave for the Hospital. We had only her word for it that the can held a litre, which we paid her ten bucks for, rather high I guess for those parts. Every month or so we would have to upbraid her for the aqueous composition of her supplies, and she would always have some excuse handy: The cow was about to calve, the cow had just calved, the cow was sick, the cow had jumped over the moon—which last she could easily have said because she spoke exclusively in Bihari, in a high-pitched contentious snarl. (That is to say, she spoke only Bihari to us, she might have known Hindi perfectly well.) Then the quality of the milk would dramatically improve after a week or so—which delay lent artistic verisimilitude to her excuse, whatever it was—and continue thus for a couple of weeks, after which it would begin to decline again.

Girija Devi had her troubles too. Her husband was a habitual drunkard who would lie in wait at the beginning of each month to take away the money we and a couple of the other doctors paid her; but she was usually too much for him. He brought the milk a few times, but I can't even recall his face. Girija Devi was smarter than Pushpa in some ways (maybe she had had more advantages): Her son, sixteen or seventeen, was in the upper echelons of the local high school. We met him once or twice. He was smartly dressed and obviously more polished than the average denizen of

M____. Of course Girija Devi's daughters, of whom she had a ragged assortment, were not sent to school. They tagged along behind her sometimes, shy and uncouth.

She was a woman of force and character, Girija Devi, and she was surely past forty and far from being dead. She seemed to have handled matters better than Pushpa had. She has sent us a couple of letters since we came away (one asking for money); she has found someone to write them for her. Pushpa, though we asked her to stay in touch and write if she needed anything, never has. It's a bit worrying. In all my letters to M____ in the last two years I've asked for some news of Pushpa, but no one there mentions her in their letters.

Girija Devi's second name leads me to think she was a Yadav. Ever since Laloo Prasad pushed his wife on to the *gaddi*, I have occasionally amused myself by wondering how different women might have adapted to such a situation. Rabri Devi, also a Yadav, has managed though not without enormous difficulties in the beginning. Girija Devi, I'm sure, would have handled it with aplomb. I don't believe Pushpa would have been able to handle it; but I don't know the depths of her courage and realism.

One Bihari woman who would have seized the chance with both hands is Laloo Prasad's biographer, Dr Neelkamal. Her book is a remarkably engineered, endearingly naïve blend of haughty self-satisfaction and abasement before the Leader, and has for me something of the relentless fascination which the basilisk is said to have for its victim. For one thing, she is quite honest about her efforts to enter politics, and what she expects from it.

No, I should have no worries about any trauma Dr Neelkamal might suffer if offered the Chief Ministership. The problem would be how to get her out of office after her term. As far as my experience goes, she is not a typical Bihari member of her sex.

*

There is no doubt that women in Bihar, or for that matter in India at large, get a worse deal than men—I am speaking very generally, you understand. From childhood on their needs of food, clothing, education are given less priority than their brothers'. Why, many of them are even denied the right to life on being born, and many more shortly after marriage.

In his collection of journalistic essays, *No Full Stops in India* (Viking, 1991), Mark Tully quotes from a feminist essay in *Seminar*:

> With Sita as our ideal, can sati be far behind? It is this overarching ideology of male superiority and female dispensability that sanctions sati and leads to its glorification, and accepts the silent violence against women that rages in practically every home across the country.

Tully himself adds:

> That statement, suggesting that raging violence is tolerated in practically every home, is surely an insult to Indian women.

Tully has of course twisted the words around: 'Silent violence raging in practically every home' is not the same thing as 'raging violence tolerated in practically every home'. But Tully has a point.

A patriarchal and in many ways basically unjust system is

tolerated in silence by the great majority of Indians. This does not necessarily constitute violence. It is a system born out of the centuries, and most Indians would feel lost without the moorings they have developed within it. For one thing, much of the 'violence' is condoned and actually committed by women—especially in the framework of the in-law relationship.

Kavery saw, in her work at the Hospital in M____, many burns cases involving young married women. In one, I remember, the woman had sixty per cent burns and was brought to the Hospital by her parents—who would not pay for or authorize treatment, because they insisted that their daughter, having been married, was the responsibility of the in-laws. While they debated the matter, the young woman died.

But Kavery also saw cases of accidents and stab wounds and illness where the grieving husband remained for days at his wife's bedside, attending to her every need as devotedly as a daughter, allowing himself rest and nourishment only at the insistence of the medical staff. One husband of a stab victim, himself thin and malnourished, was desperately keen on donating blood, and could be dissuaded only when he was told his blood group did not match hers—which was untrue, though he didn't understand the explanation anyway. '*Rishta ek hai, khoon ek hi hai,*' he kept muttering—how could their blood be different when they were husband and wife?

There are peace, and harmony, and love, and other consolations even in an order based on inequality. That is what I think too many of us citified liberals gloss over when we are too intent upon scoring points over 'the other side'.

*

A sufficiency of money makes most crosses bearable and most lives worth living; no doubt in Patna and elsewhere there are women in affluent and 'Anglicized' (why is that a dirty word?) families who live liberated and liberal lives. I do not claim to paint a picture of Bihar society in its entirety: I only write of what I've seen. I just didn't get to meet too many liberated women (other than some of the Sisters) and the loss is mine.

In 'traditional' (why, and how, is that also a dirty word?) society, it appears, a woman can be free only when she gets to the position of Matriarch. Kishan's mother was pretty unfettered. So also was the wife of Papa, the Hospital's medical director. (Papa and his wife were Catholics with a Portuguese name I was surprised to find in Bihar, but that was only my ignorance.) She was never called Mama; everyone gave her a wide berth, including Papa when he could. She had a caustic tongue and a cynical, seen-it-all expression. They had two daughters and two sons. The sons were married to sisters whom I could never tell apart. From time to time they would descend on campus, silks fluttering and perfume scattering on the winds. Their lives seemed to be less circumscribed, but who can tell?

The one class of privileged women in M____, beyond all question, were the Sisters. Of course there were divisions and degrees among them—for instance, the Bihari nuns were generally spoken disparagingly of and discriminated against by the elite group, most of them from Kerala. But on the whole they lived and ate better, and existed in more secure conditions, than their lower-caste sisters outside the walls.

But it is better for them, in every way, to stay within the walls . . . There have been few incidents of violence on the campus in the last two decades. Around 1980, two novices walking from the railway station (about a kilometre away if you cut through the railway colony) were raped and murdered; two years later the Jesuit priest of the parish was shot dead. Neither of these gruesome happenings actually took place on the hospital campus, though.

The reason there is no violence directed against the Sisters nowadays is probably because the two big local gangsters have a vice-like grip on the area. Both are Bhumihars, related in one way or another to the big Bhumihar landlords, who themselves, I've written before, are on terms of perfect cordiality with the Sisters, who in a sense exist under their aegis . . . I suppose everyone looks every other way, when they're not scratching each other's backs.

A couple of weeks after we reached M____ in September 1996, a *saathi*—someone who attends on an in-patient and is allowed into the wards—slapped a nurse. He was drunk, and perhaps not affiliated to any of the gangs, though he was reported to have been armed. The Hospital closed for a day, a silent march was taken around the town, led by Dr Kishore (who because of his political connections and Rajput family was respected by the gangsters), and speeches were made on the Hospital lawns by the Block Development Officer, the police *thanedar* and other local bigwigs. The 'criminals' need the Hospital, and the Sisters don't let them forget it.

The Order has of course the solid strength of the Roman Catholic Church behind it, which is not to be taken lightly in Bihar or anywhere else. The Sisters, as I said in Chapter Four, don't go in at all for missionary activity among the higher castes, confine their public health camps to villages and mohallas where the underprivileged and backward castes live, and do not upset the social order. They are looked upon as harmless if they do not go beyond their bounds.

*

None of my examples is representative of Bihari womanhood. Who is? Perhaps Rabri Devi? Laloo Prasad may well have intended great things for the women of Bihar (one innovation to be applauded, introduced soon after he became Chief Minister in 1990, was to sanction two days special leave every month for working women in the government services—this is from Dr Neelkamal's book), but most of his agenda for social change has been thrown off the rails.

Somehow I cannot think of Laloo Prasad as an ordinary politician. I have no doubt he meant to do a lot of good to the social order when he entered politics, and that he made his plans to carry out reforms when he first became Chief Minister in 1990. But he did not have the strength of character to hold to the straight path, which is also, always, narrow.

Ten thousand crores of rupees seems to me a small price to pay for change in Bihar—development, and empowerment, and enfranchisement, and justice. Speaking for myself (an infant crying in the night) I would let Laloo Prasad get away with it if he can deliver on his promises. A professional deserves to be paid. Let him keep the big bucks; but let him give change.

Reading, Ritin', Rimatic, and Revolution

The fourth R is Revolution

If you go south out of M____, past the Hospital, you come upon the highway, with the broad lands of the Tal spread before you. Turn right before the highway and you pass the colony of pukka houses where Laloo Prasad's government resettled the Majhis. At the other end of the colony there is a broad compound of perhaps an acre, with a couple of dilapidated buildings standing at the further end. Set into the main building is an inscribed stone which says in the chaste Sanskritized Hindi affected by bureaucrats with a feeling of inferiority, and incomprehensible to most of the populace:

> BIHAR SARKAR
>
> The inauguration of the Charvaha School of M____ was auspiciously performed [*susampanna*] by the blessed lotus hands [*paavan kar-kamal*] of the Honourable Laloo Prasad, Chief Minister (Bihar Government) at a function presided over by Dilip Singh, MLA, on 7.10.94.

Little more than two years later, the school was obviously not a temple of learning. The concrete slabs which in rural schools serve for desks and benches were pitted and unswept; in the corners of the classrooms there were unmistakable signs of inhabitation by cattle. A watchman came out of the other building to ask our business, but my companion was a government employee and put him in his place. No, the watchman said, classes were not held there any more. There was no teacher. Yes, the cattle took shelter there in the rains.

One of the Majhis we knew fairly well, a young man named Sunil, who was, remarkably, a college graduate. Sunil did some part-time fetch-and-carry work at the Hospital; that was all his degree had got him. His caste, however, had got his parents a pukka house in the colony. Sunil did get a sarkari job as teacher in a village school, but nine or ten months without a salary had dampened his enthusiasm. It was for the same reason, he said, the Charvaha school teacher had abandoned his post.

It is not uncommon for money meant for such minions of the state government to be eaten up by babus along the line. The 'commission' is an immemorial Indian custom, and villagers still have to pay a cut to get their money orders. Only, in Bihar, the percentage of the commission has been increased with reckless audacity until, as with the rural schoolteachers' pay, nothing is left at the end of the line. Sunil had been to Patna to plead his case, but an audience with even a lowly babu comes expensive.

However, one thing was clear as we talked to Sunil. His house—his parents', really—stood out in that colony of the underprivileged. It was neat, the tablecloth-sized yard was brushed and clean, and he even had a garden with roses and hibiscus probably sprung from cuttings he had taken from the Hospital. Elsewhere in the colony, pigs rooted in the filth—the Majhis are traditionally pig-keepers—and pools of stagnant water, aswarm with mosquitoes, gleamed dully among the weeds and overgrown plots of land. You could see almost as if it had been written that this house belonged to someone with an education. On our way back my companion pointed out the only other house in the colony belonging to a graduate, and it too was sparkling.

*

The Charvaha schools were a good concept, but like so many of Laloo Prasad's societal initiatives, it fell through in the execution. In M____ the school stands on the periphery of a large expanse of pasturage, where boys from M____ and some nearby villages take the cows and buffaloes out to graze each morning. The idea was that they would leave their charges within easy distance and spend a few hours being educated. ('Charvaha' if I'm not thinking of something else means 'grazer'.)

There were a few dozen of these schools inaugurated by the lotus hands of various dignitaries in many Bihar districts. Laloo Prasad did his share, for he took a personal interest in the scheme. But in only a few districts were they functioning at all in 1997, as many newspaper reports attested. Most of them shared the fate of the school in M____.

The Charvaha school was not, of course, the only school in M____. There was a parish school, under the supervision of the Church, with a nun as headmistress; there was a school run by a Marwari trust, founded by Kishan's grandfather; and there was the usual quota of government-run schools. The parish school charged fees of only thirty or forty rupees a month: trifles to us, but still beyond people like Pushpa.

The Catholic Church has always known that the best way to spread the Faith is through education, and Ignatius Loyola, Francis Xavier and their Jesuit followers founded schools which were for three centuries some of the best in the world. In Bihar, the best schools—outside Jamshedpur and Ranchi, I suppose—are still Christian. The way to spread beliefs is to catch 'em young, and it was very foolish of Laloo's revolution to neglect this.

Laloo, having himself clawed his way to two degrees, realized that education for all had to be the cornerstone of his social revolution. But there are too many interest-groups to satisfy; and 'education for all' has joined the herd of milch cows kept by a corrupt bureaucracy.

College lecturers and professors do usually get some part of their salaries most of the time. But in 1997, the universities of Bihar were in severe financial crisis. For several years past, teachers had been drawing only about two-thirds of their pay; their provident fund contributions had not even been deposited. The government, it appeared, was 'unable' to pay the required sums of money to the universities. Magadh University, it was reported, was owed Rs 111 crore.

Given such hardships, colleges and universities—or at least certain individuals concerned with running them—found ingenious ways of supplementing the pay they received.

On 11 May 1999, *The Week* reported the Vigilance Department filed an FIR against former Bihar Minister of State for Education Jitanram Manjhi, Primary and Secondary Education Secretary S.K. Negi, and Vice-Chancellor of Lalit Narain Mithila University Jai Kishan Yadav for involvement in a fake B.Ed. degree racket, later naming Vice-Chancellor of B.N. Mandal University Dr A.M.S. Abdul Mogni as well. Eighty-four persons are accused altogether; thirty colleges affiliated to four universities (Magadh and Vinoba Bhave, besides the two above) are reportedly tainted by the scandal.

It used to be common practice for Biharis to return to their state with well-sounding degrees from fictitious colleges elsewhere in the country. Now with typical Bihari enterprise, the business has been indigenized; more than that, it has almost been legitimized. A cheapjack artist sitting in an attic and turning out forged certificates is one thing; the Vice-Chancellor himself affixing his signature below the names of students who have not passed their examinations is entirely different.

That's putting it broadly. The Vice-Chancellor himself didn't sign anybody's degree certificate. What Mogni did, apparently, was to permit affiliation to the university of various private colleges, some of which did not exist, without referring them to the University Affiliation Committee. The National Council of Teachers' Education has reported that only nine of forty-six B.Ed. colleges in Bihar had full affiliation. The racket is making Rs 200 crore a year, and buyers come mainly from Andhra Pradesh, Gujarat, Madhya Pradesh, Rajasthan and West Bengal.

You can't say Biharis don't think big!

*

And they attend to the details too. The doctors at the mission Hospital in M____, all MBBSs, were forever writing the exams for admission to post-graduate courses. They never made it, not because they weren't bright enough but because they had not been trained well enough during the degree course. One of them told us how preparations were usually made for the PG exams: 'There are ten papers, so ten of us get together and pay Rs 10,000 each. With a lakh, we can bribe the university clerk who handles these things to give us seats next to each other, in the same row. Once that is arranged each of us picks one subject to learn thoroughly and then we're set.'

Copying from each other, and the use of unfair aids generally, is such common practice in the northern states that it hardly needs to be written about. A year or two ago when the Uttar Pradesh government planned to introduce a piece of legislation that would provide for stricter invigilation, students across the state protested so violently that the bill had to be shelved.

In Bihar MBBS students need some kind of advantage, because they are taught very little during the course which they cannot gather from textbooks. They commonly finish their six or eight or ten years in medical college without ever having witnessed the simplest of surgical operations, much less having performed one. A professor hesitates to pass on his skills, because next thing you know the student might be setting up a private clinic down the road from his own.

Medical students in Bihar are often married in their first or second year, as I mentioned in an earlier chapter: They need the dowry to pay their fees. All in all, it's an expensive business getting a medical degree, if you count sundry expenses such as Rs 10,000 to ensure the right seat in the right hall, and perhaps a tip to the invigilator on your way out.

It's not very much better in the south. Capitation fees, donations and so on ensure that you complete a professional degree course in debt—at least to your own family—and any ethical sense you had on starting will have been leached out of you. You get out of college wanting to, needing to make money, and you don't care how you do it. Why blame the doctors and engineers? All they are guilty of is following examples set by the leaders of the profession and of the country. And the leaders are the fellows who jet to Texas for an appendicectomy at state expense.

As some columnist recently pointed out, V.P. Singh has been in London for quite a while now for medical treatment. So he does not have much faith in the quality of Indian doctors. And what has been responsible, more than anything else, for ensuring their poor quality in the last decade? (*Postscript*: I read recently, in a newsmagazine, that V.P. Singh spends six months every year in London because he needs dialysis, and the water in India isn't pure enough for it. Why can't he use Bisleri?)

*

I don't know how many crores went down the milch cow channel with the Charvaha schools. But in October 1997, with much fanfare, the third phase of the District Primary Education Programme (DPEP) was launched in seventeen districts of Bihar, and many other Indian states. The cost of DPEP-III in Bihar alone is a little over thirty-five crores of rupees; but it's not the government's money. It comes through the World Bank, from Japan and Australia among other countries, and is disbursed by UNICEF.

I was lucky enough to get a look at primary education in one district of Bihar, because UNICEF asked me to do a report—not on DPEP but on Ujala, the teachers' training component of the Bihar Education Project (BEP), which had been instituted some five years earlier. Someone at UNICEF Patna knew the Sisters, and so . . . it was what has been called the Keralite mafia at work, you can say. Anyway, my visit to Muzaffarpur coincided with the inauguration of DPEP-III and all the associated tamasha, and I spent the best part of a week in the district visiting schools and observing teachers' training programmes, and so can offer some privileged information.

The best way to begin is to quote my report for background information. Muzaffarpur is not 'typical' of Bihar, but the extent and variety of its problems are.

> Muzaffarpur, with an area of 3,122.78 sq km and a population of 29.538 lakh, is one of North Bihar's larger and more important districts. (The Division is also headquartered at Muzaffarpur town.) It is still largely rural, and most of the workforce is engaged in agriculture, with the few industries (plastics, pharmaceuticals, concrete casting, pipes and pumpsets) centred on the one town of importance.
>
> Demographic trends are disturbing: The 1981 ratio of 963 females to 1,000 males had fallen to 904 just a decade later. Literacy rates are also not a cause for pride: In 1991, the male literacy rate was 48.3 per cent, the female 22.43, and the overall rate 36.11—all lower than the figures for Bihar, which are themselves below the national average.
>
> Among the Scheduled Castes, who at 15.72 per cent make up an appreciable fraction of the population, the literacy rate among females is a mere 4.59 per cent—lower, again, than the state average of 7.59. [Ye gods, what dismal statistics!] Though the Gross Access Ratio of 74.79 per cent and the Gross Enrolment Ratio of 74 are both considerably higher than the state averages, the Retention Rate of 22.5 is much lower—reflecting the widespread use of child labour, particularly at harvest time. [This gobbledygook refers to the child's easy access to a school, the percentage of children who actually enrol and the percentage who regularly attend school.]
>
> Social barriers to literacy and empowerment in general are conspicuous. So is gender discrimination. It was for all these reasons that Muzaffarpur was one of the earliest districts picked for implementation of the BEP, in 1992-93,

and going by figures the drive for enrolment especially has met with success.

I shall quote verbatim from the report wherever it helps, since I have permission to do so from UNICEF. But to start with,. I'll put down what the strangest part of the whole experience was: The *bhaav* which my Kerala origins generated. As the launch of DPEP–III was happening at the same time, I attended not a few functions at which Kerala was lauded as the great beacon of hope in many speeches, and in more than one song about literacy.

Also, many people were not quite clear just what my role was, and word got round that I was a sarkari babu on some kind of tour of inspection; that I had come from Kerala to see what was being done in Bihar. One headmistress even requested my intercession in some matter of transfers from her school. It was all very embarrassing.

And I was even more embarrassed when we left Bihar and moved to rural Kerala, where Kavery worked briefly in a hospital near Thekkady that we had heard shining reports of but which turned out to be run by a charlatan and a crook, who was locally revered because he invoked the name of Jesus every few minutes. That's when I realized that a high literacy rate can coexist with a great lack of social awareness; and anyway Kerala's hundred per cent literacy rate is in part just a business of juggling figures.

*

From Patna the road to Muzaffarpur crosses the Ganga by the never-ending Danapur bridge and passes through Vaishali district, which is as beautiful as its name. The national highway near Muzaffarpur is one of the most horrible roads I've been on, with great excavations pitting and seaming it and making travel an agony as you're hurled from one side of the bus to the other.

After a night at the District Education Office hostel in Muzaffarpur town I got a lift to the District Institute of Education and Training (DIET) in Muraul a couple of hours away, a really beautiful spot by the Gandak river, or rather one of its canals. Here—all the primary schoolteachers in Muzaffarpur district already having been trained—there were two batches of teachers from Bhagalpur and Purnea who had already started their ten-day training course.

I attached myself to the Bhagalpur batch, mainly because of the senior trainer, Shiv Shankar Pandey, a short undistinguished gentleman with immense belief in what he was doing. Undistinguished only at first glance, Pandey ji really had tremendous presence; and when he adjured me on the third day not to drink in my room in the evenings I obeyed at once.

The training exercises are simple games, designed to get across simple concepts. I won't describe them; there are enough professionals from many fields involved in the DPEP, including journalists. The teachers, of all ages from twenty-five to fifty, participated with gusto. The students of many of them must have been amazed to see them behaving like children. Pandeyji handled them very well.

The one concept the trainees had difficulty with—perhaps because the trainers didn't seem to believe in it wholly either—was that of Minimum Levels of Learning (MLL). Essentially, this means it's more important to bring every student up to a certain level of competence and knowledge than to coach the brighter ones and let the less bright fall by the wayside. At primary school level, I suppose, this makes sense; but in our weirdly competitive school system—through which all these teachers had themselves struggled—the glory which a good student brings offsets half a dozen who're not going to make it anyway, and will only have to write their names when they need to collect money orders or fill out sarkari forms.

In the chapter headed 'Biharis need to be kicked' I quoted Mrityunjay Kumar Sharma, the Brahmin teacher in a Musahar school who advocated spreading literacy by cutting off PDS (ration shop) facilities to the illiterate. I spoke to him at length, because he was the most impressive of the Bhagalpur batch, impressive because ambitious. Alone of all whom I met, he attempted (with fair success) to speak consistently in English. It was an uplifting and saddening interview, for he is a model of so many bright young citizens who cannot get to do what they want to do, yet do not give up hope.

Mrityunjay was thirty-one, a teacher for two years and the only teacher at a primary school near Sultanganj, with seventy-eight students in Classes I to V, ninety-five per cent of them Musahars. When I asked him why he became a teacher, he said, 'I wanted to become a doctor. But my family is very poor—my father is a farmer—and I couldn't afford to write the entrance more than once. Also I have five younger brothers and a sister.

'I needed some job, I worked for some time in an office but I didn't want to be a clerk. Since I was denied the chance to become a doctor, I wanted to do some other service. For four or five years before doing this BPSC selection I was giving English tuitions. My students did well. Some of them got into engineering, another into the IAF. He came and touched my feet. . . All this gave me the impression this is the right job.'

Mrityunjay enjoyed the training ('it gives us inspiration

from within') but wasn't sold on the MLL. 'The biggest thing for me was, I was always very result-oriented. I always gave special attention to the more intelligent boys I was tutoring. In my school too I have been giving more attention to ten good students. I devote one hour to them alone.

'Here with MLL the emphasis is different. I had discussions with my colleagues; they ask is it fair to pay more attention to certain students. I thought about it for one whole night. And I decided I won't leave those ten. They are my pride. But now I think I was doing something wrong in neglecting the others. I'll give more time to them.'

The interesting thing is that Mrityunjay personally had no caste problems about his students. Musahars are the lowest of the low—as their name implies, they are rat-eaters, anathema to practically everybody else; Mrityunjay is very much a Brahmin, wearing a token tuft with his city clothes... I only call this interesting because not being from Bihar, or indeed from a background where caste was at all important, I did not know the dynamics of such a situation. But Mrityunjay was aggressive about it:

'I was once teased by boys of the Brahmin mohalla about teaching Musahars. I told them, "Very well, you bring the brightest boys from your school and we'll have a competition." They agreed and my boys did better. Since then the Brahmins have been asking me to accept their sons as students!'

He was full of pride as he said this, not the social pride of one who has scored off the Brahmins but the pride of the teacher whose students have added lustre to his name, the pride of Drona after Arjuna captured Drupada and brought him back as *gurudakshina.* The society is strong which has such teachers; but that same society, with its bureaucracy and government regulations, makes the task of those like

Mrityunjay even more difficult than it naturally is.

'There are no qualified science teachers in any middle school in Bhagalpur,' he said when I asked what he thought of the system. 'We who are B.Sc.s are wasted on primary schools, because all postings are based on seniority. Why should this be so?

'My colleagues in the district who are my own age, we're young and eager to change things. We made a suggestion to the BEO [Block Education Officer], put those of us who are good teachers and anxious to achieve into one school, let there be one school like this in each Block. Then see what we accomplish in one year. The BEO said it was beyond him.'

The suggestion is, of course, against all such democratic concepts as MLL. But the system's reaction, and its style of functioning—however democratic—do much to ensure that quality doesn't get found out, either.

*

Two days later I visited a Musahar school. It wasn't, of course, a Musahar school officially; but other castes refuse to let their children associate with Musahars, so any school in a Musahar locality becomes quite soon a Musahar school—assuming of course that the Musahar children attend it. The headmaster of this school was an elderly Maithili named Jha; he, like Mrityunjay, had no personal fears of caste pollution. But he had faced problems from high-caste neighbours who reproached him for allowing his students to bring water from the well for him to drink, or tea on occasion. He did not have Mrityunjay's fire to challenge his neighbours to a contest; he was an old man and clearly thought education was above all these trifles.

The Musahar children were almost all unwashed and

underfed, with the straw-coloured hair and pot-bellies which accompany kwashiorkor. It was difficult to get any direct response from most of them, though one or two grinned impudently at the strangers. The one room (maybe fifteen feet square—the school had become pukka but three years ago, and the building had come from the Jawahar Rozgar Yojana) held some thirty children from four to fifteen years old. The students themselves were in Classes I to V; and it's common for school-going children in the villages, particularly girls, to take younger siblings along. The oldest girl had just been married and covered her head proudly with her pallu and would not look at us. The others had no inhibitions after a while, and when Pandeyji, for my benefit, put some of them through a rudimentary test while Jha looked on paternally, they participated with gusto.

The room was fairly clean and the walls were covered with the bright charts and pictures which properly go with the New Education. That is one blessing trained teachers have brought to rural schools. Jha was a prime mover in local cultural programmes, and the children sang out their lessons in words he had written, to tunes he had composed. He was proud of them; but he lamented their fate once they passed Class V, for they would not dare attend the local Middle School, which was in a 'forward' mohalla. However, he said, even if these children did not go beyond Class V, 'they will send their children to college'.

There was no question of textbooks in that school. But the children had been taught to recognize the alphabets, and to write their names. To find so many children in school was itself unusual, but the harvest was long over and the floods had not receded. The best time for rat-catching is before the harvest when the field-rodents are rife amidst the grain. The Musahars have traditionally performed a most useful service.

We went to at least a dozen schools in the four blocks around Muraul in four days. The others were very different from the Musahar school. Large bare buildings, the roofs usually tiled or tin-sheeted; large bare playgrounds. The children wore uniforms, though most went barefoot; the classrooms were equipped with all the usual accessories, but play equipment was largely absent except for goalposts. The DPEP, of course, targeted only primary schoolchildren, so while their classrooms were bright with charts and pictures and games the middle school still learned as I had in my schooldays and no doubt my father and grandfather had done in theirs.

The school buildings were not well-maintained; they could not be. One headmistress told me that the Rs 2,000 she got annually from the BEP was insufficient for the school's upkeep—hers was the best-kept school I saw—and she had to appeal to the local MP or MLA for doles from their discretionary funds.

In more than one school, classes were held outside. The rooms were usually leaky, or cramped, or unwholesome. The best room was usually used to store grain in—parents of school-goers get a few kilos every month as an incentive or compensation for the loss of a pair of hands in the fields. One school was fortunate to have a large banyan in the grounds, and all the children were ranged in orderly rows in its shade, with their teachers in chairs before them.

The campuses I saw were all neat and sanitary, with no toilet or garbage stinks. The lack of playground equipment was probably the worst hardship, but teachers who could devised ingenious ways of getting round this. The banyan-tree school included among its teachers an ex-Army man who was at least fifty but amazingly fit. He had induced the girls to play kabaddi, and produced a champion team.

While we were there they put on a match, junior girls against senior. The juniors won handily. They were quite good. Often denied opportunity and always denied privilege, the children were yet encouraged to make use of their talents. More than once I was told that this girl had won the district competition for best singer, or that boy was the fastest runner in five blocks. Life in the villages of Bihar is not what we know it to be in the cities; but it's foolish to think these children must be underprivileged *because* they are Biharis. Bihar is not the malaise, but perhaps a very visible symptom.

*

My visit to Muraul coincided, as I've mentioned, with the inauguration of the third phase of the DPEP in Bihar, and a number of functions had been got up with *dhoom-dhaam* and tamasha to mark the occasion. On 27 October all the schools we visited had speeches and some cultural programme to be sat through; also doubtful samosas and jalebis and very sweet tea, later in the headmaster's room. I vividly remembered the description in *English, August* of some more high-powered party: 'The green chutney which accompanied the samosas seemed to look up at him and say, "Hallo, my name's cholera, what's yours?"'

The biggest function was at the middle school in Dholi Bazar, run by a formidable headmistress named Veena Chaudhary. She stood up in front of the local politicos and teachers—all male—on the dais and made a speech saying 'We women will get our rights only when we take them.' Not a sentiment which endeared her to them, as sour looks and sour remarks testified. But there was no doubt she ran the school well, if the way she ran the morning's proceedings was any guide.

Chaudhary had a formidable record as well. She had been teaching for twenty-five years, she said; and when rural and urban teaching cadres were merged in 1978 she was the first teacher in all Bihar to leave the city for the village. In 1978, there were seventy-five students (two-thirds of them boys) in the six standards. Now, in Classes I to VIII, there were about 750. Two-thirds were still boys, but 250 of the whole were from the Scheduled Castes and 200 from the Other Backward Castes. Attendance, according to her, varied from sixty to seventy-five per cent, which is pretty good for a village.

Training, she said, had a positive impact; but as only primary school teachers are trained under DPEP, only Classes I and II benefited. 'The ones from Class III onwards are no good. They are from the city [Muzaffarpur], they can't teach and are spoiling the students. I banned them from bringing their knitting to class. I make sure they lose attendance if they don't sign in time. That's why they go around saying I'm the most *badmaashi* headmistress in the block.'

But training was, to her, a tool, and not the most valuable one either to a teacher. Listening to her I found just what havoc a rigid and reasonless bureaucracy can wreak on the educational system. 'Two years ago nine male teachers were transferred from here and in their place I got six women who are no good. I have no maths or science teachers. A science teacher, a B.Sc., was promoted to be headmaster of a primary school on account of seniority. Is there any sense in this?'

Mrityunjay had told me the same thing. Naturally, I had not known about it; but equally naturally, given the ways of government, it's bound to happen. A young science graduate who teaches science in a middle school will grow old enough to be promoted to headmastership; but he will get the smallest school going, which will be a primary school where science is not taught. The teacher the middle school gets in exchange is likely as not to be an elderly person without a degree who will be lumped with science anyway.

There is a certain beautifully screwy logic to all this, like in a badly-planned murder whose perpetrator remains undetected.

I learned a little about the problems of running a village school from Chaudhary—not least of which is how to ensure that children attend. 'You must understand that most guardians [officialese for fathers] here are small businessmen [Dholi Bazar, as its name implies, is a local market]. They don't want their children to stay on at school after lunch, but to help with work. What we do, we make them leave their books here when they go to lunch and shut the gates after them, so they have to come back.

'Besides, we don't distribute grain under the noon-meal scheme to those with less than eighty per cent attendance, or to those who run away after lunch.' Such norms are strictly beyond her competence to decide; but she had in twenty years won the guardians' support:

'At the beginning there was opposition to me because I am from a forward caste and most here are Harijans. But in '79 I called a mass meeting of the villagers and told them that I am not from any caste: Teacher is my caste. There are now students from twelve nearby villages here, and more Harijans than in any other local school.'

Training was important to Chaudhary; but she said again that it was not the most valuable of a teacher's tools. 'Primary education can only be successful when parents are enlightened. Their attitude is, "After education there are no jobs available, so why educate?"' And unconsciously echoing

Mrityunjay—and probably a host of other teachers—she added, 'We are liable to punishment if we don't work properly. There should be some such punishment for parents too.' But strong-willed lady that she was, she had won over most of the guardians of her wards. 'I tell the parents at festival time—Chhatth and Holi—if you are planning to buy your children new clothes, buy them school uniforms.' And did they? With the ghost of a smile she answered, 'They have been very supportive.'

And as a government teacher for twenty-five years, Chaudhary knew her teaching was not what made *her* most valuable to the government. 'We have so much extra work to do,' she mourned. 'Census—and not just people, livestock too; then election duty, distributing grain. . . Why can't we be allowed to just teach?'

*

I don't suppose the mandarins at UNICEF liked it very much that the teachers I found most impressive, in their philosophy and in their classrooms, I also had to report as being least impressed with the whole business of training. But maybe they had already had such reports from the other hacks who'd visited the districts; maybe no one reads the damn reports anyway.

Time after time I was given statistics off the cuff about the number of teachers who are 'born teachers', the number who can be motivated, the number who don't improve no matter what training is given. . . and these figures (apart from the first category, 'born teachers') differed very widely depending upon who was giving them and what her or his place in the training scheme was. But I'll never forget what one teacher told me, and she the most motivated I thought.

Praveena Roy handled Class VIII at a Girls Middle School (in reality co-educational) in Dholi, not far from Mrs Chaudhary's school. I'd seen her in the classroom on a visit and was most impressed by how she could be kind without losing her firmness. The best teachers are, I think, like that. She was also a strikingly beautiful woman. . . Later I saw her at Dholi Bazar during the function and Mrs Chaudhary seemed to think highly of her. Then one evening she visited the Muraul DIET.

For some reason, the trainer, Pandeyji, stuck around during most of my interview, and I couldn't very well ask him to leave. Perhaps Mrs Roy was perceived as a bit outspoken. She wasn't very well liked, possibly, also because though never trained herself under the BEP she had often attended the DIET as a trainer. This was because the former principal of DIET, one Dr J. Jha, had also been impressed by her and sought her assistance.

An MA in history from Jabalpur, she later took a two-year diploma in teaching from the same university. She had been a Bihar government school teacher since 1990. Though introduced as Mrs Roy, she wore no bindi; I heard later from Pandeyji that her husband, a local Bhumihar landlord but a progressive one, had been killed by one of the leftist senas a few years earlier.

Mrs Roy was hesitant to speak out in Pandeyji's presence. But at times she could be scathing: 'When Dr Jha was here the teachers at the DIET were disciplined. They are not now; they don't remember they are role models for the children [since Dr Jha left the institute had been without a Principal]. And there are some aspects of their personal behaviour I don't want to speak about for the record.' It's very likely that her widowhood had made her to be thought easy prey; not that the marriage tie means much to goondas in Bihar, or almost anywhere in India. But teachers are not goondas by profession.

Later she said, 'In primary school it is more important to build consciousness than to impart facts. Children run away from their books if learning becomes like work. . . Here the main problem is poverty. A boy has to collect and bring home fodder and firewood, a girl has to go to the fields and help with the harvest.

'Students have no caste-consciousness; but teachers and parents do. It's a great barrier to literacy. Caste and party affiliations . . . how do we tackle problems like these, when there is no value for teachers here?'

Why did she say that, I asked, and she echoed Mrs Chaudhary, 'There is more of a burden placed on teachers by the government than by the school. Census, Pulse Polio, elections, health tests—all these paper horses (*kaagazi ghode*) are more important than teaching, apparently.'

Yet she was happy teaching. 'I could have had a wide choice of professions, with my education, but from when I was a child my father told me, You will teach children. And I never want to do anything else.'

When Pandeyji had quit the room—someone called him—Mrs Roy was bitter about teachers who thought of their work as a job, and of their salary more than their students. Her view was that if you need to undergo 'motivational training' to do your job well, you had no business taking up the job in the first place. Of course, she was from a background which obviated any necessity to work for a living, and far too many teachers are not.

Earlier, seeing her reluctance to comment on Pandeyji's enthusiastic support of training schemes such as Ujala, I'd ventured to say, 'I think Praveenaji is not a great believer in sarkari projects. . .' She had only nodded then, but when

Pandeyji was away she said with vehemence, 'I have no belief in any project. Motivation is from the individual; communication has to be with another person. After all, language is that which the other person understands.'

I'm supposed to be a writer, and I thought about that for a long time.

*

Shiv Shankar Pandey himself was very keen on training, and not I think because his job behoved him to be. In the absence of a principal he was the senior man at the DIET; though headmaster in Motipur, he had been for over a year on permanent deputation at Muraul. He had been a teacher since 1977; in 1996 he had taken his BA in Hindi and also been one of thirty-odd resource persons chosen by the BEP in a state-wide competition.

He lived very simply in one of the small houses allotted to trainers at the DIET. When I visited him there one evening he seated me on the bed, offered me refreshments, and called his teenaged son and daughter in to touch my feet because, he said, 'it is our custom.' He followed all the rules of his caste and family as strictly at home as he disregarded them outside; or, rather, in the classroom his caste was 'Teacher', the same as Mrs Chaudhary's.

I'm not going to relate any more of what I was told about training; but Pandey's ideas of his role as teacher chimed well with Mrs Chaudhary's and Mrs Roy's, and are worth giving:

'The point is to make oneself a model that children will respect and follow. For example, here I get food in the mess for myself because I work here. But I don't get food for my family: That is not ethical. From my own daily routine—in the mornings I can be seen working in the garden, or collecting firewood—I try to set a model for the trainees, be they adults or children.

'My attitude is this. Say I'm training, at one time, thirty-five teachers from fifteen schools; then at least 1,500 students are going to be influenced by one word I say. I have more responsibility here; that's why I opted to leave my school and come here.

'After all, a child is a bank draft for one crore or one *arab*—who knows what it will become?'

He had had the same problems in his village which other Brahmins have when they teach lower-caste children. 'The Brahmins of my village once threatened to deny me food and water [the local form of excommunication] because I interacted freely with the Musahar children. I don't take them seriously. Refusing food or water because it is unhygienic is one thing. Caste has no place in schools.'

*

Once teachers leave the cloisters of the DIET and return to their schools, I can imagine that the first fine careless rapture imparted by training—the games, the concepts, the fellowship, the community of idealism—begins to evaporate a little. There is the intolerable burden the government places on them every month or so: Officiating at elections, keeping records . . . each involving much weary paperwork.

Then there are the local problems, the old ones of caste and community; persuading children to come to school in harvest time; coping with leaky buildings; managing without textbooks, blackboards, sports facilities.

And on top of all this is the heartrending fact that the sarkar is mightily uninterested in their hard work. No one from the District Education Office bothered to turn up, I was told, at any of the DPEP-III functions in Muraul block; also there were no inspections, no guidance, no answers from anyone in that office at any time.

And then think of the middle school headmistress whose science teacher is transferred as headmaster of a primary school just weeks before the yearly examinations, on account of seniority. Think of the fresh and eager B.Sc.s who are set to teaching six-year-olds while science is taught to those about to enter high school by old-timers with Intermediate degrees dating back thirty years.

With all this, indeed, Why to Teach?

*

The last two people I interviewed in Muzaffarpur district were unusual in being highly qualified yet working in a field which did not appear to give them opportunities commensurate with their ability. The first was a thirty-year-old trainer, Nagendra Kumar Paswan, with vision—and ambition—seemingly beyond his scope. He had taken his MA in Economics some ten years earlier, taught in a private college for two years and in a primary school for four before joining the BEP, where he had been engaged for two years in training. (Much as I hate to bring this up, his caste—he was a Dalit—had probably made it difficult for him to get a better job: He was not only ambitious but also very intelligent.)

He began by saying, 'There's too much emphasis on training teachers and not enough on training the community. VEC [Village Education Council] training was different in the beginning when we had just a few schools in each block. Now that we're broadbased, VEC training is non-existent.

'What happens is that the *mukhiya* [headman] or some other powerful person grabs hold of the VEC and packs it with chamchas. Or teachers manipulate its working to get decisions in their favour.' (The VEC is meant to play an important advisory role. Mrs Chaudhary had earlier told me how she had swayed opinion within it, though she was the wrong caste, by force of argument and personality. This can cut both ways.)

After detailing his views on training, Paswan went on to motivation. 'Ten per cent of teachers are born. [How often I'd heard this phrase by then!] Even without training they're effective. Other teachers don't want to work. They're into politics or *dalali* [touting], or they're MPs' or MLAs' men. Or else Teachers Association men—they're all *kaamchors* [shirkers].

'It's true what the slogan says—when you educate a man you educate a man, but when you educate a woman you educate a family. The Mahila Samakhya [these Samakhyas are organizations of women in the villages who set themselves certain social tasks; I have heard good reports of their work even in the Champaran districts] is a very strong concept; but here most members are themselves illiterate... Attendance [in the schools] is still very low, about forty to sixty per cent on average. But it's still a start, and it's improving all the time, because our commitment is genuine.

'Look at it this way: You need community and social awareness to bring about total literacy. But you need literacy to bring about awareness. You see the problem?'

That had already occurred to me. But the fact that the problem has been solved elsewhere means that awareness can be produced among the illiterate. Think of the Independence movement; think of Kerala. (I put into my report to UNICEF some thoughts on my home state which might have been true, but which I may have put less idealistically after what I was to experience there quite soon. . .)

I met twenty-eight-year-old Amarendra in Muzaffarpur town the morning that I was setting back for Patna and thence M____. His qualifications were quite stunning. An MA in economics from Agra, he had also taken a Ph.D. in rural development from the (highly esteemed) A.N. Sinha Institute of Social Studies in Patna; and he now had a deferred Fellowship to work on a comparative study of poverty in South Asia at the Woodrow Wilson Institute in Washington, D.C.

What is really stunning about all this is that you don't expect to find someone with qualifications like these in a small Bihar town, and then to be told he is only an Assistant Resource Person in the BEP, while practically overseeing teachers' training in the whole district. This is where seniority-based norms for promotion and the generally red tape-snarled functioning of the BEP at the government level gut the system—for Amarendra told me, off the record, that he *was* bitter about his lack of opportunities, despite some backing from UNICEF, and that he would be leaving to take up his Fellowship pretty soon. He's across the black waters by now, I guess, and will he ever come back?

I asked Amarendra why he had decided to work in the field, and he replied, 'The hypothesis of my Ph.D. was that poverty alleviation programmes have not made a dent on poverty in Bihar. There are several broad reasons why: Poor implementation; the structure of society; the lack of awareness . . . But to my mind primary education is the key factor. For instance, the uneducated cannot know what schemes are available for their benefit. I wanted to get first-hand knowledge of this lack.'

Did he think people are overly dependent on such schemes and projects, on the *mai-baap* sarkar? 'No, the reactions of the people at large are always that the government will not do anything for them. What we do—if we are messengers of change—is to make them do it themselves. We are only catalysts.'

Amarendra, at my request, then defined the Minimum Levels of Learning (MLL) more clearly than I'd ever heard it done; he also spoke about the lack of resources: 'In Muzaffarpur district we have set a target of 300 more teachers by the year 2000. You see, in DPEP-III the World Bank has set a condition that any existing vacancy should be filled by the state government. Future vacancies will be filled at the Bank's cost. To this extent, we are dependent on the Bihar government. Yet they treat this project as another source of money, while we deal in faith.'

He added, 'Caste and social problems have diminished in the last few years, since the backward castes were empowered. The main problem as I see it is that teachers are aware of their responsibilities but don't *want* to teach. For them, it's a job—not a mission.'

*

This chapter is very different from the impressionistic style I've perforce used in the rest of the book, and maybe I've gone to such lengths just to show I *am* capable of conventional journalism. Maybe not. I know there are a number of journalists and social workers and NGOs who have been associated with DPEP all over India, and I'm sure they would be interested in what's going on in Bihar.

But having caught some glimpses of the work that's going on, I am intensely interested too. Surely there is truth in Amarendra's contention that primary education is the key to poverty alleviation, even if it's not the whole truth.

Above all, I've quoted at such length from my UNICEF report to show there *is* good work going on in Bihar, and no scarcity of motivated workers. Those who write off the whole state, those who persuade themselves nothing can be done, are doing so for selfish reasons.

No, there is no dearth of schemes and volunteers. The thirty or so women who were raped by goons of a local politician in mid-1999 had assembled at the local centre of one such scheme for training. And despite their experience, volunteers will still come forward—as they are doing in Rajasthan, in Andhra Pradesh, in Mozambique, Nicaragua and Vietnam.

As I've been saying in every chapter, Laloo Prasad's coming to power in 1990 was the first ray of hope for the underprivileged in Bihar. He has, unhappily, let his chances go, and his time is so taken up now by just staying alive that every spot of brightness on his original agenda has been dimmed and dirtied by its use as a weapon in the battle against his enemies.

Laloo Prasad is still the most important man in Bihar. But he is not synonymous with the state—except to media analysts with fifteen seconds' worth of wisdom for the camera. Someone else will turn up. The things that have to be done will be done.

Bihar rides the two-headed tiger

All the ills of democracy can be cured by more democracy.
—Alfred E. Smith

Indeed, you won the elections, but I won the count.
—Anastasio Somoza, replying to an accusation of rigging

1. The sixty-percenters

A Bihari gentleman wrote an angry letter to my paper after my first essay on living in Bihar had appeared in its pages: 'Who is this fellow, where does he come from, and are things so wonderful where he is?'

Touché. No, things are not wonderful anywhere. It was after our Bihar experience that we moved to my home state of Kerala, and there are a lot of crooks there too. There's a lot of violence everywhere in India, and there's a great deal of corruption. But nowhere else I've been have the two settled down so happily together and begun to raise a brood of healthy children.

The jewel of my collection of clippings from the Patna *Times of India* was pinched by someone at a party in New Delhi in '98. I recommend a search of the files for 1997 to anyone who can. I won't remember names, but the gist of the news report was that a group of 'intellectuals' were in a state of terrible indignation and planning to complain to the

Bihar Governor and the Supreme Court about a minister in the state government. (He was in charge of either Public Works or Human Resources, or maybe something else.)

The 'intellectuals' had met the minister to protest about the high incidence of corruption in the departments in his charge. The minister had yawned and told them in a friendly way, just instructing them about Life, 'See, graft is all right up to sixty per cent. If it exceeds that only do you need to complain.'

I don't think Kerala could beat that.

*

Laloo Prasad Yadav, in his seven years as Chief Minister, did many good works for the disadvantaged of Bihar. Among the most important affected the fundamental machinery of democracy.

Prior to 1990, polling booths at election time, in most of rural Bihar, were located in the mohallas of the 'forwards'. The Yadavs and Dalits were saved the trouble of walking to these areas and standing in line for hours in the sun: Their voting was very kindly and diligently done for them.

It was only after Laloo became Chief Minister that polling booths were established in the 'backward' mohallas as well, thus literally enfranchising those who had had no say in government. And if this was done, in some instances, at the expense of the 'forwards', I don't think it was any great loss.

It is also true that Laloo's personal feeling for the disadvantaged is deep and genuine. His own travails as a boy herding cattle, insulted and *used* by the landowning castes, are vivid in his memory and responsible for much of his original political agenda. There are stories about how, when he drives out of Patna through the Majhi slums by the Ganga, he stops and asks after the residents by name . . . 'Phuluwa Bai! How is your son? Good, good. Tell him to keep going to school, there's nothing like education. *Haan,* look here, I'll be coming back this way in the evening, so take this hundred rupees and get a chicken and make sure you've a good dinner waiting for me.'

This is powerful stuff. Does anybody think Phuluwa Bai and all her neighbours won't vote for Laloo Prasad without thinking?

And yet that is—or was—not why he did it, not just to get votes. There is a profound empathy between him and his constituency. And his gestures towards their aspirations, their empowerment, have also a touch of the dramatic which we Indians cannot resist. I have heard that he once turned out the Patna Fire Brigade and dispatched them to a Majhi mohalla to give the inhabitants a good bath. Clean water is hard to come by even on the Ganga's banks.

But how did Laloo Prasad come to power in 1990 anyway, if the dice were loaded against him? How did he enfranchise his constituency when they could not cast their votes? He did not have the vision of a Jayaprakash Narayan or a Mahatma, the moral power to inspire a non-violent mass movement. Quite obviously—obvious to him—he used the weapons of the power elite against themselves, and those weapons are not lightly cast away once used. They have a tendency to stick to your hands; if you drop them, they will be used against you. He who rides the tiger does not get off it again with any degree of impunity.

Stories of rigging, booth capturing and even assassination are easy to come by in Bihar in election time. Also large scale bribing. Essentially, the power brokers were bought over—and don't tell me high-souled statesmen like

V.P. Singh knew nothing of all this (I'm speaking of 1990). Where those who controlled the election process could not be bought over, the unempowered were empowered, literally—they were given arms and told to go out and seize their democracy. A resident of a Dalit mohalla told me of how he and his neighbours were woken up at midnight and given fifty guns and as many bombs.

Laloo Prasad's tactics enabled his fellow Yadavs to be just as brutal, exploitative and undemocratic as their former oppressors. And not to them alone: For the Yadavs are just as much part of the caste hierarchy as the Bhumihar-Rajput-Brahmin-Lala ('Bhu-ra-ba-l') coalition, and when they got the chance they turned quite naturally to oppressing those *below* them, the Paswans and Majhis, the Doms and Musahars, as well as the Brahmins and Bhumihars above them. There was good cause for the bitter rivalry between Laloo and his former henchman Ram Vilas Paswan; also for the battle between Laloo and Nitish Kumar, who is leader of the Kurmis who are also backward.

That second rivalry does not qualify for the term bitter; Laloo Prasad does not appear to have abandoned the Kurmis as he has the Paswans, he's just shelved them. In a speech in the Bihar Assembly during this year's NDA fiasco, he is reported to have actually said (*Outlook*, 20 March 2000) that Nitish and he had been 'like Billa and Ranga, but unfortunately, you left me'. (What on earth does that mean? That they were both confessed rapists and killers, but Nitish Kumar reformed?)

However, though Laloo Prasad had the votes of his fellow Yadavs and other traditionally depressed castes, he could not have brought them to his side without enlisting the support of a portion of the power elite. Here, of course, V.P. Singh, from a former royal family, and other 'forward'

Janata Dal leaders helped him immensely. And there was no way he could just dump them once he came to power; no way, then, that he could ensure a completely successful social revolution.

With a corrupt power elite in place, corruption remained the force behind government. The newly powerful too used corruption to cement their hold on power: Corruption became a means of ensuring social justice; it also became the end, the proof that a just society had been constructed. Any Bihari patriot can point to a newly rich Paswan or Yadav and say, 'This is successful democracy.' Bombay exhibits much the same evidence of a democratic system's success. By the standards we have set for ourselves, our democracy is a success because anyone, regardless of caste or creed, can use corrupt means to rise.

Kipling called India, in *Kim,* the only democratic country in the world. But the fact that a Muslim can deny a Hindu his vote, or a Jat swindle a Bania, or an Oraon murder a Bhumihar—or a Sikh convert a Christian—is not proof of an equal or just society. It's merely proof that human nature can transcend social boundaries.

Corruption is a great leveller. In Bihar it is slightly more inevitable than death and a great deal more so than taxes. Anticipating my Bihari correspondent's rejoinder, Yes, there is corruption in every state of the Republic, but nowhere in so pandemic a form as in Bihar. We all got so worked up over Bofors ten years ago, but what were the takings there?—a measly sixty crores or so. The fodder scam alone has been worth a hundred times that to the men who have governed Bihar in the last decade and a half; and that means not only Laloo Prasad but everyone since the forgotten Karpoori Thakur.

*

In every chapter of this book, corruption—the use of money and therefrom power—is the principal character. It pervades every sphere of life, every field of activity. Bofors! It was the centre of national attention for half a decade. But in an earlier chapter on education I have quoted the National Council of Teachers' Education as stating that the fake degree racket in Bihar was worth Rs 200 crore a year. And it doesn't even make the front pages.

Why is there no popular resentment of the level of corruption? That's easy to answer. You only hear the privileged grumble about the scam, because it's their money—or money which would have been put to use for their benefit—which is being eaten up, and the privileged are relatively few in Bihar. The poor do not pay taxes and have no use for civic amenities, and the all-pervasive graft is usually scaled down to within their means by the time it reaches them. And the well-off do no more than grumble for one of two reasons: Either they have their own little piece of the action, however infinitesimal; or to do more than grumble would swiftly invite a look-in by the other head of the two-headed tiger the state rides, which is violence.

When I was working in Bombay, ten years ago, I was told that there was placed on the Chief Minister's table in Mantralaya every day one crore rupees in *hafta* money; cash. I have also met a printer and sometime journalist in Delhi who carried one lakh in cash in a briefcase to the bedroom of a former Finance Minister, even now a big shot in the Congress (I), as 'commission' for having been given the contract to print the Party's election posters. One lakh over two decades ago means a lot though it sounds like chickenfeed now. The biggest problem with journalism in this or any other democracy is that you can't print all you know, even if you want to . . . but we'll go into that later.

Yet despite the emasculation of their democratic power almost everyone you meet in Bihar is politically sensitive to a point which seems ridiculous to an outsider. I wonder how many who read this would be able to name their MP and MLA, let alone those of a dozen neighbouring constituencies. In Bihar chance-met citizens will tell you all the names of all the area's politicos, trace their antecedents—political and genealogical—and confidently state what particular pie each of them has got his hands in up to the elbows. This is a staple of everyday conversation.

At the Hospital in M____, too, political talk was common. Soon after we got there the fodder scam became big news, and we heard references to bullocks riding scooters and tankers full of cattle some weeks before such items made the national press. Dr Kishore, our neighbour, was a politician's son, and Kishan, the medical representative, was always full of the latest gossip from his frequent trips to Patna, and we were kept well-informed. They would drop a dozen names in the course of a quotidian dialogue. Yet, is this political *awareness?* It means nothing; it only begins to matter when people use their knowledge to do something for themselves.

The bachelors who dwelt in single rooms upstairs were, I think, all or almost all Dalit converts to Christianity, who most of them worked in the community health department of the Hospital. They did not speak much in front of the doctors, but as an outsider I struck up a rapport with one or two of them. I accompanied the community health team on several visits to nearby villages: This was always refreshing and taught me more than the drawing-room gossip ever did.

One of the villages on the regular menu I shall call Mailpur, and it was fifteen kilometres away. A dull and bumpy drive in the hot season; but in the big floods of every ten years or so, an infinitely more adventurous trip by boat. We drove one morning, after an early breakfast, some three kilometres in the department's jeep to a point where the road became only a thin cart-track; there Ashok, the driver, left us having been adjured to return at 3 p.m. A boatman from some nearby village had already been engaged, and we climbed into his craft: I know nothing of boats but this was a flat-bottomed scrap saved from the junkyard, some fifteen feet long and five or six in the beam.

I have described in a previous chapter how the Tal is one vast lake during the big flood, beautiful and useless. It was pleasant in the morning to sit in the boat—on the thwarts; there were no seats—and talk. There were seven or eight of us: two Sisters, two of the community health 'boys' and two or three nurses and I. There were also two boatmen. By the way, it was no rowboat, it was a punt. For some distance there was enough clearance for the skipper to use his fifteen-foot pole, but as soon as the main channel of the flood diverged and strayed among the fields, the first mate had to get out and tow. Those twelve kilometres from our point of embarkation took the best part of the morning.

It grew hot, too; there was nothing much to see except water and more water and spoiled fields, and desolate pump housing—before flood-time the wise farmer unbolts his pumpset, if he has one, and takes it home, or it will be stolen.

Now and then in a tree we would see a long brown snake coiled among the branches. There was no other sign of life for miles. We came to a village at last and drew past it, and the ladies muffled their noses. The name of the village I have forgotten, but the *ladki-log*—as the 'boys' referred to the nurses—changed the sound of its name very slightly and called it 'Paijna', which is crude dialect for 'toilet'. The smell was incredible, and the flood waters distributed its cause impartially.

There was nothing to do for three hours but talk, and wonder at the unbelievable waste of water. A few months ago the parched hectares had been crying out for it, and now they cried against it. The rains had ceased, but the land would not be cultivable until the water had evaporated in the fierce sun. And soon after that water would be scarce again. Even now the dry districts to the south needed water.

How easy to build and maintain a simple irrigation system, a few canals and dykes and bunds. In Tamil Nadu, I remembered, the tanks and 'anaicuts' built by the Cholas were still in use after more than eight centuries. The Ganga plain had been cultivated for even longer. Surely in Asoka's time the blessed water had not been wasted like this.

It wouldn't have taken much money to do it, but all the money was being eaten up. And things were worse every year. As I was writing the first draft of this chapter I heard floods in Bihar in the 1999 season had claimed 221 lives, and that's only what the government was willing to admit. And what about the loss to property, what about the invisible and incalculable loss because the water is not used?

Akhilesh, the leader of the community health youths (who taught me much about Bihar) was thinking the same thing. 'Yes,' he said, 'a few canals to carry the water to where it is needed, and both that area and this would benefit. Then,' he added half to himself, '*yahan sona ugalega, sona.*' Gold will grow here.

I remembered the Manoj Kumar song:

Mere desh ki dharti. . .mere desh ki dharti
Sona ugale, ugale heere moti. . .

Only in college we foul-mouthed and lustful youths used to sing it differently:

Mere desh ki dharti, khul gayi dhoti
Dikh gaye heere moti . . .

I wondered if people like Naipaul and Nirad Chaudhuri had been correct; if this was a land that had been raped so often its cultivators had no longer any rights, if its inhabitants had lost that essential spark of humanity which provokes people to fight back for themselves, to better themselves.

It had been a rich land and productive until—until when? For more than two thousand years successive empires had made their centres of power here, armies had conquered and conquered again and always the land had tempted, because the Ganga brought its riches every year. The sixty-percenters had always been lured here, and always lifted the dhoti and taken away the family jewels . . . Democracy had changed nothing, at least not this corrosive brand of democracy, born of blandishment by banditry, a brew of taxation and pillage so finely blended one could not be told from the other.

What was illegal any more when a minister, having taken his oath to the Republic and sworn to protect the Constitution, could tell a delegation of public figures that sixty per cent off the top is only reasonable?

II. The other face of the tiger

> The conquest of the earth, which mostly means the taking it away from those who have a different complexion or slightly flatter noses than ourselves, is not a pretty thing when you look into it too much.
>
> —Joseph Conrad, *The Heart of Darkness*

I'll write about what went on in Mailpur elsewhere; but our voyage back was much swifter and more comfortable than the journey out. The wind was in our favour, and the skipper and his mate jury-rigged a kind of mast and attached to it something like a ragged bed-sheet, or perhaps his spare dhoti. This worked remarkably well, and no punting had to be done.

More than two-thirds of the way back, just before we drew into the swollen main channel again, I saw something round and white, with black strands attached, lying in some reeds at the foot of higher ground. Akhilesh had seen it too, and he said with an uneasy laugh, '*Kisi ka sar kaat diya*'—someone's head has been cut off. It was indeed a skull, and a woman's presumably from the long hair; it had been cut off, most likely with a sword, and though the cut seemed clean the lower jaw appeared to be missing.

We passed perhaps five metres from it, and all our eyes were fixed on the ghastly object. No one said anything. What was there to say? Swords are common enough even in this age of Kalashnikovs; and in Bihar you don't have to go particularly far out of your way to see an intimation of mortality. There wasn't any point in going to the police, of course; they had enough fresh corpses to ignore or inter.

> PATNA, June 27. At least 88 human skulls were seized at Patna railway station today, according to police.
> The Government railway police officials told PTI that the skulls were found in a polythene bag lying unclaimed in the room of ticket collectors. They said so far no arrests have been made. An investigation had been ordered . . .
>
> — A 1999 newspaper report

The staid dictionary I subscribe to doesn't admit it, but I'm pretty sure 'skull' was once used as a colloquialism, in either the US or Britain, for a ticket to a show or game. Perhaps some connection with scalper, too. . . How fitting, how *congruous,* to find eighty-eight skulls in the ticket collectors' room.

I've seen many weird things at Patna Junction, but never a skull in the bare sense of the word. This grisly news item reminded me at once of the skull in the fields I'd seen almost two years earlier. Eighty-eight skulls all in one bag could have almost any explanation in Bihar; from being the fetishes of some grotesque cult to being the relics of passengers whose train had suffered an unusual delay.

Of course the truth, which a newsmagazine later made clear, was more prosaic. This bag was only a token of the racket which supplies medical colleges with portions of the human anatomy. It was illegal, naturally, and no one claimed the skulls.

But I wondered, that day sailing back from Mailpur, if we had seen not one skull in the field but eighty-eight, what would we have done? I suppose we should have reported it: Even in Bihar, eighty-eight skulls in one spot takes some explaining. But say five or six?

I'm not sure. I guess we'd have sailed on by.

I just hope those eighty-eight human beings were dead *before* their skulls were detached.

*

Violence was something we could expect every time we stepped out of the Hospital Campus. I don't say it ever happened; but it could be expected. It wasn't unlikely. One evening Kavery and I were walking outside the quarters when we heard the rapid chatter of automatic gunfire from the town. We stood outside, waiting for Kavery to be called to the operating theatre; but in a few minutes two of the boys who lived upstairs came screeching back through the gates on a scooter. William Williamson, whose scooter it was, was a Tamil from Jamshedpur who had just recently joined the Hospital as X-ray technician. He was unused to the pace of life in M____ and was ashen and stuttering:

'I'd just gone to the market to buy eggs. I'd given a ten-rupee note to the shopkeeper when someone opened up at the top of the street. He was firing down it in our direction. The shopkeeper downed his shutters at once, we just jumped on the scooter and fled.'

Ranjit, the laconic and handsome local on the pillion who worked in accounts, was clutching a bag of groceries and was more casual about the whole thing. 'It was just some guy skylarking,' he said. After half an hour I heard them drive off again to get the eggs. The shutters would have come up again in five minutes if it had been just someone skylarking, and Ranjit was right.

We had heard stories about the violence in M____, and in Bihar generally, before coming, but we had had no idea how common it was. We had reckoned on occasional murders and dacoities, not things that went bang in the night every other night.

Everyone, even in the south, has heard stories of the violence in Bihar. A classmate of mine in college, Krishna—this was fifteen years ago or more—got his first job after graduation with an engineering company which was putting up conveyor belts at some power plant in the Dhanbad area. He had an old Bullet then, which he had spent much time and money on maintaining and was keen to take with him. I remember he used to go out to the Marina with it and practice making U-turns in the sand in top gear; because, he said, he'd heard the *dakus* in South Bihar specialized in blocking a lonely road at night with a felled tree, and the only thing you could do if you came up against something like that was to turn right round and make tracks in several opposite directions.

In our time, the roads were so bad it wouldn't have been any trouble making a U-turn. You never would be in top gear, even if you were foolish to drive alone on a lonely road at night.

Krishna didn't take his Bullet with him, but he came back with a few stories. He told us of how the tribal people were being corrupted, how they were persuaded to sign away their rights to the land for a few cases of country liquor. I'd only read about that before, with the American Indians and the Polynesians.

Some days after we'd first reached M____ in '96, a shopkeeper in the market was shot dead in his sweet shop, in broad daylight, for a few kilograms of *mithai.* Five men had come to the shop and asked for the sweets, then refused to pay. The shopkeeper naturally, but stupidly, refused, at which angered by his lack of bonhomie—it was the festive season—they shot him point blank.

I went into M____ many times, to buy this or that, to catch a train to Patna or a bus to Begusarai, usually returning after dark. I never had any trouble, but it wasn't really advisable for a foreigner to do it. The gods who look after fools and madmen and drunkards guarded me. But there were many times, especially on the trains, that I felt violence only a hair's-breadth away.

More than once there was a dacoity on the railway line the day after one of my trips. In one of these, a doctor from the Hospital was among those robbed. Of course nobody on Bihar trains carries much money: He lost a couple of hundred bucks, and his watch chain being unlinked it had ridden up his loosely rolled sleeve so the dacoits didn't see it. After that I carried most of my money in my shoes, and wore a cheap watch; but I kept something, 200 rupees or so, in my wallet so that the dacoits wouldn't shoot me out of frustration.

With Kavery I went by train once to Delhi and twice to Calcutta (the first time we had been to that lovely and paradoxical city, which I hope is never renamed Kolkata because that's a rice ball Tamils eat). To Calcutta the first time we went second class, and if Kishan hadn't been there to see us off we wouldn't have got our berths. They were occupied, but Kishan with his usual chutzpah—he was only five foot four or so—rousted out the big man sleeping on one of the berths and bullied him into going elsewhere. The second time we travelled AC sleeper.

Our tickets to Delhi I found to my horror had been booked second class in one of Kavery's moments of mental aberration. It was too late to change, and we risked it. We must both have been mad, I more than she because I'd enough experience of Bihar trains, mad for she actually wore jeans and a T-shirt during the journey. I almost got into a fight to save her *izzat*—izzat is a very precious commodity among us Biharis—but I'll tell that story elsewhere.

*

Train dacoities and fights are small-time stuff. The real violence was in M____, almost palpable at times even in the cloister we were residents of. There were two gangs of 'criminals' in the town, and when trouble flared up between them a hush fell over the Hospital campus too. We became used to hearing the rat-tatatata of automatic arms, often in the middle of the night, sometimes soon after dusk, once or twice around dawn.

After the first few such incidents we became resigned to the fact that Kavery would almost inevitably be called to the operating theatre. 'Oh shit,' I would mutter as I got from under the *razai* and out of the mosquito net and stumbled towards the intercom while Kavery got out of the other side of the bed and struggled into her clothes, saying, 'I hope they're dead.'

This is not really as nasty as it sounds, for on almost every occasion those killed and injured were 'criminals'. On one horrific morning it was different. We heard the gunfire very early, long before a winter sunrise. One of the gangs had ambushed the other. Among those killed was an eleven-year-old girl who had been brushing her teeth on an upstairs terrace and had leaned over the parapet to see what was happening. But usually the gangsters were considerate enough to only eliminate each other. There were plenty of willing, and able, replacements.

Other people shared Kavery's sentiments, and some of them had been put to more trouble by the gangsters' activities than merely being routed out of bed at two in the morning. In late 1996 the lieutenant of one of the gang leaders, a much-wanted man named Ashok Singh, was brought by the cops to the Hospital with two bleeding stumps where his hands had been. He had been carrying a couple of country bombs to do a neighbour a good turn, but they'd gone off early as often happens.

Ashok Singh was also, it transpired, a Calmpose addict, but Kavery didn't know that as she looked down at him and saw the glazed, desperate look in his eyes. The police daroga outside the theatre told her casually, *'Marne deejiye usko.'* Let him die. She retorted, 'That's your job, mine is to save him,' and went in. Later—after an operation which consisted of tying the blood vessels and nerves, trimming the forearm bones and closing the stumps—as she went on her rounds she found his mother and brother with the still unconscious Ashok Singh. They were both well-dressed and respectable. The mother was weeping but not in the turbulent rustic way. 'Doctor saab,' the brother burst out in the policeman's own words, 'let him die.'

Ashok Singh was removed to Patna Jail. For all I know he's there still. If he ever gets out—he had a few murders to his name—he's unlikely, without hands, to find an opening in his trade again.

*

Thinking about it, why should Ashok Singh have been carrying country bombs? The gangs are equipped with the very latest weapons, and they're quite cheap. They tote AK-47s and even –57s while the police go around with the equivalent of Lee Enfields (the only relatively well-equipped police force is the Patna Armed Police, and even they don't have Kalashnikovs). Everyone in M____ knows where the arms dropped in Purulia a couple of years earlier went.

But country bombs are also popular, and there is an unfailing demand for them. One morning in late 1997 a boy of about fourteen was brought to the Hospital with a gangrenous hand. It was obvious that the original injury was the result of an explosion. It had not been treated for a while, and the wound had become septic and was now actually crawling with maggots. (This is not uncommon in rural areas, where hospitals are resorted to only when it is too late.)

Questioned, the boy said a firecracker had burst in his

hand. But Divali was still a month off, and the doctors dragged his story out of him a word at a time. He said he had been working in a bomb factory.

Much has been written about child labour in the fireworks factories of Sivakasi; should we be surprised to learn that children are cheaper to use and more dispensable in the manufacture of illegal arms as well?

The boy's story was backed by such strong circumstantial detail that it was impossible to disbelieve. He said homeless boys like himself were picked up in the cities and brought to Bihar. He himself was from Old Delhi—a curious instance of reversing the flow from the villages to the town which everybody deprecates.

The boys were set to work in groups of two or three beside the Ganga, each group a couple of hundred metres from the next in case of accident. And there were many accidents, quality control not being terribly important to the manufacturers. When something went off bang and the workers were injured, the Ganga was a handy means of disposal. This boy had somehow escaped and got to town whence some Samaritan had brought him to the Hospital. Of course, his hand was a write-off, and he was told most of his arm would have to be amputated. He protested, but the doctors told him there was no alternative. Next morning he was missing. He had probably slipped away in the middle of the night to catch a train to Delhi.

Arms manufacture is a cottage industry in Bihar, and probably—like the fake degree racket—brings in crores of rupees. It's a lucrative business, since there is no tax, and no bribes to be paid to government inspectors. Not two kilometres from the Hospital campus there were shacks by the Ganga where a single-shot pistol could be bought for Rs . . . But why should I give that away, or the method of manufacture? I might want to go into business myself one day, with the help of friends who're qualified engineers. Or I might want to eliminate someone, and the way things are going in this country that will be sooner than I would want to think.

By single-shot, above, I mean the pistol can only fire once, after that it's unusable. But one shot is enough to settle a feud, that is if the thing doesn't blow up in your hand. . . Either way the feud is settled. Sophisticated weapons are also cheap: You can buy an AK-47 in M____, if you have the right credentials, for just about what a handgun costs elsewhere in India if acquired through legal channels.

But simpler weapons are still used. I have seen reports of tribespeople using bows and arrows to kill gangsters who had threatened them (chapter one). The senas of the landlords and the left both have the very latest in automatic hand-held weapons, but their victims are often reported as having been hacked to death (. . . this is an interesting Indianism. In my childhood the mofussil pages of the newspapers were never complete without one or two reports to the effect that 'Periasamy Gounder had hacked Chinnasamy Gounder to death.' The weapon was usually an *aruval* or hatchet. But we're getting on. In a recent report in *The Week* on vigilante killings in Bengal, the term used twice was 'lynched to death'. I searched the page in vain for the method used: Ah, the mysteries of Indian journalism) . . . or sometimes burned alive. I have never asked anyone in a position to state the reason with authority why they should use such antiquated implements, but I would imagine it is simply to make a point and frighten the victim's friends. God knows there is nothing soothing about bodies riddled with bullets, but what can be done by an imaginative person with a sharp edge, or fire, is much more horrifying, as we saw in the Graham Staines 'incident'.

But in M____ we quickly grew accustomed to all this. At least I never had to see the victims of the gang wars, and those who work in a Hospital are very soon inured to human suffering. If they don't learn to shake off what they have seen when they go off duty—that is if they haven't already been conditioned by medical college—they quickly find other jobs.

Kishan—our medical-rep friend—though he once had his troubles from one of the 'criminals', was not the man to go in awe of anyone, and he was friends with some of the gangsters. I suppose if your town was M____ you had grown up and attended school with some of the guys, or you did business with them in one way or another. They might have bought aspirin from him, or arsenic. The day after the Divali of 1997, Kishan came to the Hospital on work and dropped by at our flat for a smoke. He was quite hung over, which is usual for the day after Divali. They'd had a wild time the previous night, he said. Early in the evening they'd run out of fireworks, so they set some bombs in a row and touched those off. It had been a jolly Divali.

How many people do you know who can procure country bombs when the fireworks run out on Divali night? Bihar certainly broadens the mind.

*

Sher Shah Suri was the last good administrator to come out of Bihar, though contemporary old-timers speak wistfully of the days of S.K. Sinha, Chief Minister from 1946 to '61. Sher Shah was from Sasaram—better known now as the late Jagjivan Ram's Lok Sabha constituency.

To Sher Shah as to all absolute rulers violence was a tool.

He used it to drive Humayun out and establish his short-lived empire; but once he was the monarch there is every evidence that he was fair. Besides, he had worked his way up through the ranks of the Lodi and Mughal revenue service, and used his insider's knowledge to thoroughly reorganize and revitalize the administration. It's much the same system we have; Akbar and later the British only improved upon it (from their point of view), they never saw the necessity to change it altogether.

Perhaps that's what's wrong with it. The system was not designed for a democracy, it was built to serve an autocrat; so why should we be surprised or stricken when it throws up one autocrat after another, each using violence as a tool? To be fair to Sher Shah, none of his successors has approached his own high standards as an administrator.

Tigers, as far as I know, do not sustain a democratic system for themselves. You can scarcely expect those who ride tigers to do so.

O ladies who have seen the light

The nuns at M____ belonged to an order of Sisters of Charity, and like all such orders derived their mission and its laws from Vincent de Paul, who had the bright idea (at around the time the Three Musketeers were performing their inconceivable deeds) of enlisting lay women to help in nursing the poor and sick.

Until then all religious orders of women had been cloistered; nuns who took the solemn vows stayed within their walls and were dead to the outside world. But to de Paul's help came the wealthy ladies of Paris, some no doubt getting a kick out of Causes as socialites do today, but even so they gave of their wealth to establish hospitals. With one noblewoman, Louise de Marillac, de Paul founded the Daughters of Charity, whose combined strength today numbers over 50,000.

The Daughters of Charity formed a congregation of the laity and not an order of nuns. But all the various religious orders of Sisters of Charity have sprung from within that fold, and all have done praiseworthy work among the sick and poor and war-wounded. For some reason the Orders of Charity have been especially popular in North America, and the Sisters at M____ belonged to an American order I will not specify. Mother Teresa's Missionaries of Charity also derive from de Paul. The younger nuns at M____ were a trifle disparaging, or else uncommunicative, when I asked them about the Calcutta-based order. They were not, they implied, such publicity-seekers. Or perhaps I imagined it.

Vincent de Paul was canonized in 1733, and Louise de Marillac a century and a half later. Quite an amazing chap, de Paul, when you read about him. In his youth he was captured by the Barbary pirates, which (as anyone who has read Rafael Sabatini, or *Ben Hur*, knows) meant hard labour for life at the oars of a galley. He escaped after a year.

He would have been quite at home in M____.

*

Kavery had first made friends with two of the nuns in medical college. They were much older then she, having taken their vows and a baccalaureate before being sent by the Order to learn medicine. They had also been to the Mother House in the States for training, and in the college mess primly ate bananas with knife and fork until they were laughed out of the practice. The other girls used to hang around outside their rooms to catch a glimpse of what they wore under their wimples. '*How* d'you solve a problem like. . .'

When we were both feeling somewhat unsettled, in Madras, one of these nuns—Sister Alberta, I'll call her—wrote from M____ asking Kavery to join their Hospital as head of surgery. Kavery had been there many years earlier, when the last of the Americans were in charge of both Convent and Hospital, and remembered her brief time there with fondness. I too jumped at the chance to leave the city. Also, there was a thrill—it cannot be denied—about going to *Bihar*, something today in the name which permits you to put your chest out and lends a swagger to your walk.

I was impressed as all hell, too, by what Kavery told me about the nuns. I'd not studied at a mission or convent school or lived in Kerala, any of which privileges some understanding of Sisters. We knew they were devoted women, living simply, working for the downtrodden, healing the sick . . . and all this in Bihar . . . Wow.

*

The sisters from America had come to M____ fifty years earlier, at the request of the local Jesuits who saw there was good work to be done here by women. M____ in those days had nothing but a railway station and a ferry across the Ganga, both vital to transport of goods and passengers within Bihar. (Now it has no ferry, but it has, or used to have, the best hospital for fifty kilometres in every direction.)

Some time in the '30s a Briton, who owned one of the small railway lines in those parts which carried coal and timber, had a vision of the Virgin Mary. He built a shrine to her which is still the focal point of the Parish. When I first saw it I gasped: It was as if the Taj Mahal had littered and one of the brood had been brought up by a preternaturally Presbyterian architect. But we got used to its looks in time, and since The Shrine (as it was always referred to) was surrounded by some dozen acres of landscaped, well-tended lawns and flower-beds with paved walks and pavilions, it was the favoured evening pleasance of all the denizens of the Convent and Hospital. It was very soothing of a sunset, with tall trees limned against the western clouds and great flocks of fishing birds arrowing across the sky, returning from the Ganga.

The annual festival at The Shrine, held every February, is one of the biggest in Bihar. In '97 we watched busload after busload of pilgrims drive through the campus, swinging past the doctors' quarters (narrowly missing the gate) and on to The Shrine. I didn't go there during the festival, but I was told at least 50,000 Christians had come from Hazaribagh and Ranchi, from Gaya and Siwan and Dumka. So had big shots in the Church from Patna and Delhi and Kerala, and even a papal legate from the Vatican. (*The Times of India,* Patna, which is a newspaper always worth a laugh, actually referred to him in a photo caption as Mr Papalnuncio).

It was a vast mela. The grounds around The Shrine had been looking their best, with the black poppies which we so loved and the huge roses and dahlias and the smaller flowers in all their glory. When the pilgrims left everything had been trampled down and the grass had turned brown. But the Parish priest and his men quickly cleaned up again, though the flowers were through for the year.

About the Sisters. . . In the ten years following their arrival they had established their Mission and built the Hospital. We have talked to some of the nuns who were novices then, and it was a wild and dangerous place, without electricity but with plenty of snakes and scorpions and jackals. The jackals can still be heard not far from the campus, howling in the night. They were brave women then who came from the USA, and brave women who came to join the Order from Kerala, and if I do not agree with their ideas of what constitutes salvation, of what is right for India and Indians, that's my business—but I admire their spirit.

But by the time we came to M____ things had changed a great deal. The Hospital was now run by young Sisters in their thirties and forties, mostly Malayalis with a few Mangaloreans and the odd Goan or Tamil or Bihari, with degrees in hospital administration and finance and management usually from the US where the Mother House had its own colleges. Perversely, the better qualified they were to run the Hospital, the less motivated they were. The service ethic had withered.

I'll illustrate what I mean with an incident which jolted both of us. Two months after we'd been settled in M____, a young girl (about seven years old) was brought in with burns suffered in a Divali accident. She was the elder of two little daughters of a Punjabi family in Barauni, where her father worked at the refinery. Her name was Anjali but she was called Sweetie, she had all the angelic looks of Punjabi girlhood, and in a very few days she was the pet of the Hospital. She had a private room in the burns ward near the office of the nursing superintendent, Sister Namrata, who looked the type you wouldn't want to meet down a dark alley. Nurses off duty would gather in Sweetie's room, nurses on duty would try to get assigned to her ward, and doctors too would find an excuse to visit her. She had a sweet nature, as well, and we all gave her gifts for her birthday (I wrote her a poem in Hindi, the first such composition I'd attempted since leaving school).

But she was quite badly burned—about sixty-five per cent of her body area, with only her face unscarred—and quite deeply too. Kavery did her best, and at first Sweetie seemed to respond. But with children you never can tell, because you can't explain things to them too well, and after a month or so she began to rebel against the incessant torture of her body. She had to be bathed, and her dressings changed, every day; and that was unbearably painful to a child who cannot tell why the adults are subjecting her to such torment. The corridors rang daily with her shrieks, and her parents and the more soft-hearted nurses could not take her reproaches any more. Only Kavery could bear to be strict with her. She did three skin-grafts, but Sweetie had lost the will to live. She contracted septicemia and died after more than two months in the Hospital. To coin a cliché, I should think there was no dry eye on campus that night, and enough Masses must have been said to float her soul to Heaven had the angels been on strike.

A month or so after that another burns case was brought in, a young man who'd had an accident. In a place like M____ any in-patients are put in the general ward until they ask for a private room (as I've said earlier, you can't tell who's rich in rural Bihar by the way they dress or live, because ostentation is sure to attract crime). Later that day the family asked Kavery to get him a private room, for they were well-off. Kavery was quite sure he would recover with skin grafts, and so passed on the request. It was more money for the Hospital, after all.

Next day she was flabbergasted to hear the young man had left, 'Against Medical Advice' as the jargon is, but really because he had been refused a private room. She couldn't meet Sister Namrata that day, but I had the opportunity (I was a privileged outsider with access to the Hospital and Convent; perhaps it hasn't turned out a good idea, from the point of view of the nuns anyway) and brought up the subject innocently.

'Oh,' shuddered Sister Namrata, lifting to her brow an arm which could have knocked me flat with one back-handed swipe, 'I couldn't give him a room in this ward. No,' and she reached for her handkerchief, 'I can still hear Sweetie screaming, and I don't want another burns case near my office.'

Many months later, when we were on terms of almost daily confrontation with the nuns, I brought up this incident while I was arguing with another Sister, and asked what about the service motive, what about *caritas*, which is the root of 'charity' but in Latin means something closer to affection, and is a word to be found in the mottos of most orders of Sisters of Charity. She said nothing, just changed the subject. What about it, was the answer.

*

I was going, in a wicked moment, to call this chapter 'Mercenaries of Charity'. But that would be unfair and untrue. Many of the Sisters, of the younger generation as well, were our friends, and decent and honourable people. The trouble was, as in any other walk of life in this Management Age, the decent and honourable nuns were sidelined. They never got anywhere near *running* the Hospital itself, and most preferred it that way, for they knew that power corrupts. They were satisfied with using their undoubted talents to run the department which their talents best fitted, and the administration was content to leave them that way.

There is certainly going to be much in this chapter which will suit the priest baiters of today. But I will not leave it out on that account. It is a chapter central to the book, because it is about the people who brought us to M____ and with whom we spent much of our days. Had this book been about my brushes with Hindu, or Muslim, or Sikh missions and their attached fundamentalists, I would be just as honest as I know how. I am against all organized forms of religion—if anybody is interested—which seek to dominate others or taint them. It's one reason to keep writing.

After all, why would I spend two years on this book if I didn't believe it was worth it? I have enough ego to think my work is important—if not as important as that of the Sisters who work in social causes, certainly as important as the work of the Sisters in administration. Tom Wolfe put it well in an essay on journalism: If a writer isn't convinced that his work is among the 'most important activities going on in contemporary civilization, he should move on to something else that he thinks is' . . . Like hack work for a house magazine, or editing the stuff in other people's websites.

Kavery once worked for a hospital in Uttar Pradesh run by a Hindu mission, a great and famous foundation which has done wonderful work all over the world in the name of its founder's teacher. The founder had believed implicitly in the communion of worship and of humanity. One of the tenets of the mission itself was not to recognize caste. Yet on feast-days, at the meals provided for the public, Dalits were fed apart from the higher-caste Hindus. When Kavery remonstrated with a Swami about this, his answer was, 'Yes, *we* believe it is not so, but we must respect public sentiment.' Only those without self-respect put public sentiment ahead of their own.

Once again, Kavery—she was why I was in Bihar, so you're not going to escape her presence in this book—attended a medical college run by Catholics, and most seats were reserved for students who had perforce to attend Chapel and Mass. But there was also a special hour set apart one afternoon a week, again for the Catholics, which they were reticent about. The other students couldn't discover what transpired during that hour until a sheet of paper fell out of a Catholic student's diary. Cyclostyled on it was the topic for next week:

HOW TO SAVE OUR HINDU SINNERS.

There was much hooting, and finally the authorities were

shamed into abandoning the project.

How to save any of us? And preferably without damning the rest?

*

Kavery, because she worked in the Hospital, was soon brought down to earth by the essential if somewhat mechanistic—or should I say ritualistic—pragmatism of the Sisters, but I had to find out for myself how naïve I had been in Madras. On our reconnaissance in May '96, the Sisters had been charm itself, and had either assented readily to all our requests or—invaluable gift for a manager!—given the impression that they assented without actually committing themselves to anything.

The first time I became personally aware that my naïvete had foundered on the rock of the Sisters' cynicism was in the matter of the jeep. We'd had one in Madras, which it was impractical to bring to Bihar; but I didn't want to spend the five years we'd promised ourselves in M____ without ever being able to drive. So in May I'd very nicely asked Sister Supriya, the administrator, if I could occasionally use their jeep when we were settled down at the Hospital, and very nicely she'd said yes.

Once we were settled and I asked to borrow the jeep for a weekend trip to Patna, Supriya equally nicely said it wouldn't be possible. She said the Parish priest had asked to borrow it, she'd checked with Sister Cassandra (the assistant administrator and as tough a cookie as you'd want to meet) who'd told her it was against the rules . . . She appeared to feel so bad about it that I found myself consoling her for having let me down. Only much later did I realize I'd been had, and using classic management tactics too. Supriya was the good guy and Cassandra the bad guy, and *she* was hard as nails and didn't mind being the bad guy. These tactics are common in any organization, but what brought me down to earth was that not even nuns would scruple to tell lies. Supriya had said we could have the jeep, to get Kavery to the Hospital; now that Kavery was safely there, she could say we were not to have the jeep.

I never drove in Bihar until I went back for the elections in February '98 and took the Ambassador's wheel part of the way back from Madhepura.

Of course, that was purely a private affair, and perhaps you'll think it trivial, as Kavery does. But it meant more to me than just not being able to drive. I felt . . . as you would if you were lied to by someone whom you'd not only trusted but looked up to. As I said, what Sister Supriya used is standard management strategy, and the history of the Catholic Church for a millennium and a half quite clearly shows it has never believed the means are unjustifiable by the end. But there were many more things besides ideology wrong with that Hospital which Kavery fought in vain against.

One thing was the very Hospital building itself. The original building, which Kavery remembered, was suited to the climate: brick and plaster and high ceilings and lots of windows. The new building was a concrete monster with low ceilings and the general appearance of a honeycomb. From March to September you sweated in there, and froze in winter. We found that some German foundation had donated the money for the building on condition that the design be theirs, and the architect had gone ahead and planned something with central air-conditioning, and the Sisters had had to take it or lose the money.

The sensible thing would have been to refuse it, for there

was no chance of getting an air-conditioning plant fitted. Anyway the new building together with the old would hold almost 200 patients, and that kind of demand simply did not exist. One more old-style block added to the original buildings would have been ample.

I wonder if they tried to convince the donors about the unfeasibility of centrally air-conditioned hospitals in rural Bihar. Sister Supriya said they had, but I now suspect they didn't want to see the money get past them and would wait twenty-five or fifty years for another sucker to come along with money for the air-conditioning.

Plenty of this money flows into Asia and South America, mainly from rich Catholic individuals and organizations in the US, Germany, the Netherlands. . . usually countries with a Protestant majority. I suppose it's the insecurity of the minority that leads them to propagate the faith. Silly sods. Once or twice teams came to the Hospital from, presumably, donor organizations, to see that the work was being done. On such occasions everybody put on their Sunday clothes and participated enthusiastically. Of course, the donors are not primarily interested in the medical facilities; what they want to see is evidence of *mission* work, and as Hindu sinners we were not privy to those meetings. . . but we'll go into mission work later.

Sister Supriya was an excellent front for the administration, tall and slim and perpetually smiling, with a ready gift of tears when called for. Like all the Sisters, she spoke excellent English—in this case, Bluegrass Malayalam, which does not compare with Oxford Punjabi for the pleasure it affords connoisseurs but can sound very sweet. Sister Cassandra was the real steel in the combination, and she didn't mind being blamed for things the administrator couldn't help doing, which was most helpful to the administrator—as in the case of my promised jeep.

There were about thirty Sisters and novices who worked in the Hospital, and all but the Sister on duty went back to the Convent for meals and at night. There were some twenty-five more Sisters who resided there: Some worked in the Parish school, some taught the novices, some had more or less retired, the rest had assorted duties. The nun in charge—titles like Mother and Superior had been abolished—was a really efficient and (once you got to know her) likable person, Sister Beena, who ran the community health department attached to but not part of the Hospital.

I forgot to say that none of the Sisters wore habits any more. No wondering what was beneath the wimple. That had been done away with some ten or twelve years earlier, and now they all wore saris or the occasional salwar-kameez. Though many wore the simplest saris—the beige variety which is seen on nuns all over India now, even in the south, or simply printed cottons and polyesters—some were dressed quite expensively. Nothing flashy, of course, but then neither does Sonia Gandhi wear flashy saris. When Kavery asked one or two of them about their wardrobes, they said, 'Oh, our families gift them to us, how can we refuse?' 'Bloody hell,' she told me later in the flat, 'I can't afford to wear saris like those to *work.*'

There's a tailpiece to this. One of the older Sisters, a quiet and self-effacing type who was the senior gynaecologist at the Hospital, had an accident and broke her arm a few months before we left. She had to wear her arm in a sling for some weeks, and naturally being unable to get it through a blouse-sleeve, switched to salwar-kameezes, of which she acquired quite an extensive collection, for we never saw her wear the same one twice in two weeks.

Very many of the Sisters were from Kerala, as I've said, and some from Tamil Nadu and the Konkan coast; but for the last few years there had been a steady decline in the supply from the south and west. So the locals had had to be recruited. We didn't meet too many Bihari Sisters, they were in their novitiates mostly; but we gathered that the senior Indian nuns looked down upon them.

Our apartment had only Indian-style toilets, and I have a troublesome knee, hard-earned from four years of football in college. As of course the existing facilities could not be ripped out and replaced with Western-style pans, I asked Sister Supriya if the Hospital maintenance staff could rig up an appropriate movable arrangement for me. She agreed, and said with a look of distaste, 'In the Convent all the toilets used to be Western-style, but now with these Biharis coming in we're having to replace them with Indian-style commodes.'

That was a rare instance of one Sister commenting about another, or others. In general they kept their mouth shut about their sisters' doings—as when I mentioned Sister Namrata's reaction to the burns case—and quite rightly so. What are fraternities and sororities for if they can't keep secrets? But here, though I was not a Catholic, I was a Malayali who could use Western toilets and be witty in English and use a fork and knife—not all at the same time of course—and that put me higher, in Supriya's estimation, than a Bihari Sister; though that was not very high.

Do you think I'm being mean? Then just contrast my expectations, when I left Madras for Bihar, with what I found among a community whose members I had already placed on a pedestal. Some amount of religious disagreement I had supposed would take place, but I know my Bible well enough (better, it turned out, than some of the Sisters did) and the question of divinity apart was ready to acknowledge the message of the New Testament. But the Sisters had no thought of doctrinal discussion with a kaffir.

To look at it another way, among any small community whose members are brought together not by commonality of interest and shared sympathies, but by laws held in common, you can expect to find friction. Shouldn't dissensions, however, be secondary to their mission, especially when it has been proclaimed noble and sacred and they are sworn by solemn oaths to honour and protect it . . .? But who am I to preach to the converted.

I have written in an earlier chapter, how the American Sisters, not having that fundamental grasp of the caste system native to all of us Indians, treated Bhumihar and coolie the same. With most of the Indian Sisters the caste hierarchy was naturally the basis of their interaction with anyone. After all, Christians, Muslims and even Sikhs in India for the most part follow the caste distinctions of their Hindu ancestors; I even had a Parsi landlady in Bombay who asked me my caste when she first interviewed me. So when a Sister in the Hospital, on hearing that one of the junior doctors had applied for a government job, told Kavery slightingly, 'He won't get it, he's low-caste;' or when another Sister whispered to us about a gynaecologist who'd just joined the Hospital, 'Actually she's dhobi caste, no one else will take her,' we shouldn't have been surprised.

Or should we have? Should we expect people who have devoted their lives to serving a faith which is supposed to make no distinction between man and man (woman is, of course, still 'the weaker vessel') but which has really built and perpetuated a hugely powerful empire by simply and with sophistication playing upon those distinctions—should we expect such women, many of them poorly-informed and ill-read, to shrug off, to extirpate from their conscious and subconscious minds their vicarious centuries of training? The question of their motivation in devoting their lives to the faith needs to be considered, and I do that a little hence.

Looking at it another way, the Sisters were simply affirming the reality of their society, they were being true to it as the American Sisters could not (in India; in their native land, I'm sure, most of them could as easily lose their thirty or forty years of Indianization). There is undoubtedly some virtue in pragmatism; but I do not think it goes well with any belief in social and gender equality, in *justice* if you will. Unhappily, journalists who believe in justice and still have to report on social realities are caught in a cleft stick, and the Indian media are making no attempt to find their way out of it. I'll treat this subject more extensively in a later chapter.

In many of the older Sisters, and in a few of the younger, I did find that spiritual element which I suppose I hunger for and which hunger prompted us to answer the Sisters' call. There was a Sister who lived in the Convent: quite a senior nun (she had been the Provincial many years earlier) who would periodically travel to one of the various Houses of the Order all over India to organize spiritual retreats. As she was also in charge of the Convent's library—which contained much matter of a secular nature, ranging from old *Reader's Digest* condensed books to *The Godfather* and *Peyton Place* (almost embarrassingly non-ecclesiastical)—I met her to get the key to the library about once a fortnight, and when she could spare the time I enjoyed talking with her.

Sister Teresa Rose had come to M____ some thirty years earlier from the US; she was from Arkansas and we discussed Clinton once, though she had left the state at around the time Clinton had smoked pot and not inhaled. But she would never speak of controversial subjects—not that I ever dreamed of debating the infallibility of the Pope with her, of course, but even when I went to take leave of her before we left M____, and I spoke of what was happening to their Order (becoming somewhat emotional as I usually do in such situations) she would not say anything, though I'm sure she thought and felt much. She was one of those persons immersed in a Greater Cause who will not waste their energies upon the trivia that detract from its efficacy; though I do not consider such circumstances trivia, and think they harm the goodness, the essential morality of the Cause as well as its greatness, I cannot help but admire such people.

She also lent me two volumes of a fictionalized history of the Order, taking it about as far as the War Between the States; it had been written by a Sister with Papal approval or whatever and I found it insufferable in its attitude to the pagans (our Hindu—and Protestant—sinners). But it helped me understand them.

There were two even more elderly Sisters we got glimpses of now and then when they visited M____ for some meeting or the other. One of them had, at the age of eighteen, been part of the original American shipment fifty years previously, when the party had been accidentally split into two and two or three of them, without any escort, had made the five-day journey overland from Bombay while the others rounded the sub-continent by ship. This lady, though practically living history, was still working in the field, near Gaya—one of the most dangerous districts in Bihar—and the other Sisters would tell me admiringly of her adventures, as how she had alighted from a bus which had broken down somewhere in the wilds and hitched a lift on a passing motorcycle. But most of the younger nuns, though they spoke glowingly of these exploits, were far too happy cocooned in their Convent—involved with Hospital administration or balancing the budget or whatever they were called upon to do—to emulate those in the field.

Motivation too has an economic side to it. The American Sisters, one can safely assume, were all, or very nearly all, those who had heard the Call and joined the Order. In India, in Kerala, large families with ten or twelve kids, half of them girls, and not much to spare for dowries, produce a different motivation. One of the Malayali Sisters herself, one with whom we both got on well and whom I would sometimes visit in her department, told me of this economic angle. (Other nuns, of other Orders, have since told me the same thing.) She also told me that respect for nuns in Kerala was waning: Non-Government and voluntary organizations were doing better work and demanding less *bhaav.*

Families in Kerala, I suppose, also tend to produce fewer children these days, and more of the girls are going in for professional courses. The Church's grip on the state is just as unrelenting as it has been for forty years; but it's the Fathers who represent that strength, and the people behind the Fathers. . .

So it is in Bihar, though they don't have that kind of power yet. Father Jose, the Parish priest (who lived in the same house from which Father Martinsek had been summoned and shot twenty years earlier over the theft of a generating set) was a pleasant, inoffensive man we always liked to talk to. But he had a dangerous job, and my belief is he would have been a lion when it came to fighting for his Faith—though they don't use that kind of language outside the seminaries. The Church picks out her bravest sons for lands inhabited by savage infidels, and the Jesuits are even more careful. They also have their pick of the best young men.

While the nuns, for the most part, stay behind walls and

carry on their work unobtrusively (free medicines, education, that kind of thing) the Fathers proselytize more aggressively. To be fair, they are doing a lot of work which needs to be done and which few others are doing—certainly not those who protest most violently against conversions—like helping tribespeople and Dalits obtain their rights, organizing them to fight against the oppressing classes; and they get killed doing it. When we were in M____ a priest in one of the southern districts was hacked to death by members of one of the leftist armies, who have abandoned their own objectives of class war and are getting rich from extortion and the timber racket; also, a priest who taught in a school in Dumka was paraded naked around the town for allegedly sexually assaulting a student.

I have a photograph of that, from a newspaper clipping, and it sickens me how humans can do that to a human being. The faces of the crowd are visible around the edge of the photograph, and they are grinning. . . Since then, churches in Gujarat have been burned and desecrated, Graham Staines and his sons burned alive and Arul Doss impaled by arrows. . .

The fact is that these priests are doing good work, and work which needs to be done—leprosy clinics, educating and organizing the poor and marginalized—but there is also no doubt that they are proselytizing. Does it matter so much? The people they work with will not be helped or allowed their rights by the higher-caste Hindus, the very same men who compound their crime of omission by another of commission—of murder and assorted acts of terrorism.

Gandhi once said, 'If all Christians in India behaved the way Christ teaches them to behave, there would be no Hindus left here.' He was of course being ironic; but if it could ever happen, there *would* be no Hindus, and a damn good thing too if Hindus are expected to behave like those apes in Dumka. But why malign the apes? Dara Singh may or may not be guilty of the atrocities attributed to him; but his name has become an icon of the kind of man, Hindu or Christian, whom we can do without.

*

There is no point in going into the details of our confrontations with the Sisters—or, rather, the Hospital administration, for we had little quarrel with the Sisters as such. Suffice it to say that Supriya and Cassandra were running the Hospital into the ground. I've often seen that people with MBAs and the like, if they lack creativity, turn out to be actually destructive.

The Hospital had a capacity of almost 200, and the census rarely rose above half that. (The surgical wards in Kavery's time were almost full.) People were set to jobs not suited to their skills—for instance, there were two Sisters who had been trained in radiology, and one was put in spiritual care and the other in charge of stores. Those who were not Sisters were not given the facilities or equipment they needed, and doctors were often treated demeaningly. Even the locals were being alienated, and towards the end of our stay were almost literally up in arms.

It was as if the Sisters were destroying the Hospital—to which patients came from a hundred kilometres around—on purpose. We heard of new and modern hospitals opening in nearby Begusarai, the trading post. Modern facilities, modern prices: There's plenty of money in Bihar. When we said to the sisters that we ought to change with the times (not going high-tech for the sake of it but generally streamlining procedures) because there would soon be competition, one of them (the maddest of the lot, I've thought) exclaimed scornfully, 'Compete! Why should we compete?'—as if they held some divine charter.

Sister Supriya's sweetness didn't last long. Five months after Kavery took her post she went to the administrator to ask for some of the perks she had been promised verbally the previous May. Supriya not only denied all knowledge of them but said, 'You should have got everything in writing; otherwise you might come back after three months and ask for even more.'

The administrator, though a local bigwig, was pretty low down the pecking order. The affairs of the Province—India and Nepal—were run from the Provincial's office in Patna, and the Provincial was a Sister whom Kavery had known earlier and trusted to be fair. Though she was shattered by Supriya's remarks I got her to write a letter to Sister Bridget in Patna and things were soon set right. After all, the Sisters had asked Kavery to come up to M____; it wasn't as if she had begged for a job.

But the whole business didn't do much for our relationship with the administration. Supriya took on a syrupy dangerousness, and as I never can resist a confrontation she must soon have come to loathe me heartily. Kavery's relationship with most of the nuns continued to be affectionate, and when she fell ill, as she twice did, they nursed her with genuine love. And I wouldn't say I wasn't on good terms with the Sisters: After all, I came back from Bihar thinking I had had a good time, so it couldn't have been bad, could it?

*

'There's no inviolability about conversions. You can buy religious adherents just as you can buy votes. For a poor person it really doesn't matter.'

—Fali S. Nariman, senior Supreme Court advocate, when he resigned as the Gujarat Government's standing counsel to protest attacks on Christians in 1999.

Rice Christians. What a wonderfully evocative term. I understand it carried the same connotation in Eastern Asia, Japan and the Philippines and coastal China, when the Church first sent its missionaries there in the sixteenth century. It means converts who become Christians not out of belief in what the Church teaches but for the advantages the Church can give. And to be quite honest the Church does not teach that all men are brothers, but that the sufferings undergone in this life will be made up for in the next world. It does not offer Dalits and Adivasis a chance to rise above their lowly social status in this world; but it does give them a chance to better their economic condition.

Those who had been trained by the missions and accepted the pre-eminence of the Church made wonderful workers. Like the operating theatre staff at the Hospital. The discipline, the routines established by the earliest American and Irish doctors were still followed unswervingly, without cutting corners, and Kavery said it was one of the best she'd worked in. Though much of the equipment they used was a quarter-century old, it was maintained in excellent condition. The staff comprised some eleven women, all tribal converts, all smiling and silent, held together by the will of 'Sister' Bernadette—not a nun but we used the honorific since she'd been there forty years and knew the work as well as any doctor. I've watched her order things into place, waiting for the surgeon's next demand, with just a move of her head. . . But those who chafed under the discipline, who were not willing to be just obedient servants, saw things differently.

The half-dozen 'boys' who lived upstairs and worked with Sister Beena in the community health department or (one or two) elsewhere in the Hospital were bright chaps, mostly Dalit converts who had a sense of self-worth, partly the result I suppose of Parish school education but very much the legacy of Ambedkar. But they were still ordered around by Sister Supriya, the administrator, and her gang; put to any odd jobs which someone had to do.

I don't mean sweeping and washing clothes, of course. I mean like fixing the stage for a function, or getting something done in Patna, or some piece of equipment repaired in town. Hardly community health work, unless you mean the nuns' community. They were always addressed familiarly as 'tum', but showed no resentment. These were bright young men; one had an LL.B., another wrote and designed skits for the community health department and, in a major competition in Patna which teams from all over north India attended, was adjudged best director.

The chap with the LL.B., Akhilesh, I got quite friendly with, and he gave me a lot of information about life in Bihar. He wouldn't say anything about the nuns—not because he was scared but because he had his pride. But through him I met a few young men like him, one of whom (a bit more firebrandish) I shall call Anand—also a Dalit and a convert with a B.Com. and an LL.B. and a go-getting attitude.

Anand was loosely associated with some NGO or voluntary outfit which was doing something in the outback, and his ambition was to set up an NGO of his own. After that he would be in silk and lavender for the rest of his life. (This is a common ambition in Bihar, I discovered.)

I didn't understand; but then I've not had much to do with NGOs, which become important only in an area where the government is doing nothing, which is most of Bihar. Anand explained to me the rationale behind setting up NGOs:

'All you have to do is register your organization, and to do that you need a recommendation from someone already established in the field—like the Church—which is a non-profit organization. Then with their contacts you get in touch with some foreign foundation which has an interest in the field you have said you're specializing in. They give you annual funding; you use about ten to twenty per cent for your work and keep the rest for yourself. You can do enough with that much to impress them, because they don't understand that a dollar can buy much more here than in the West.'

He told me about people he knew who lived in what were practically palaces, owned three cars and 'ran hospitals' using this essentially simple method. All you needed was a glib tongue and a persuasive manner, and both are anyway necessary adjuncts to success in this Management Age. They probably did good work with the percentage of 'donations' they put to use, and perhaps it was nearer fifty than ten per cent. Fifty per cent of a dollar donation, tax-free, goes a hell of a long way in this country. As Cecil Rhodes is reported to have said, 'Philanthropy is all very well in its way, but philanthropy plus five per cent is a good deal better.'

As for the institution which made the recommendation, he said, its fee, off the record, was ten per cent of the original subscription. In Bihar this was collected on behalf of the Church by. . . but I won't name names. It's a Father who is probably one of the most powerful men in the state and certainly is very powerful in the Church, much more so than the Bishop himself. If he's still in Patna, I think a lot of people will understand whom I mean . . . a Malayali of course. I don't think he took it for himself, but the Church also needs money and has trained its fund-collectors well. It's also true that ten per cent is, in Bihar, very small skimming off the top.

If the Church can do it, argued Anand, knowing it's against the law of the land and against Christian morality, why can't I?

Anand—and many other Dalit converts I met at one time or another—were especially bitter about Malayali priests and nuns. In the Christendom of Bihar they were kingmakers, if not actually kings. 'Why,' asked Anand, 'do they not ordain more of our people?' It was a legitimate question. Four centuries ago it had been asked of European priests in every land from Peru to Macao, Goa to Kyushu. The answer invariably was, 'You are not yet ready, my son. The very fact that you ask the question shows that you are not ready.' That was the answer the Bihari Dalits got now, from the Malayali Establishment.

For the Church needs uncomplaining, unquestioning obedience. It does not need foolish martyrs; it needs clever ones whose martyrdom will further the Cause. Its institutionalized shrewdness sometimes makes me shudder.

Small wonder the younger Dalit converts were angry. They were given no role in the Church; and with their education and convent English—and especially because of their caste, or lack of it—they were fitted for few roles outside the Church and institutions run by the Church.

Now they, too, had seized on to the reservations idea. When the idea of reservations was first mooted as a Constitutional proviso, identifying the communities/tribes/castes who would enjoy the new facility became an enervating and sometimes very enriching task. The Church nobly refused on behalf of all its congregation. But now the Bihari Dalits feel they were defrauded.

Had they, or their fathers, not converted, they might even be better off. Representations had been made to the Bishop of Patna, who was a Dalit, but the Church did not like the idea on principle. Now the Dalits, some of them, were actually talking of a march to Delhi. 'The Church,' said Anand and his friends, 'doesn't want us to have reservations because they're afraid that if we get any political clout we'll go against the Church.'

There is small fear of that in the present—er—*fundamentally* surcharged atmosphere. As Christians—and very likely as Dalits—they will be mistrusted by the propagandists of Hindutva, who have already announced that they are against reservations for Dalit Christians. (At the time of the Pope's visit in November, one of their rallying cries was that this demand be withdrawn.) Dalit Christians are unlikely to get reservation without support from the Church. There are sections in the Church who support their demand, but it is a political demand and therefore dangerous to anyone with power.

Anand and his brothers were Christians but had no say in the Church; Dalits but had no political power. They wanted something and they were damned well going to get it. Words haven't come to blows—yet; because they are outside existing power structures and lack a godfather.

*

I said earlier that foreign donors to mission foundations are not as interested in the work of medical institutions as they are in evidence of conversion. It's the hot topic of the last decade of John Paul II's papacy. I've got to watch what I say here, and am not going to quote authorities; but delve a bit into this business and you'll find clear proof that there is, literally, a bounty on the heads of converts. I've heard how much the bounty is, too, and it's not insubstantial. Just ask yourself why priests of the Eastern Churches in Kerala, who have all along prided themselves on their descent from some one of the 400 Nambudiri families converted by St Thomas, should suddenly, these days, be talking of their work among the 'tribals'...

And since John Paul II became Pope, too, the distinction between various Churches has become nebulous. India is seen as fertile ground, No Man's Land, ripe for claiming by either a benevolent Church or—as they see it—by the savage hordes of Islam. Remember the Pope's parting words after his visit to India last year—about the 'third Christian millennium' witnessing 'a great harvest of faith on this vast and vital continent'? That he could say it at all argues a power not likely to turn aside.

And so much for that, and not that I give a damn anyway about who converts to what. I'm against *all* forms of organized religion. And before you start throwing stones at me for Sangh Parivar talk ('He who is not with me is against me'), just toddle along and check for yourself. And remember that for the sake of peace I have not recorded some of the worst abuses of religion I have witnessed. The half hath not been told thee.

*

To return to the Sisters of Charity, Catholic Christianity as I suddenly saw it after so many years—I hadn't been into a

Church since I was a child, and only dimly remember anything about the appurtenances of the religion—was amusingly adapted to the local paganism. The nuns all wear saris in Bihar; the priests, at Mass, wear a saffron shawl-like vestment over their white robes, which are also redolent of the East. And talking of redolence, they use Indian lamps and *agarbattis* liberally (though of course the Catholic Church has always gone in for censers and dousings of holy water; in fact much of its superficial appearance is like Hinduism, and reminiscent of its Eastern origins). I went to midnight Mass one Christmas—of course I didn't take Communion—and felt quite at home. It wasn't all that different in substance or tone from some ceremonial you might have witnessed in a *math*.

Then, the laity—Hindu or Christian—were encouraged always to use the salutation 'Jai Yesu' to the Sisters and Fathers. But in sermons it was never 'Yesu', but 'Prabhu'. Local festivals were also adapted. Kavery told me of how, during her first stay at M____, she heard a Divali sermon: '*Is din par Prabhu dharti par aaye* (On this day Prabhu came to earth)'—an ingenious formula which also incensed her. I took it as it came and it afforded us some fun.

The funniest part of the Rice Christian angle in the Hospital was provided by the spiritual care department, staffed by two or three Sisters at least one of whom was mental. On our brief visit in May '96 this lady—let's call her Sister Eliza—had entertained us with witticisms like this one:

'This'—holding up a forefinger—'is Abdullah. Now what's this?' and she would waggle her finger up and down. We all professed not to know.

'It's Sheikh Abdullah!' and she would dissolve in gales of laughter, more decorously echoed by her Sisters.

Now Sister Eliza took her job in spiritual care very seriously. No PJs there. She and her two somewhat more subdued partners in crime would tour the wards—after the doctors had done so; all the doctors except Papa, the medical director, were Hindu—and preach to the patients for hours. They would also leave behind printed material which was so crudely evangelistic no one could have taken it seriously, of the 'Believe in Christ and you will be well' variety. (But many who *are* Christian take it seriously, as we found in Kerala.)

I suppose some of the victims of spiritual care were driven out of Hospital sooner than medical opinion would have thought possible, which is a cure of a sort; some others must have taken it resignedly as another affliction to be endured. But some young men of M____ who happened to be in-patients used it creatively. They would pretend to be influenced by the drivel Sister Eliza droned out, and later when the fancy took them they would leave the ward. When stopped by the nurses on duty they would say they were going up to spiritual care to listen to some more preaching, and naturally they had to be allowed out. Then they would walk out of Hospital, take a rickshaw to town and enjoy a good day with their friends before returning in the evening much refreshed. The doctors soon found out and put an end to visits to Sister Eliza by in-patients, though they could do nothing about her visits to them.

Sister Beena's work with the community health department I will leave for another chapter. But no chapter on the Hospital will be complete if I don't write about the nurses. The duration of the nursing course was almost four years, and then the graduates had to serve a bond of one year. So there were some two hundred girls aged from sixteen to twenty-two staying on campus, mostly in a tall barracks next to the Convent. The earlier batches had been made up almost wholly of Malayalis, but the state government had a year or two previously stipulated that at least half of each batch of forty or so should be locals. It was no trouble to attract girls: The nursing school is one of India's best, and its graduates attract starting salaries of almost Rs 4,000 a month (plus free board and lodging) in the best hospitals of Calcutta, Lucknow and Delhi—while their poorer cousins back in Kerala are lucky to get half that and are more often than not cruelly exploited by quacks.

They were therefore very bright girls; and life in M____ made them hardy as well. It's no easy job for a twenty-year-old girl on the night shift to control a ward full of Bihari men some of whom are drunk and many of whom have pistols tucked into their waistbands. And at the same time to look after their two or three juniors assigned to the same shift and ward… Did I say they were well-trained? The nuns taught well, and were strict but affectionate as if to younger sisters. There were fines for any breach of discipline: for instance, speaking Malayalam on duty. Only Hindi and English were allowed. At least Hindi is a compulsory subject in Kerala schools, and though the nurses' pronunciation was sometimes funny they didn't have much trouble with grammar—apart from the objectionable habit of addressing the locals as 'tum', which the Indian Sisters had initiated.

Of course, the girls were in much the same situation as girl boarders at a convent school—except that their duties in the Hospital were much more onerous than PT—and broke rules and giggled and teased the nuns as girls will. We enjoyed being in their company, and made it a point to call the girls of each batch home for high tea at intervals of a month or so.

That was really fun. In the first place, it was no easy job in a room about fifteen feet by thirty—already cluttered with three cupboards full of books, a hugeish dining table, a cane sofa set and assorted items we hadn't found room for anywhere else—to seat thirty-five or forty girls. I had to tidy the room, one of the tasks I most enjoy but only when in the mood for it, and make the seating arrangements. Durga (Paswan, who for a time ran our errands) would have been sent earlier in the afternoon to buy hoards of samosas and cake and mixture.

Some of the girls were naturally shy; some were made more so by my presence, or Madam's; but there were always a few really smart ones to keep the conversation going, or to sing. Some sang very sweetly, but usually modern Hindi film songs. I would urge them to sing old Malayalam classics. And at their prompting I once sang that Malayalam film song delighted in by connoisseurs which goes

Ente kanmaniyute kavulil oru dimple;
Aa dimple-*inte kumbilil oru* pimple.
Ente kaamugi nee etra etra simple!
Ninte kannukalil twinkle twinkle little star …

but I could see they didn't believe the song (which had been recorded long before they were a gleam in their mothers' eyes) existed. Of course they were accustomed to a vastly different standard of Malayalam film music. For that matter, I only half-believed the song existed myself until we heard it wafting from a wayside radio in Munnar last year.

Then after sufficient entertainment and gossip we would make tea and hand around the eats. We would have somehow dredged up enough plates for the whole bunch, but there would be drinking utensils for only about half. So when twenty or so of the girls had had tea I would take their plates and cups/tumblers/glasses into the kitchen. Invariably a dozen or so of the girls would crowd in after me and begin washing up. However much I protested that only the cups needed to be done, the rest could be left for Pushpa in the morning, they would ignore me and relentlessly scrub everything in the sink. On one such occasion I cried out to Kavery, who was talking with the other girls in the drawing-room, 'Kavery! Help!' but I was swept aside and out.

The girls would leave in time for dinner, which I am sure they did justice to though they complained loudly of its quality. Growing children—and that's what they were, though when you think of the work they would be doing in a very few years, and the training they were then undergoing for it, you have to wonder at the spirit in them.

They were well-looked after by the Sisters, and given ample opportunity to show their extra-curricular skills as well. For a week leading up to Nurses' Day (Miss Nightingale's birthday, 12 May) there were competitions and speeches. There were as I've said many excellent singers among them, and the nuns—most of whom of course sang like angels, having been trained in choir—coached them as much as they had time for.

One nun, Sister Cassilda (I've never been sure of the spelling) had an especially enchanting voice, and had even studied music. One Christmas eve I had accompanied Supriya and some other of the Sisters, including 'Cassie', to Patna on a shopping trip in the Hospital's Tatamobile. It was dark before we were halfway home, and the nuns began to sing carols. It was lovely: Their voices and the cold and the darkness and speed somehow created the Christmas spirit, conjured it out of our souls, though it was different, but then

Christmas always is different ... Cassie sang a carol I'd never heard before, about a little drummer-boy, and all through the Christmas season if there was any carol-singing I begged her for it. I didn't sing in the car, I can't sing, but my facility with arithmetic helped a bit with the Partridge-in-a-Pear-Tree one.

Sister Cassilda also surprised me one day when I dropped by her office to say hello—she was then in charge of accounts—and when we were talking of music she praised *Jesus Christ Superstar* and sang a snatch of it. I'd never expected someone of the Church to talk highly of that musical, and it rounded out my admiration of her voice and good nature.

The Nurses' Day functions ... There were skits and 'fashion shows' and dances. Many of the girls had been trained in classical dance, especially bharatanatyam; but the Sisters would not allow them to perform dances set to Hindu *stutis*. We thought that intolerant, and besides there is nothing more pathetic than a poor girl in classical attire dancing bharatanatyam to some impromptu nonsense in praise of 'Yesu'. So most of the entries for the dance competitions were filmi dances, set to filmi tunes; and though the girls did them well, with a verve and abandon that might have been envied in Bombay, to us (brought up in a more prudish age) there was something obscene in these sixteen- and eighteen-year-olds gyrating on stage *a la* Madhuri or Urmila or Shilpa. The nuns did not disapprove, and I think they were at fault. Even a stuti to Ganapati or Devi should be less offensive to the Church than the effusions of whoever has the option on vulgarity in Hindi films these days.

*

When they came, they had the Bible and we had the land.
Now we have the Bible and they have the land.
—African saying

I have said, and am going to say, many things in this chapter which will be unpalatable to modern secularists. A religious majority has, I agree, a moral duty to be more tolerant of the customs of minorities; but the minorities also have a responsibility not to use that advantage to excess. Time after time I have noticed at 'secular' institutions that Hindus are expected to, and do, attend Christmas celebrations and solemnly acknowledge Christian sentiments; but Christians on the whole stay away from functions held for Divali and Vinayaka Chaturthi.

It's no skin off my nose; as I've said, I don't care who worships what as long as they stay off each other's back and off mine in particular. But institutionalizing this kind of intolerance rubs my nose raw. I'm sure there is evident, in this chapter, a certain malicious glee at the misfortunes of the Sisters in M____ and of the Hospital since Kavery left. Too bad. I'm sorry for it; but I'm being straight about how I feel.

I hate generalizations, especially when I make them myself, and when I say 'Hindus' or 'Christians' I mean 'most' or 'many'. I must add that my observations of Christians—and Hindus, for that matter—are more relevant to the backward districts: Idukki in Kerala and the region around M____, for instance.

I sincerely shared the attitudes of the newspaper I write for until I went 'home' to Kerala—we were in Idukki—in '98. That experience has disabused both Kavery and me of certain notions which go with the Establishment secular attitude, for there I saw how both secularism and Christianity were *used* by the Church and those who control it, how the mass of Christians were owned and their minds and attitudes perverted by the rich. It's too much to go into here, and one observation about Kerala will inevitably lead to another irrelevant to this chapter ... A Malayali friend of mine has suggested that I write a book about Kerala entitled *The Last Malayali*.

I have not been to Bhagalpur, and since I did not go to Bihar as a journalist I made no particular effort to find out how Muslims and Hindus lived together, but I was never conscious of any friction—it may be because I wasn't looking for any. In M____ there was a sweeper named Ghulam at the Hospital, who had attached himself to the household of Dr Kishore—who lived in the flat opposite ours—in an *ex-officio* capacity. Ghulam greeted us traditionally at Divali, and played Holi, and we greeted him traditionally at Id and respected him for his observance of Ramadan. But I never thought I should subsidize a trip to Mecca for him...

Kishore told me that during the strife of December 1992, when there was evidence of trouble in the Muslim mohalla, Ghulam took refuge with him for a couple of days. During that time he did his *namaz* in the puja room.

Incidentally, as I have written elsewhere in this book (but you may have skipped it) there was no trouble in M____ in December '92 or since. The 'criminals' issued a fiat that Muslims were not to be touched, and that was that. Presumably they had orders from Patna. The Janata Dal was one big happy family then.

I can bring myself to understand the feelings of those who sincerely deplore the skewed secularism which deprives Hindus of self-respect. But I cannot begin to understand those who channel these feelings and use them for their own purposes. Hindu or Muslim or Christian, we are our own worst enemy.

*

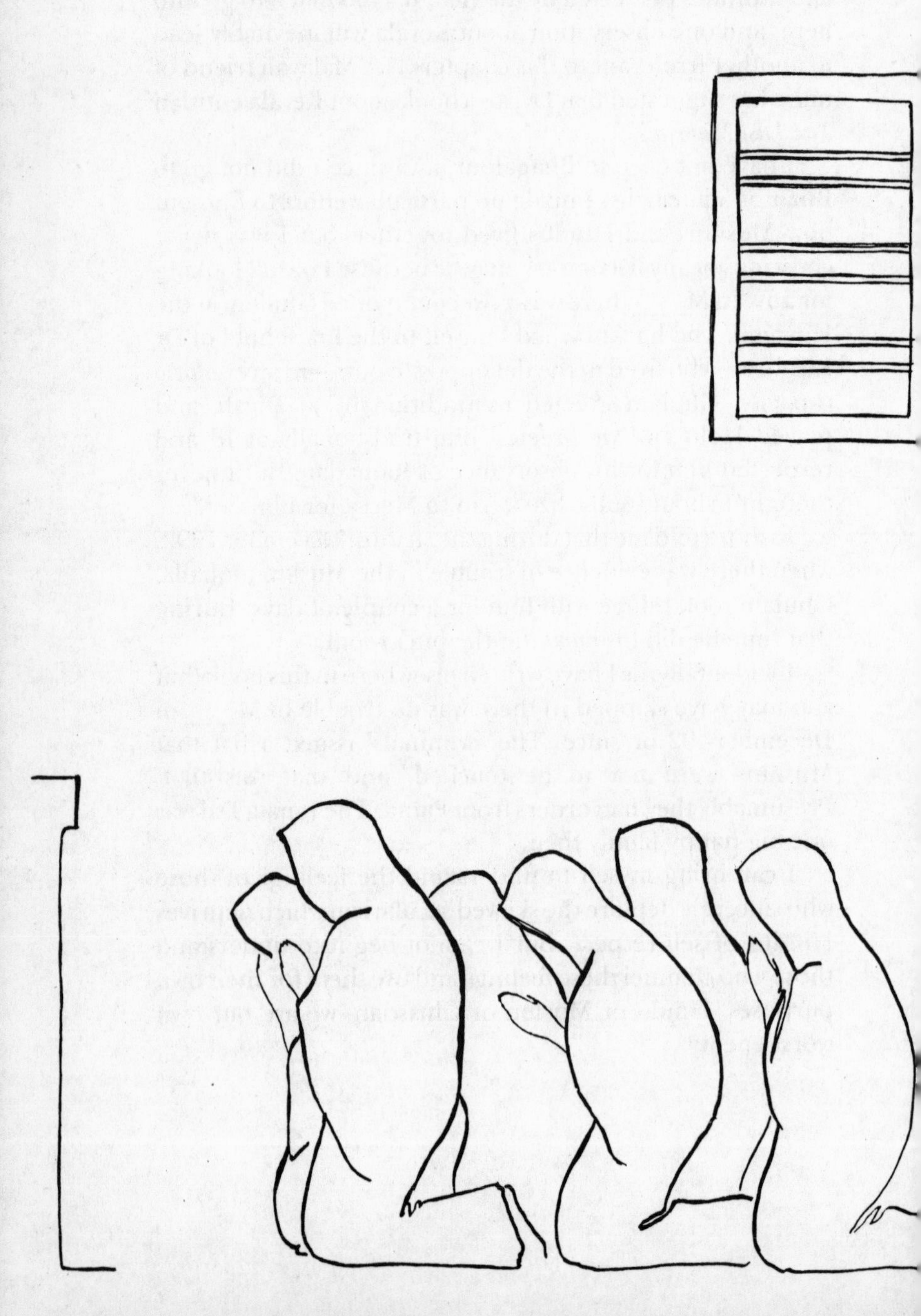

The doctors at the Hospital in M____ both resented and feared the nuns. Besides Papa (the seniormost), Kavery, and the two nuns who were the senior gynaecologists, there were six or eight younger men and the junior gynaecologists who were all of a different persuasion from the Sisters. Dr Kishore had been there longer than anyone but Papa, and though he disliked most of what the Sisters did they had a hold over him and he was not above carrying tales to them. He hoped to be medical director some day. Papa was due to retire, and he was only medical director because he agreed with everything the administration had to say.

(*Postscript*: I might as well say that Dr Kishore had a certain addiction problem and since [as theory has it] excessive dependence on a drug is caused by low self-esteem, he had not enough faith in himself to break free of the Sisters and the security afforded by a job at the Hospital. The nuns used it, too; Sister Eliza from spiritual care was a regular visitor after a bad spell and spent hours alone with Kishore's wife Ratna, presumably telling her to Believe. Ratna was too scared to tell Eliza to get lost.

(Supriya tried it with Kavery once, asking her, 'Why does Vijay drink so much?' Kavery told her it was none of her business. And as I have no problem with self-esteem except perhaps an excess of it there was no reason I should fear to confront Supriya whenever I thought the need had arisen.

(I'm glad to report that Kishore has recently resigned and set up shop in M____ itself. He won't lack customers.)

Not to put too fine a point on it, the Sisters in administration treated the junior doctors with the elegant contempt they felt they owed them. They were not Catholics; they were Biharis; their English was halting and often faulty. Medically speaking they did the best they could given the limitations of their background and training. The

Sisters were much more respectful to Kavery and me (and those not in administration were truly affectionate), because after all we had opportunities. We didn't have to have their damned job. And after my first essay on Bihar appeared in *The Hindu*, they were *perhaps* a little afraid of me. At least I'd like to think so. Journalism is an area of dark and awful mystery to the layman.

The juniors for their part were always writing exams and attending interviews, desperate to get an MD seat or a public sector job. 'Sit on your arse for fifty years and hang your hat on a pension'... yes, but when there are no choices how do you get the security you crave?

Kavery stood up to the Sisters' unreasonable demands whenever she had to, which was too often to suit her temperament, and the three juniors in surgery soon perked up. It was sad to see how eager and anxious they were to do the simplest procedures, how little opportunity they had been given in college. But they were sharp enough; by the time we went south on annual leave in mid '97 they could handle an appendicectomy. Gunshot wounds and emergencies and almost all elective cases of course had to be referred to Patna in Kavery's absence, by taxi if it could be afforded. The Sisters had an ambulance, the Tatamobile, but it was kept for their own uses. I suppose it might have been foolish to hire it out on the ninety-kilometre drive to Patna; besides, it had enough to do as things were.

There was one of the junior doctors who did stand up to the nuns. Dr Arvind had an irascible nature and an intense pride. Any affront to his dignity would be met with a flare-up. He didn't hesitate to tell the Sisters what he thought, and that made them a little wary of him. He was a little man, like our Marwari friend Kishan, but without his extroverted verbosity. He was a nice chap when you got to know him, and Kavery thought highly of his potential. He is one of the two people then in M____ who still keeps in touch with us.

Well, more than two years have gone by since we left M____. There's a new administrator, Sister Cassandra, the former assistant; most of the Sisters we loved and respected have left the Hospital and gone, as they had wished, to farther-flung areas, in Bengal and the North-East and the hills of Uttar Pradesh and south Bihar. Amelia in the lab, who was an accomplished herbalist, is still there as far as we know; but Rose in physiotherapy who also practised homoeopathy, and Beena of community health, have both left to do work which is more real.

Only one of the junior doctors we knew is still there. One or two of those who have left are in private practice (which means a clinic in the village; but what else can they do?) and Arvind has joined a hospital in Kishanganj as senior resident in surgery, which is great news; one has got into that public sector haven called the Coal Board, which the doctors used to talk about as the Crusaders talked about Jerusalem. The senior nurses Kavery worked with and cared for are all over the North, and a few in the Gulf perhaps; an occasional letter flutters in from one of them to Madam.

Papa has retired after over forty years at the Hospital. Dr Kishore has left. The new medical director is Sister Alberta, who was Kavery's classmate and who first wrote her in Madras asking her to come to M____. She was in Garhwal when we were in Bihar; and on one of her visits to the Mother House I remember spending an afternoon telling her of all the ills the Order had brought upon itself, even quoting Matthew 7:3 at her. She must have thought it was the Devil himself, and she later wrote Kavery sorrowfully, 'You let your husband influence you too much.'

The punchline is Arvind's. In his last letter, just before leaving M____ and joining the Kishanganj hospital, he wrote us that 'the whole Hospital is deteriorating day by day and future of this Hospital looks dark', which doesn't surprise me in the least. Then he added:

'Now Dr Alberta is new CMO of the Hospital. After seeing Dr Alberta's behaviour I am surprised that she was your friend ...'

*

Postscript: I'm unhappy with this chapter, there's no denying it. I do not relish the possibility that I may very well have provided ammunition to the egregious but puissant idiots who are vitiating our national, societal and cultural integrity. Maybe when I'm older and wiser I'll figure out a way to be the kind of writer I want to be without hurting anyone's feelings. But methinks I do protest too much . . . What I have written I have written.

'Hum Maxim mangta hai!'

There was damn all to amuse ourselves with in Bihar. We didn't have a TV, on principle; the Patna edition of *The Times of India* was highly amusing but for the wrong reasons; and we didn't particularly want to visit the local movie hall, where during the intermission the manager paced the aisles with a gun in his hand to deter presumption. The girls—that is, the nurses—often went, but only during the day and in large groups.

Kavery would often be filled with an urgent desire to see a movie, and while I can leave Hindi fillums strictly alone it would be a break even to get to Patna for a weekend. We would borrow the community health jeep or the Tatamobile from the Sisters (for a fee per kilometre plus some standard charge: It worked out to less than Rs 300 for the weekend) and the driver too, and set off usually Saturday morning before it had become too warm and the chill off the Ganga was still in the air. Winter drives were lovely, the fields on either side of the road golden with mustard and a glimpse every now and then through the trees of the silver river pushing at its banks less than a kilometre away.

Shivkumar, the driver of the Tatamobile, was a weatherbeaten and taciturn chap who'd seen it all but whose rare grin lit up his face. The drive to Patna was accomplished with all possible speed, which means a thirty kmph average.

We usually broke the journey halfway, at the Sisters' house in Bakhtiarpur. There was a small hospital there, the in-patients all being women in labour; it was a place for hard-working nuns. I remember the towns en route to Patna: Barh, Bakhtiarpur, Atmalgaula, the bridge across the Punpun with a colossal and crudely coloured statue of Bajrangbali next to it, Fatuha (which always reminded me of Salman Rushdie) . . . strange names to a southerner and romantic too. There was another bridge before Fatuha, an old stone structure where the road curved slightly, with low stone walls sloping up from nothing and down again to nothing. It was very old, no one I asked knew just how old, and I could imagine Clive riding across it. It was a long and weary way from Pilasi to Avadh, though the roads would have been better in his time.

Patna must be the ugliest and most squalid state capital in India. Monuments of tourist interest include the shopping complex owned by Shatrughan Sinha and the several-storeyed mansion of the chap who built the Sulabh Shauchalayas, which I was told has twenty-six bathrooms . . . I never made it to the Museum, which has some exciting Buddhist relics; I was always thinking (until it was time to pack) that we'd be in Bihar five years, there'd be another chance.

But there is one building in Patna which is surely unmatched in any capital city anywhere in the world: a huge grey breast rising some dozen stories from a hectare of land. It is a granary built by a British Resident, John Garstin, in the nineteenth century to provide, in times of plenty, against famine. The natives, bearing their baskets of grain, were supposed to troop up a staircase which winds round the granary, empty their precious burden through a hole in the top, and troop down a corresponding staircase. I don't know if it was ever used. I seem to remember reading somewhere that it couldn't be, because the doors at the bottom opened inwards. The whole thing's monstrously Freudian; or, alternatively, it looks like a stupa with a malignant growth.

When we went to Patna together, making a holiday of it, we'd check into some midmarket hotel (all the deluxe ones are called Magadh and Maurya and Gupta, but they're for people who want to keep Patna out) and after complaining about the plumbing, trying to get the TV fixed and wangling a clean towel or two we might go to a movie or to dinner. I remember at one classy restaurant I saw a largish cockroach walking along the back of Kavery's chair, and I drew the headwaiter's attention to it. With a catering-institute smile he simply reached out and plucked it away in his hand, then made off for the kitchen presumably to return the creature to its native habitat. Maybe it was a pet of one of the cooks. We left that place hurriedly and without tipping, though I turned at the door to see Kavery trying to slip the waiter a tenner. I stopped that, but she was protesting all evening that it hadn't been his fault.

This irreverence to Hygieia is certainly not peculiar to Patna. When Kavery was a child in Delhi her father once took the family out to the Ashok—then New Delhi's only deluxe hotel—for a pineapple juice (seven bucks; this was in Nehru's austere days). Her mother expressed a wish to inspect the kitchens. They entered, inspected and left; at the door her mother turned just in time to see one of the chefs pause in marinating a chicken, lift his finger to his mouth and lick it appreciatively.

Not that the private sector is any better. When I worked in Bombay ten years ago our office-boy (a round-faced Shiv Sainik named Janardhan who still owes me 600 bucks) moonlighted as a waiter at a major hotel. On his first evening there he cleared a table, bore his tray to the scullery (or whatever they call it at fancy hotels: La Scullerie perhaps) and began to wash the silver in soap and hot water. Up came the head-waiter, his moustache bristling with indignation, and snatched the fork out of his hand. '*Maa ke laude*,' he said, 'do you think we're paying you to waste your time like this? This is the way to do it' and he wiped all the silver clean on his napkin with a few brisk strokes. It was a good lesson Janardhan taught me; I guess it was worth 600 bucks.

Back in Patna, the movie houses weren't much better. At one—was it called Elphinstone?—we stood sweating in the black hole they called a lobby until the previous show was over and the previous herd trampled all through us. Kavery and I got seats at opposite ends of a long row. The film was *Raja Hindustani* ('*Pardesi, pardesi jaana nahin*' was all the rage then, the nursing students at M____ sang it constantly) and I simply had to get out and breathe some fresh air when it came to the final scene. (Later, when we saw *Dil To Pagal Hai* in a much better-appointed Calcutta theatre, I realized it hadn't been the movie house which had made me sick.)

After the show Shivkumar would invariably be waiting outside with the car. He'd have had a good time in some downmarket theatre, watching a refreshing *dishum-dishum* film without frills.

We could do a little shopping in Patna: at the Khadi Bhandar, and at the couple of good department stores, dating from the Raj, which are on the Dak Bungalow Road-Bailey's Road corner if I'm not mistaken. That's where we got cheese and sauces and cosmetics and stuff. A whole bunch of modern, glitzy shopping 'plazas' have sprung up in downtown Patna in the last three or four years; there's plenty of money there, most of it black and much of it certainly having been made in politics. The salesman ethic in the shops is still, however, 'Take it if you want and get out of here.'

When I went alone to Patna it was a more adventurous journey. The distance by railroad is about ninety kilometres, and an express usually does it in two and a half hours. Leave home early in the morning, catch one of the expresses on the Howrah-New Delhi line between 6.30 and 7.30, and return by express late in the evening, was the general idea. However, early during our stay in M____ I once got to the station about ten and was foolish enough to take a passenger instead of waiting an hour for an express.

Dante's ninth circle of hell was nothing to that ride. The train took four and a half solid hours of sweltering summer (that should be 'liquid hours', I guess) to cover ninety kilometres, and it stopped thirty-four times on the way (not counting Rajinder Nagar and Patna Sahib in town). Of course there aren't thirty-four railway stations between M____ and Patna; mostly there was just a wooden pole stuck in the ground with a crude hand-lettered placard on it announcing 'Jayaprakash Narayan Halt' or 'Laloo Prasad Halt'. These 'Halts' are common all over Bihar—once in late '97, to my delight, I saw a 'Rabri Devi Halt' near the UP border.

The 'Halts' are another sign of rural empowerment during Laloo's Raj. There's nothing official about it, of course; but any passenger train driver who doesn't stop at one of them is risking a stoning. And chain-pulling is also routine, even on the expresses; it's so common and unremarked upon that a couple of times I was tempted to have a go myself. One day I'll do it when I've nothing to lose; I think the thrill is cheap at a thousand bucks. It's only the 'or one year's imprisonment' which deters me. Bihar is the place to do it in if you're similarly tempted.

The passenger train had also been thoroughly and completely vandalized. Not a single light fixture or fan remained, and I'm not too sure there actually were any alarm chains. The electrical and hydraulic lines (am I getting it wrong?) between bogies are also often stolen. (Once there was a general hold-up at the railway station at M____ because the Deputy General Manager, Railways, was due on a visit and the cables of *his* train had been severed somewhere down the line.) Many times I've returned from Patna, late in the evening, in the kind of darkness which should be accompanied by wailing and gnashing of teeth. Carriage after carriage was dark—even on expresses. Nobody gnashed his teeth, and there's wailing only when a dacoit gang seizes the moment.

You're lucky if you get a seat on one of these trains. If you're travelling unreserved—and most are, even on the expresses—you've to get to Patna Junction early and hope for the best. Some of the expresses are intra-Bihar and less crowded; the thing to do is get to the station early, buy a ticket and wait. (I did most of my waiting at the Embassy hotel—or is it the Ambassador—next to the station, where there's quite a decent bar with a lot of fish floating around in a tank.) There's never much of a queue in the current booking office, as most people travel not only unreserved but ticketless. I never saw a ticket inspector on the Patna-M____ route but once, and that was when my sorry passenger reached Patna.

Patna Junction is not a great place to wait. When we went to M____ in May '96 we had return tickets from Patna, not M____, and they were only on the waiting list. I'd got a senior journalist in Patna to confirm them, and he told me he'd spoken to the Deputy General Manager. Of course they weren't confirmed; our fellow-passengers laughed at me and said you needed at least a minister to get it done. The Sisters had offered to get the tickets confirmed (or should it be consecrated?) by the Bishop of Patna, but in those days I had far too much faith in the power of the press . . . Anyway, waiting at Patna Junction I thought I'd never seen such a foul railway station in my life. There was no order, no cleanliness, no fresh air, no reservation charts, and I had to keep my hand on my wallet all the time we were there. But they had done up the station next time I visited it. Platform 1 is all tiles and marble and litter bins now, and the red splotches are cleaned up almost as soon as they appear.

You won't find litter bins *anywhere* in the city, so don't look. Dak Bungalow Road and Bailey Road and Rajendra Prasad Nagar and Anne Marg, the road leading to the airport past all the big shots' houses, are clean enough (though there aren't any bins there either) but the rest of Patna is steeped in squalor. Gandhi Maidan, about which I'd heard so much, is a vast dust bowl, but I never had the luck to see it during a rally.

Patna was once a lovely city—for the British. An English correspondent of Kavery's, on learning we were in Bihar, wrote her a nostalgic letter: 'It was such a beautiful city [in the '30s], so well-maintained . . .' Some of the British flavour, but very little, lingers near the junction where the old-time supermarkets are, with old-timers in colonial moustaches and their wives in print dresses occasionally sighted in the shops. Perhaps it's to be found in the clubs as well.

Once when I was travelling back to M____ an elderly gentleman in coat and dhoti, followed by his wife and a porter carrying their cases, got on at a mofussil town. Apparently there was some back-chat from the porter about his fee, for suddenly the old chap's voice rang out: '*Hum Angrezi zamaane ke hain* (we belong to the days of the

British).' His rates of pay must also have belonged to those times; the porter looked at him contemptuously and said the obvious: '*Woh zamaana guzar gaya* (those days are gone).' You do see these old fossils about, though I never got to meet any. Those who really rule Bihar belong to a much more ancient era than the British, but they're not fossils.

Traffic in Patna is not too bad—well it is actually, but otherwise it's not too bad. The roads are lousy; but the way to travel is by cycle-rickshaw. (Autos are usually on a shared basis—you say you want one all to yourself and the driver rapidly revises his charges upwards, and even then will ask if it's okay to pick up a passenger on the way providing he sits in front.) Swaying along the road from the junction, wheel to wheel—often actually scraping wheels—with another rickshaw pedalled by another scrawny citizen suffering from not enough nutrition and more than enough brown sugar, scooters weaving in and out of the mayhem, and lungs full of Patna's dust: It's really not such an unfamiliar experience in India, but it sums up Patna.

*

As the suburban trains are Bombay's most significant expression of its psyche, so are the express and passenger trains Bihar's fundamental expression; by which I mean to say that the quickest way to understand and appreciate the complexities (and simplicities) of Life in Bihar is to do a course of rail travel. It's no more dangerous than Bombay; and far cheaper, since you don't have to buy a ticket unless you want to.

The 'Biscuit Bandits' who figured in southern dailies and magazines in the latter half of 1999 made their first appearance two years earlier in Bihar. Their technique is simple. Gang members fall into conversation with fellow-passengers and since, on express trains in India, second-class travellers soon become more intimate than friends, it is natural to buy each other tea and share each other's food. A packet of biscuits is broached, the Bandits take a couple and proffer the packet to the mark, who takes one and wakes up in the Railway Hospital in Patna, or Khagaria, or wherever, despoiled of all his wealth.

As this modus operandi became known and biscuit-offerings began to be refused, the gangsters became Banana Bandits. They'd inject whatever tranquilizer they were using (Lorazepam is the drug of choice) into some of a bunch of bananas, eat the safe ones, and . . . Soft drinks were also thus treated, especially those that come in tetrapacks.

There are more directly physical ways of coming to grief on Bihar trains. The first flashpoint comes at daybreak, when short-distance commuters who've just got on to a sleeper car in an express rouse those who've reserved their berths and are enjoying the last, blissful half-sleep of dawn before they have to get up and brush their teeth: '*Uthiye, uthiye, chheh baj gaya*! (Get up, get up, it's gone six o'clock!)' Peaceable Bengalis who'd got on at Howrah, Dilliwalas and southerners traversing Bihar for the first time, may object; after all, they've paid for the use of the whole berth all through the journey. Their resistance is met with a genuinely baffled '*Yeh kya paagalpan hai*? (What madness is this?)' The Bihari simply cannot fathom the attitude of a man who is taking up five feet of sitting room when two dozen commuters are crowded between the toilet and the sleeper-car partition.

This kind of 'adjustment' is intensely irritating to someone from the south or a city-dweller, but it is an endearing Bihari trait when you become familiar with it.

Sure, the Bihari will insist—to the point of using physical force—that you share your seat with him, but he does not bear a grudge; and two hours later when he fishes out his *parathas* and *achar* he will hand you a share with a twinkle in his eye. He is very like the rural Jat in these matters. The difference is that in most of India you will only meet with this kind of adjustment on the slow, mofussil trains; the expresses speed between Bangalore and Madras without a thought to the other India. Bihar's geographical position, and the compulsions of the Railways, bring the two Indias into collision.

The hell with it. I'm sounding like William Dalrymple or some other jumped-up Fleet Street hack sent on a two-month mission, all expenses paid, to bring back 'the message of India'. No two Indias for me. I don't believe in retailing wisdom like 'Our India is not as real as Their India' or echoing Gandhi's wistful 'The Real India is in the villages' or resuscitating that amber-preserved '*timeless* India' which Nirad Chaudhuri kept as a pet until it died of nostalgia in Oxford.

Where I am, where I have been, what I have seen and heard, there is my India.

To come back to 'adjustment': It's a very popular Indian word, and it has taken on shades of meaning which range far beyond the dictionary definition. In Karnataka you can hear '*Svalpa adjust maadi*', in Delhi '*Thhoda adjust karo na*'. I heard, at the Hospital in M____, the community health worker Akhilesh and our neighbour Dr Kishore discussing the South, to which they had each been on a month-long trip. One of their grouses was 'No one will *adjust* on the train.' Indeed, I thought, imagine asking anyone on the Brindavan to move over a bit, unless you're pregnant or have a limb missing and medals on your chest.

We travelled long-distance on second class only once in Bihar (apart from two overnight trips to Calcutta, which don't count) and that was when Kavery by some oversight or overconfidence booked us second class returns to Delhi. The train was bulging at the seams and only Kishan's aggression got us through the clutching, grasping, elbowing, screaming ten-foot deep flesh at the door and into our compartment. Once there he cleared enough space for us to sit, with a little extra for Kavery; not even he could clear two berths, and given his Bihari upbringing it would have gone against the grain to attempt it.

There were about twenty people sitting—five or six of them on the upper berths—and maybe ten standing in that compartment, and we soon got to know the principal personalities. Sitting opposite us was a smiling, dark-eyed Marwari matron with whom we soon became friendly. Standing in the aisle was an elderly gent in white dhoti-kurta who, soon after the train started moving again, began to expatiate upon the evils of not *adjusting*. 'I've travelled all over India,' he said with baleful glances in our direction but apparently speaking to the air, 'and Bihar is the best state for railway travel.' I was stunned, but soon got his drift. 'Only in Bihar are there *sajjan* who *adjust*,' he continued. 'Nowhere else. In the South, they're very bad.' I gathered that he wanted Kavery to uncross her legs and shift nearer the window so he could sit down. Attack is the best form of defence, so I began a soliloquy of my own. 'Yes,' I said, 'in the South we believe in buying tickets and confirming our reservations in advance. That's the problem with Bihar. Nobody buys tickets.' The young man next to me started laughing, and the old chap soon faded away. He probably hadn't bought a ticket.

Much later, in eastern UP, two 'maharaj's in holy ash and

saffron, complete with trident, entered the compartment, and—India hasn't changed much from the days of *Kim*—everyone moved over to give them room. The Marwari matron opposite, with whom we'd been having a diverting conversation (her ancestors had gone to Delhi from M____ and she might even have been a distant cousin of Kishan's) at once switched her attention to the swamis.

They said they were going to Ayodhya, which immediately increased their unholiness in my eyes. Recent reports have shown that a lot of bogus characters have gathered there since '92. *The Week* has even carried pictures of supposed *sants* gathered around a bottle of rum; and while I'm certainly not against drinking, there is a touch of puritanism in me which tends to Dr Sukumaran Azheekode's views on holy men doing it.

But the Marwari matron, a devout woman, had no doubts. The garb, for her, sanctified the wearer. I remembered Totaka's verse in *Bhaja-Govindam*:

> The ascetic with matted hair; the shaven one; the depilated one; the one who assumes various robes of saffron—the fool sees and sees not that these disguises are only for the belly's sake.

In fifteen minutes she was prattling on about the spiritual discourses she helped organize in her colony in north-west Delhi and the various maharajs who had blessed the congregation there. The holy men nodded sagely and partook of her parathas. And then, to our horror, she was giving them her Delhi address and inviting them to stay and sanctify the colony.

I hope she's still alive.

*

Returning from our touch of culture in Delhi the train wasn't crowded until we reached Bihar. There was a group of young men in the compartment, in jeans and sneakers, and a middle-aged man opposite me in the window seat. The young men were friendly and polite. They had a curious but enterprising line of work. They would scour the bazaars of Delhi for novelties of any kind, get a good lot of them at a discount, and flog them in Bihar at 200-300 per cent profit. This time—it was getting close to Divali—they had acquired some wonderful firecrackers, with attributes it needs a Hans Christian Andersen to describe: fireworks, they solemnly assured Kavery, which would perform in the sky like a *Brahmastra* and settle in your hand like a dove. They would make a killing from Bihari businessmen eager to please their children, and were in good spirits.

The gentleman opposite was going to Monghyr, further down the Ganga, where he had a small business. He soon began to exhibit an embarrassing interest in us. Where was I from? Where was she from? What did I do? What did she do? It's only polite to display interest, and I tried to reciprocate. Finally he asked, 'Was it a love marriage or an arranged marriage?' at which I snarled '*Ki farak painda*!' and returned to my book.

This inquisitive gentleman was responsible for a near-fracas after Patna. One of the young men had got out there to get a snack, and the train started without him. Patna onwards, of course, it was treated as a local, and the compartment filled up. One of the standees, a young tough with a denim cap and hanging from it a face I disliked on sight, claimed the vacant seat. The middle-aged gent objected, and soon there was a face-off, both standing with clenched fists and noses touching. The sensible thing, I now realize, would have been to let him have the seat until and unless its possessor returned. But the heat and the long journey had got on everyone's nerves.

At this point Kavery, who should have kept her mouth shut, was unwise enough to intervene on our fellow-passenger's side just as the young tough was telling him, '*Jaa, jaa, tu budda ho gaya* (Go along, you're an old man)' and he turned on her and said '*Chup*!'

Now honour called on me to stand up for my wife when she really should have been spanked. A woman simply does not thrust herself into an affair between men—that's one of the ground realities in India—at least not in Bihar, and not when she's dressed in T-shirt and jeans. But what could I do? *Mardangi* had to be fulfilled. So now I sprang up with my blood hot and it was an embarrassing couple of minutes before we all took our seats, the young tough as well, which we could have done long ago.

This matter of fights precipitated by wounded honour is a fascinating subject for study. Some sociologist should go into it. In my first year at college a street-smart Malayali classmate from Delhi told us Southies how such fights were conducted in his part of the world.

First the exchange of insults, which may peter out with no harm done. But when one of the parties decides that things have gone too far for his honour to be placated without blows, he flings his head up and sticks out his chest and curls his lip and yells, '*Chhodo mujhe! Chhodo*! (Leave me! Let me go!)' At this his comrades seize his arms and hold him back while he makes ineffectual lurches towards his opponent, whose comrades are doing the same comradely thing by him.

This is how most street fights end in the light of day. But if the affair really is serious—or more to the point, if one of the parties decides that it is—he gets his gang and goes round to the offender's house after dark and hacks him to bits. In Bihar or anywhere else. Queensberry Rules? But honour comes before pride in conduct. Or rather, honour *is* pride in conduct.

This is something to remember very, very carefully in Bihar. And it applies in politics as well, as I said in the first chapter.

*

Bus journeys are very different. I only made two in Bihar that could be called long-distance, when I went from Patna to Muzaffarpur to do a report on the Bihar Education Programme and when I returned: Those were made in the lap of luxury (relatively speaking) except that every few minutes I'd be precipitated vertically out of my seat and come down with a bump. Occasionally the ruts were so close together—this was on a national highway—that, coming down into the lap of luxury, I'd meet myself going up again. But I made several trips to Begusarai by local minibuses, to buy provisions unavailable in M____ yet not worth going to Patna for.

They were short trips, made at top speed, of forty-five minutes to an hour and a half for some twenty-five kilometres. Pleasant trips too when I got a seat, for the road crossed the Ganga on a bridge almost two kilometres long; and the industrial township of Barauni, comparatively well-planned, lay en route. Standing, naturally, was no fun.

The ticket those days cost nine rupees; it must have gone up by now. The interesting point was that you could travel atop the bus for half-price. I never did, I was too scared; but a saving of Rs 4.50 is still a great deal for many people in our wonderful era of liberalization.

Passengers were not supposed to be carried on the roof, of course; and there was always a five-minute interlude at a police post near Barauni when the man with the tickets went in to pay his dues.

*

Six days after Divali comes Chhatth, the peculiarly Bihari festival. A puja to the sun, by a river, is especially auspicious; and those living by the Ganga, as all inhabitants of M____ do, are triply favoured. Every family, and each member of the family, may make offerings to Surya—but while the men don't really have to, every woman, maiden or matron, absolutely must. Kishan had invited me to accompany his family in '97, and I was very glad, because it was a rather special gesture of more than friendship.

Chhatth is a very big deal in Bihar. Even Laloo Prasad was let out of jail (such as it was) to offer *aarghya* to Surya along with his wife, as a photograph on the front page of *The Times of India*, Patna (8 November 1997) attests. I reproduce the caption, word for word:

> It was happy but temporary reunion for the fodder scam accused and national president of the Rashtriya Janata Dal (RJD), Mr Laloo Prasad Yadav, with his chief minister-wife, Rabri Devi, and children at Pahalwanghat on the banks of the Ganga on Thursday. The occasion was the annual offering of *aarghya* (milk to the Sun God) on the occasion of the two-day Chhatth celebrations which ended on Friday morning. Laloo had been granted special permission by the Patna High Court to participate in the festival.
>
> Rabri Devi is the first chief minister to offer *aarghya* in the Ganga. She came barefoot to the Ganga in a bullet-proof car with her children and a large number of relatives on

both days. Security was tight. Laloo arrived 15 minutes later to a warm welcome. The CM's family watched the proceedings from a specially erected red cloth enclosure.

The photograph had a headline above it: 'Laloo's day out'. It was my day out too. I walked the long road to Kishan's place, setting out at five in the morning. The road was unusually clean: I heard later that the local gangsters ensure it is so, and indeed do the work themselves, abandoning their Kalashnikovs and picking up brooms. But there are always a couple of them on guard; what better time to wipe out a rival gang than when they are engaged in cleaning the gutters? The road was brightly lit, tubelights strung on wires along its entire length. I reached the Marwari mohalla and Kishan's house by six, and changed from jeans into dhoti, worn Kerala style, not as they wear it in the north. After tea and snacks—Kishan's mother subscribed to the view that guests perish without regular nutrition-supplements— we set out for the Ganga.

On the way Kishan pointed out several buildings; practically everything of a charitable nature had been built by his grandfather. At the riverbank there was already a goodly crowd; it was just before sunrise, and families were already wading out into the river. Kishan took a number of photographs, one of which has been reproduced in *The Hindu*.

The Ganga was lovely, with the sun just rising to our right (the Ganga made a bend there) and the denizens of M____ all gathered around to meet it. They were dressed in their best clothes, especially the marriageable girls, who were all silk and gold, and the young men. Kishan wore jeans. I waded out into the water with him and his family, my dhoti doubled to my waist. I didn't offer aarghya, but helped (with my elbow mostly) Kishan's mother and sister through the throng. Families didn't try to outdo each other in the ostentation of their offerings as so often happens in India. We were at the general ghat; a little upriver was where the Bhumihars did their bit. And some eighty kilometres further still upriver, Laloo and Rabri were doing theirs.

*

In the last chapter I briefly mentioned Sister Beena, who was in charge of the community health department at the Hospital. She was to us, when we first met her, an unremarkable woman who wore thick glasses. She was in charge of the convent (in the post of what used to be called the Superior) and was therefore a person with some responsibility; the community health department was also in many ways independent of the Hospital administration. However, we found out all this only much later, and only after a few months did we begin to appreciate Beena's common sense and fundamental goodness.

My first outing with a Hospital group was to the mela I've written about in the first chapter, where Laloo made an appearance. My next was when I volunteered for the Pulse Polio programme; I was bored of sitting at home and wanted to see the world. It was an excellent idea. All the nurses and students volunteered, of course, and most of the twenty or so Sisters who worked in the Hospital. They were divided into some thirty-odd teams, to be distributed among the surrounding villages. Akhilesh, Sister Beena, Supriya—the administrator—and others who could 'organize' toured the area through the day, tallying statistics and doling out more vials of vaccine as the need arose.

I went on three Pulse Polio campaigns, each time to a different village with a different team, and remember each time fondly. First the gathering early in the morning (7 a.m. in December is just about sunrise, and quite chill) when names were read out and people assigned to various teams; then the getting-to-know-each-other: I knew most of the Sisters, of course, but the girls were always shy to begin with; then the distribution of drugs and packed lunches.

And then the jolting journey in the Tatamobile or a hired minivan, over fairly good roads at first but then village roads and finally cart-tracks, as one team after another got out at its 'point'. We'd find our post, usually at the village school or some panchayat building, commandeer a room and spread out our trinkets as we waited for the natives to arrive.

And arrive they did. The villagers in the Ganga plain may be illiterate, but there's a great deal of social awareness among them; which is also traceable to Laloo's Raj. Laloo took a personal interest in the Pulse Polio programme, and though there are the usual allegations of racketeering—in 1997-98 it was variously reported that several thousand vials of the precious vaccine were broken or out of date or spurious, and 'deaths due to polio drops' set off an alarm in Bhagalpur Division—the campaign has attracted tremendous response in Bihar in the last few years. (I was surprised when we got to Kerala to find that it's no big deal there; anyone who wants a child immunized has to bring it to a government hospital. No wonder Kerala is touted as such a model in Bihar.)

The immunization itself was not a very exacting business. The girls took care of the actual administration of the vaccine; once or twice I took a hand. One important job was the collection and tabulation of data: Name of child, age, father's name. This was necessary because the vaccine has to be given twice, about six weeks apart; so if those who came on December 6 did not come again on January 17, they might as well not have come the first time.

It was the backward villages we covered, mostly, and mother after ill-nourished mother would come, baby in arms, often with one or two scrawny (but bright-eyed) children hanging on to her sari. It was tough getting facts out of them:

'*Bachche ka naam*?'

'Tuntu.'

'*Pitaji ka naam*?'

Here the woman, sari pallu already half covering her face, would draw it completely across, turn coyly away, titter and tell her neighbour, '*Tu batao*.'

Sometimes the neighbour would be just as reluctant, and some male hanger-on—there were always two or three of those—would either give the information or, if he didn't know the family, bully it out of the woman.

The customers came in waves, and at times we were hard put to it to keep up with the flow. At other times the bright rectangle of the door would be empty of silhouettes—there was never any artificial lighting in the rooms we occupied—and the hangers-on would be sent to drum up business. Then I would wander over to the edge of the village, never very far away, and smoke a meditative cigarette as I studied the brilliant gold of the mustard fields and the long, soothing miles of green, broken only by a silver cascade from a pump or the deceptive shimmer of the videotape which ingenious farmers string around their plots to scare away the birds.

The villagers were always hospitable. It was necessary to their honour to feed and water and tea us; and although we would have brought along our lunch—samosas and mixture, maybe sandwiches and a slice of cake (either pre- or post-Christmas) we would have ample contributions of *litti* or *tekwa* as well.

These delicacies are pretty much indigestible to a non-Bihari stomach, and it took me some months in Bihar to get used to them. Kavery, though, loved them at first taste, and she was especially fond of the Bihari staple, *sattu*, which is just ground roasted dal and gram. The poorest simply mix it with water, as the Highland Scots used meal; but even the richest use sattu as a stuffing for their rotis. Both of us missed it in our chappatis when we came south.

On, I think, my second Pulse Polio expedition, there was a novice (Sister) from Tamil Nadu with us as one of the volunteers. She was terrified of anything Bihari, and though I talked to her in Tamil, she was just as terrified of me. One of the better-off families in the village where we were posted called the team home for tea, and we sat on rickety chairs in a walled-off courtyard maybe ten feet square and talked about this and that. When the tekwa came, it was due to our honour and our hosts' to eat it all, but the Tamil girl just could not. She gagged and ran out, and we all felt ashamed.

But the Malayali nurses had no such problems. (Litti and tekwa were probably ambrosia after the mess grub anyway.) Some were shy, of course, but not maladjusted; and some joked and laughed with the villagers as if they were boon companions. They were a wonderful advertisement for the Hospital.

So was Sister Beena. On that memorable boat ride I have described in an earlier chapter, to conduct a free clinic at a backward village named Mailpur, we saw a couple of snakes coiled in a thorn tree to get out of the flood. 'Have you eaten snake?' she asked. None of us had. She had eaten snake, however; she had also tried frogs, termites and grasshoppers. Most of these dishes had been sampled in the North-East. I forget now whether she had tried the local delicacy which the Musahars live by, but it wouldn't surprise me at all if she had. Not that any of these would make my stomach heave; I just haven't been lucky enough. I wouldn't *go after* fried field-rats, but if a Musahar invited me to lunch I'd go along happily and take pot-luck.

The Mailpur trip was noteworthy to me for the boat-ride. The clinics were held twice a month and it was old stuff to the community health boys and the Sisters, but they would take along different nurses each time to let them have a feel of real rural work. When we'd got to Mailpur the boat was moored at a crumbling bank and we disembarked and clambered up some steps on to firm ground. We went through the village, filthy like all the Bihar villages I've seen where 'backwards' live, with the waterpump surrounded by garbage and pigs rooting in it.

We were taken to the mukhiya's house; I never made out who he was but perhaps he was away. In floodtime the practice of agriculture has to cease, and it's a good opportunity for the men to earn something in the city. It was a two-storeyed pukka house; a couple of cows and a frisky bull-calf were tethered on the ground floor, just inside the door, and we had to step carefully.

The clinic was conducted upstairs on a terrace—really of course a room which had not been completely walled or roofed over but would be when funds sufficed. The patients trooped up, most of the village population it appeared, all with minor complaints like sores and itches and eye infections. There were lots of flies. We had no doctor with us, so anyone suffering from something serious was asked to come to the Hospital. Sisters Beena and Rose (who ran physiotherapy) were both experienced diagnosticians, however, and doled out judicious quantities of the less expensive medicines. Akhilesh and I had nothing much to do but take down names and walk around the village.

I know very well I would not like to live in a village in Bihar. Could I do the work the community health department was engaged in doing? No; it was all very well as a day's outing and as a journalistic experience. As I wrote earlier, you need the right mix of pragmatism and idealism to do such work without thinking of profits—as I had discovered several of those who run NGOs do.

*

We left M____ for good in the first week of January '98, so I could only go along for the first phase of that winter's immunization. Our team got a village on the Patna highway for a change, and we were assigned to a large school building right on the road. When, in mid-morning, our second batch of vials was being unloaded from the Tatamobile, two young men from the village came over and accosted me. Was the campaign, they asked, being funded by any foreign country?

I dissembled. '*Yeh sirf Bharat sarkar ki yojana hai, bhai saab,*' I said, though I knew the funds came from the World Bank and UNICEF and Japan and I don't know who else.

They were satisfied. 'If there had been any foreigners involved we would not support it,' they said. They seemed to be hard-core swaraj types, typical of this paranoid era, who won't do anything about the ills of their society but won't let anyone else do anything either.

Later, when business was slack, a robust muscular chap in his forties ambled over and asked if I was from Kerala. He was a merchant sailor on leave, and many of his mates were from Kerala and Tamil Nadu. He'd often been to their houses—in Kochi, Alleppey, Tirunelveli, Tuticorin. The Malayalis and Tamils, he said, were both great drinkers, but the Malayalis knew how to hold their liquor while the Tamils did not . . . I had, regretfully, to cut short this promising conversation and attend to customers.

The Pulse Polio programme is an excellent introduction to our villages. If I had my way the government would put in a little money of its own and ferry teams of college students across India to volunteer in some state whose culture is as far removed as possible from their own. You could even get corporate sponsors; after all, they fund those inter-college 'Festivals' which are increasingly beginning to look and sound like the same synthetic cyber-kitsch whether in Lucknow or Bombay or Gummidipundi.

*

The last few months of our stay in M____ were marked by several high points. There was the Jubilee of the Sisters' Order in India, two days of festivity; there was the Christmas Mass I attended, and the old-fashioned procession of carol-singing nurses with the tableau of the Holy Family; and there was the brief revolution against the Sisters which the medical representative Bipan (*see* 'I was kicking someone') attempted to spark, for which he tried to enlist our support. I still have the pamphlet Bipan had printed:

Hon'ble Administrator of ____ Hospital

Sir,
With all respect we the people of M____, draw your kind attention on the declining services of ____ Hospital. This Samavitan Qutfit is playing with the health of suffering masses as one cuts Vegetables The shortcomings of the ____ Hospital are as follows:

- Mount of defects in Hospital Administration.
- Misconduct with patients and cases of slappings with the attendants.
- There is installation of Ultra Sound but all without a Radiologist.
- Operation theatre but all without an Anaesthetist.
- The hospital but all without a Surgeon.
- The hospital without Blood Bank.
- No ambulance facility for the patients to be carried in emergency cases.
- Exodus of good doctors from the hospital is frequent.
- Bungling of medicines in the pharmacy Department is at the zenith of malpractice, i.e supply of medicines manufactured by fake companies.
- 11% tax charged on the medicines supplied by the Hospital Pharmacy. However, 7% tax is applicable in Bihar.
- No electric (power) facility after 10 p.m.

We the people of M____, kindly request you to make a kind perusal of the problems aforesaid and help the suffering masses recover their health instead of going to the grave all due to medical neglect.

With regards
Yours faithful prayees

Bharat Press.

I was impressed by the diction. Points 3, 4 and 5, for instance, could easily be a paraphrase of *Ecclesiastes*. Some of this stuff was true, but Bipan with his political ambitions and unstable temperament was not very reliable, and I suppose Bhim Singh and the other Bhumihars who controlled the area must have shut up their clansman.

This was Bipan's first foray into politics. His elder brother, if I remember right, was with the Samata Party (Nitish Kumar's local number one he said, but that might have been exaggeration) and Bipan was throwing his lot in with someone else because (he said) he'd wanted to meet Nitish Kumar once and hadn't been granted an audience. But there was probably more to it than that. Powerful families prefer to have alternatives, and Bipan and his brother joining rival parties is analogous to the custom among the nineteenth-century English gentry and nobility to send the eldest son to Parliament, the second into the army and the third into the Church.

But I divagate . . . I've been waiting two years to describe in print the wedding of Kishan's brother Gopal, and am not going to deny myself. I have mentioned it a couple of times earlier, just to tantalize you. But here's the full story.

Gopal, as I've said, was very unlike Kishan. Kishan was mercurial and energetic; Gopal was merely stolid. But he was the Elder Brother, and deferred to in everything. His marriage was arranged with the daughter of a Marwari family in Patna, a graduate (he was not)—and everyone on the campus and indeed M____ was invited. Finally only three of us could make it: our neighbour Dr Kishore, the serious and soft-spoken Ranjit from accounts, and I, who of course had no work to do and could always saunter off anywhere at any time.

The three of us got to the Marwari mohalla pretty early in the morning—by six I should think. Kishan's house was abuzz with activity: Assorted relatives were brushing their teeth, washing, dressing up; inside, the ladies were adorning themselves and through the curtains we caught stray glimpses of splendour. Of course we had to have tea; our overnight bags were labelled to be put on the bus (I still have the label attached to my bag, which I discovered that night had 'DUMBISAN' carefully and painstakingly inscribed on it by one of Kishan's more literate henchmen).

The three of us travelled in state, with the bridegroom,

his suit on a hanger and the obligatory little boy (Kishan's sister's son) who figures in the baraat, in a white Maruti van. We left before the bus did—the indefatigable Kishan was 'organizing' as we drove off—and stopped at a small Bajrangbali temple on the outskirts of M____ for good luck. As we were coming out to get into the van I was stung on the ear by one of a small, angry swarm of bees. Dr Kishore promptly pulled out the sting, and procured Cetzin at the next chemist's; but my ear swelled up all the same. Later, in Patna, the small boy with us—let's call him Rakesh—pointed out to everyone how funny Uncle's ear looked, which I thought very mean of a brat who'd spent practically the whole journey in my lap so as not to rumple Gopal's white churidar-kurta.

We stopped at some kind of motel on the way, naturally, for refreshments, the bus catching up with us. Then on to Patna, the sun fiercer (though it was November) and my ear itchier. Before the Punpun bridge there is the dargah of a Muslim saint, and here Gopal deftly flung some coins into the space enclosed by the railings. Not for the first time I wondered at how impartially ordinary people in the North use both Hindu and Muslim shrines.

We reached Patna well before eleven, and drove to a dharamshala somewhere in the City (the City is old, squalid and commercial Patna). It was a newish building, with a lot of fake marble tiles, and very light and airy; the men went to their floor and the ladies to theirs. Tea of course; after a while an enormous and excellent Marwari lunch with six varieties of everything, and we all staggered to our rooms and crashed.

The baraat was to set out shortly after dark, so by four in the afternoon things were beginning to hum. I wanted a bath, and got my things together. First I went to the toilet and it was filthy; so I filled a bucket with water and sluiced it down, up and all around. Some of my fellow baraatis watched with amusement. 'Arre, why do you do that?' asked one, a tough dark guy who was obviously the dada among Kishan's mates and regarded me as an effete outsider. The others called him Guru. 'The sweeper will do it,' he said. 'Yes, day after tomorrow,' I answered. Having a shower was also fraught with difficulties: First, there was no shower and second, there was nowhere to hang my clothes. But as an old campaigner I managed all right.

When I got back to the room I found Gopal looking rather heavy-eyed after his sleep (and also no doubt due to the thought of the coming night). I advised him to have a bath, and he almost acceded, but the others were set against it: 'You have to sit on the horse for three hours, you'll catch cold,' and he agreed to just wash his face and behind the ears. I was a bit shocked. Imagine getting married without being bathed.

The room was full of men stripped down to vest and underpants, displaying various degrees of hirsuteness. No one else, I think, except Ranjit, bothered to bathe. A shout now went up for 'maxim'. '*Maxim kiske paas hai bhai?*' '*Arre maxim mere ko do.*' '*Tere baad mujhko dena.*' I was wondering what this 'maxim' was, was it a private word for a whisky bottle? '*Yeh kaunsa maxim hai*?' I asked Ranjit, but he was clueless as myself. Kishan sidled in in his usual secret service manner, bearing, he said, two more bottles of 'maxim'. I got closer to the action and discovered what all the fuss was about. It was Lakmé Maximum Moisturiser, pale pink goo in plastic bottles, which everyone liberally smeared on face, neck and hands. It took the place of bath, talc and after-shave. Some even put it in their hair. Two or three were painting Gopal with it. What an ad, I thought, why are those fools at Lever spending lakhs shooting Lisa Ray in soft focus through rose-coloured filters when their biggest market's here, in rooms in Bihar dharamshalas full of hairy half-naked baraatis who're afraid of cold water? '*Hum Maximum mangta hai*!'—what a line. It's copyright: If anyone at Lever's wants it, they can get to me c/o Penguin Books.

A little while (and more tea) later we found ourselves in another room with a full-length mirror, where the leading baraatis were struggling with their collars and ties. Guru was apparently the only chap there who could get the knot right, and he was knotting the ties one by one around his neck, loosening them and passing them back to the tie-ee. I was in a kurta and waistcoat; after so many years in the north I still don't see any point in dressing in suit and shoes to sit cross-legged before a sacred fire.

Kishan, again with the Mata Hari air, came in carrying a crate of beer and whisky, upon which inroads were rapidly made. Guru, seeing the way I tossed off my drink, revised his estimation of me upwards (or at least sideways), and we had a couple more but secretively—Kishan's father was against drinking. But that is a standard baraat story, it's only in slurpy 'family' films like *Hum Aapke Hain Kaun* that the baraatis don't get shown pushing their glasses under the sofa.

We trooped out and assembled outside the dharamshala finally, the white mare was brought and Gopal mounted it with Rakesh (cutely dressed—ugh!) before him; the band began to whoop and the baraat set out. I was walking by Gopal, doing the duties of a responsible baraati—adjusting his stirrup, smoothing out his trousers, and so on. It was worth it to observe the regal air with which the groom is supposed to receive such attentions (as his due) faithfully maintained by Gopal. After a while it began to pall, and under the influence of my potations no doubt I went to the head of the baraat and fulfilled my responsibilities there too, with a particularly suggestive twisty kind of step I'd perfected in Bombay but hadn't needed to use in seven or eight years. When I was through Guru came up to me, also flushed and sweating, and shook hands. 'Thanks, yaar, that was a boss dance.' After that I was one of the guys.

The baraat took two full hours to reach the girl's house, a distance I afterwards discovered could be covered in fifteen minutes; the band took advantage of every crossroads, and there were a couple of roads we must have gone up and later gone down again. It was on this journey that I witnessed the memorable spectacle of a patrician lashing a plebeian with a horsewhip (*see* 'I was kicking someone').

We got there at last—I was really pooped, for apart from the walk and the constant attentions to Gopal's trousers I'd danced a couple more times, and I was out of practice. The house was an old two-storeyed building, with a short drive, and absolutely *packed* with people. We made our way upstairs, beheld Gopal and his bride-to-be seated in state (*see* 'I will be dead by forty'), ate a little and then Ranjit and I looked at each other and agreed to head back to the dharamshala.

We found a game of *jua* in progress, Guru and his cronies intent on the cards. I've never been a betting man but joined in and was soon cleaned out. I went at it like poker, bluffing even when I had nothing, but was soon disabused of my notion that Flash is anything like. The other players were a little—not much—distressed at my recklessness, and even let me win a hand, at which I protested. I lost what was in my wallet—only 300 bucks or so—and, refusing a loan, watched for a while. Ranjit played safely but cannily and won something. Then I went back to our room, where Dr Kishore was already asleep along with the sober members of the party, and crashed. It was 3 a.m. but I was up at 5; we had to get back to M____ as early as we could, and I woke Dr Kishore and Ranjit.

Gopal and his bride came by before we left to touch our feet and ask our blessings. Kishan said the marriage party would be returning later in the day but we made our way to the station, bought tickets on an express (the doctor and Ranjit paying; I had only a few ones and twos on me) and were in the Hospital campus by early afternoon.

*

It is unfortunate that to have a good opinion of Bihar you have to have lived there.

Laloo puts it to the touch

He either fears his fate too much,
Or his deserts are small,
Who dares not put it to the touch
To win or lose it all.
—James Graham, Marquis of Montrose

For the first time I was travelling to Patna by air. The Bangalore flight had landed late at Palam—I had literally run from Arrivals to Departures, for the final call had already sounded—and if a buxom booking supervisor behind the Indian Airlines counter had not assured me that she would switch my suitcase on to the Patna flight, I would have missed it. Not only did she give me a confident promise, she kept it; ten days later, on my return, I was glad to find her on duty and to be able to thank her.

On board, the attitude of the airhostesses to the passengers was enlightening. Like waiters and shopkeepers, airline stewardesses have an uncanny eye for a customer's status. On blue-ribbon flights like Bombay-Delhi and Bangalore-Bombay the stewardesses are (mostly) sweetness and light; on the Patna flight they are brusque and schoolmistressish. More than one passenger had his feet up on the seat, and more than one, without the stewardess's eye on him, would have lighted a bidi.

To the left for a large part of the flight stretched the

Himalayas, glorious in the afternoon sun. I had been away from Bihar less than six weeks and already I missed it, especially the honesty, the often brutal frankness. The district of Kerala we had landed in, we'd already found, is the kind of place where the natives wear ingratiating smiles on their faces and speak honeyed words while lifting your wallet.

Patna airport is a small shed-like structure, and I was soon out of there and on my way to the government-run hotel for tourists, where I'd been booked in by the veteran journalist who'd agreed to take me under his wing. My room was large but bare and with the general appearance of some fulminating dry-rot behind the plaster and the woodwork. As it turned out, I didn't spend much time there.

*

Patna in February 1998 was steeped in apathy. The hirelings of the various political bosses did their part, and there were the formulaic rallies and tamasha, but there wasn't much enthusiasm. Usually the mood in any city before election time can be gauged from the auto-rickshaw and taxi drivers: They form a powerful guild and have something at stake, like revising fares upward. In Patna the rickshaw pullers didn't give a damn. Some told me, 'Who wants to vote? Why should we take the trouble?'

Nobody wanted an election again so soon after the last. Voter turnout was five to ten per cent less than in '96. And the results in Bihar depended almost entirely on a pro- or anti-Laloo wave.

Patna and the district towns were teeming with spies and agents of misinformation, and I'd have been suffering from a lot of delusions had it not been for the veteran journalist I was accompanying. Let's call him The Journalist: He was an old-timer with over fifty years' experience, mostly in Bihar, and with all the journalistic virtues and skills we only talk about now. He could smell a story and write it and back it with evidence if required; and there would be no apologies from the editor the next day, either.

We drove to Madhepura next morning with another journalist, an agency man we referred to as Garu. Dressed in dark suit and dark red tie, anxious to file copy every evening, he neither drank nor smoked and was obviously out of place, or else we were. In the front seat of the hired Ambassador were a couple of The Journalist's Patna sources, one a distinguished elderly Panditji in kurta and dhoti.

The first part of the journey was familiar territory to me; we bypassed M____ and drove on up the highway to Begusarai, where we stopped to interview the local Hindi agency stringer whose wife was principal of the local college. There was no sign of her, but we sat in her office, the stringer in the principal's chair, and flunkeys brought tea and 'snakes' and hung upon his every word. In Bihar a woman might officially occupy the more powerful position, but her husband will run her office—look at Rabri Devi.

The Journalist and Garu took notes as the stringer expounded the political realities in the district. To a features writer, they didn't mean much. The caste break-up was extremely important, I realized; the stringer could quote off-hand what percentage of Bhumihars, Rajputs, Kurmis and 'backwards' existed in each of the neighbouring constituencies, and all these statistics were taken down verbatim.

I was more interested in his report on Sonia Gandhi's rally in nearby Lakhisarai. 'More than a lakh of people,' he claimed, 'attended, and were very enthusiastic in their response.' Later, in the car, The Journalist said caustically, 'One lakh people can get together in Lakhisarai only if the Ganga dries up. Where is there such a big maidan?' I realized this was true; I should have thought of it myself. Keul and Lakhisarai are twin towns not far from M____, separated by the Ganga. They are not even towns, just villages which are self-important because they are on the main railway line. Again my fatal tendency to take people at their own estimation; which is why I guess I'm only a features hack and not an investigative reporter.

After Begusarai we left the highway and went north-eastward. The roads were reasonable by Bihar standards, which means pretty damned awful; the countryside was pleasant and green most of the way, but there were no signs of development anywhere. It was much as it must have been two hundred or two thousand years ago except for the vehicles and the power lines (serving God knows what use as almost without exception villages in such far-flung areas are without electricity). As in so much of Bihar—even UP is richer in comparison—you feel like a foreign tourist, tempted to take pictures of pretty poverty and fling coins to the village urchins. I had to study an English poem in the tenth standard, contrasting railway travel in Britain and India; two lines which always made me grind my teeth were:

> . . . And little brown-skinned boys and girls
> Who wonder at the moving train.

Travelling by car to Madhepura was the first Indian experience that made me think there could be any truth in that description even today.

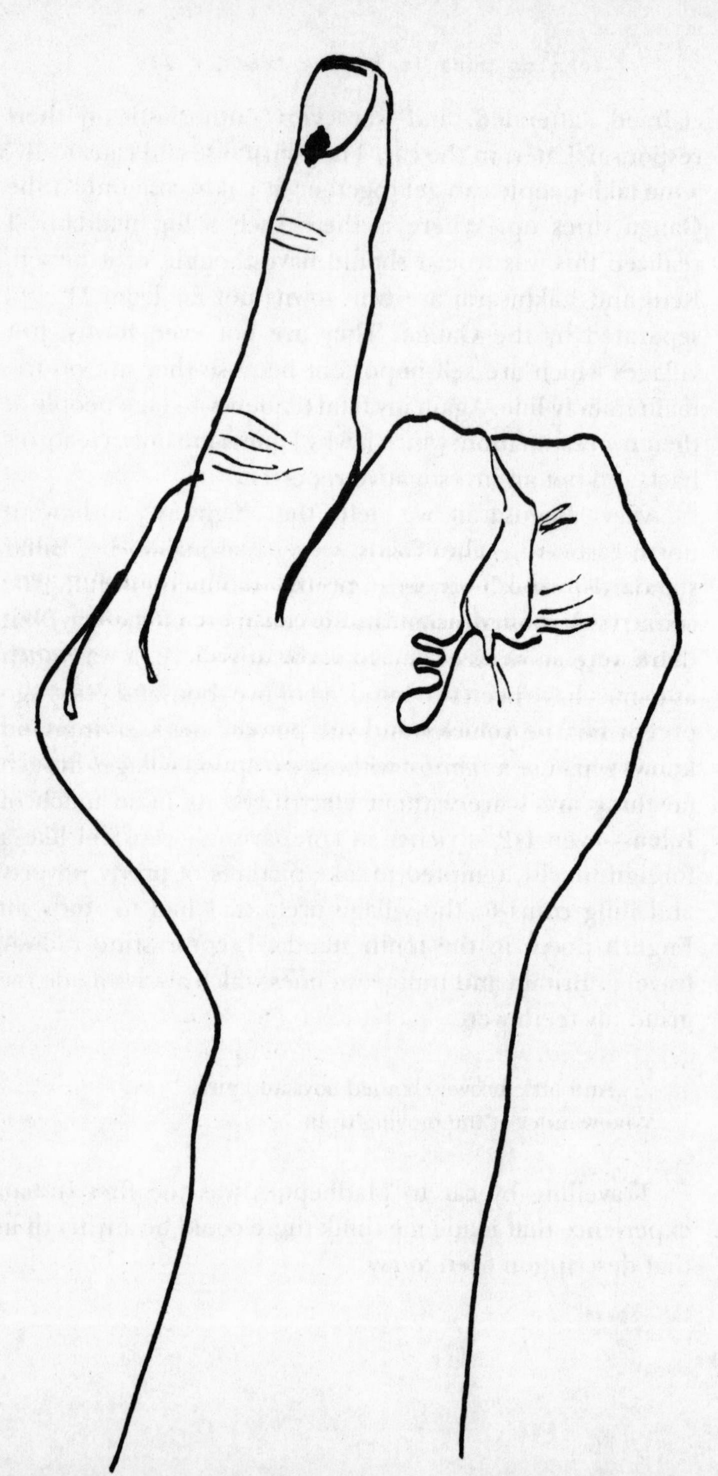

After a while it grew too dark to see the potholes, and our average speed fell drastically. We juddered and swayed across what were no doubt state highways, took all the right turnings though the driver was a Patna-dweller named Aziz, and got into Madhepura around eight, after a journey of eleven hours. It's a small town—a very small town, not even a district headquarters, not fifty kilometres from the Nepal border and only one district removed from West Bengal. There's one main street with a couple of hotels, a college or two and a government dak bungalow or guest house (what used to be called a Circuit House) a little out of town; the usual small shops on the main street, none of them selling anything which would excite a visitor from Patna.

We found our hotel quite easily, and The Journalist and I shared one room which was quite clean, even the toilet. After some refreshment we sallied forth to seek what we should find.

As The Journalist and Garu sought more vital facts, I wondered at how the streets of Madhepura blazed with light. A citizen in a tea-shop grinned and told me, 'It's never like this. We hardly ever have power. *Lekin Laloo khade rahe hain na?* (But Laloo's standing, isn't he?)' Laloo's newly acquired election symbol was the *laltein* (kerosene lantern), which was more appropriate to his constituency. I remembered a play I'd seen in Delhi many years ago, called *Blindman di Laltein*...

Madhepura has nothing to recommend it; it's a remote and unimportant outpost not only of India but even in terms of Bihar. Why should Laloo Prasad abandon his political base among the Yadavs of the heartland and travel here to contest a Lok Sabha seat?

The answer, as it so often is in Bihar, was mardangi. Laloo Prasad had been deposed as president of the Janata Dal because of the charges of corruption against him, and his place had been taken by Sharad Yadav; so Laloo felt slighted and was out to avenge the insult.

As Bihar politicians go there is probably not much difference between the two Yadavs. But Sharad Yadav has a clean image conspicuously lacking in Laloo's case; even in late 1999, when he became Union Minister for Civil Aviation (traditionally a plum post for junkets abroad) he delegated all foreign trips to his Minister of State so as not to jeopardize his record of not once having travelled abroad by air in twenty-five years of politics. But he also noticeably lacks Laloo Prasad's charisma and gift for public relations; when, soon after he had become Civil Aviation Minister, an eight-year-old girl was trapped in an escalator at the New Delhi airport and killed, Sharad Yadav as soon as he reached the spot offered five lakh rupees as compensation to her family. Laloo would never have done that (at least not in his palmy days; now he is sore beset)—he would have shed tears.

Laloo Prasad was an outsider in Madhepura. The Yadavs of the Ganga plain are poor and backward, but the Yadavs of Madhepura are another matter altogether; landed and feudal, they often take the role which the Bhumihars play in central Bihar. But then Sharad Yadav was an outsider too; his roots are in Jabalpur in Madhya Pradesh, not in Bihar at all.

Bravado has marked many of Laloo's actions in his over thirty-year political career, which began when he was General Secretary of the Patna University Students Union. In the landmark '77 elections, JP picked him for the Chapra seat in western Bihar, near his origins in Gopalganj. He could easily have contested again from there. But if the bravado which mardangi compels is his forte, it is also his foible.

Laloo Prasad has never been afraid to put it to the touch. His career evokes the same sort of uneasy wonder which is evoked by the chap in the circus who puts his head into the lion's mouth. The difference is that the freak with the lion is only endangering his own prospects, not those of a hundred million others as well.

*

The morning after our arrival in Madhepura Sharad Yadav was due to address putative constituents in town and then adjourn to the government guest house to meet more important people, representatives of the press among them. I gave the rally a miss but went along to the guest house. The lawns were crowded, there was 'security' everywhere (not all of it official) and Sharadji was late. I left my fellow tradesmen in there and adjourned for a cigarette. Though only February it was already hot.

A couple of jeans-clad youths sat astride a motorbike nearby, and we fell into conversation. My ordinary working garb of white kurta and jeans and dark glasses on a chain around my neck (which I'd adopted before Laloo Prasad became a media icon, though it provoked a number of unnecessary comments on my return South from Bihar) advertised that I was an outsider and probably a presswala. The youth at the handlebars of the bike approached me as such.

I gathered that he was, in order of importance, son of a local politico, president of the students union of the local college, and fervently anti-Laloo. This was not surprising; several inhabitants of Madhepura had conveyed similar sentiments, but less openly. There was something, however, curiously shifty-eyed about this students' boss which I thought The Journalist would be better equipped to discover the meaning of, and I invited my new friend to our hotel after we had taken leave of Sharadji.

Sharadji had arrived, and through corridors and even doorways packed with people we were led into his presence. Several aides sat close by with their eyes and ears open; 'media' can soon become a dirty word in electoral politics. The Journalist and Garu asked stock questions about prospects and policies, and Sharadji delivered stock platitudes. I wasn't much interested but very alert. Of course I'd interviewed big shots before, but never a Lok Sabha candidate in a contest which made headlines every day.

What I wanted to find out was Sharad Yadav's opinion of Laloo Prasad, his former mentor. But he was evasive and shifty, not answering a direct question—why burn bridges you may very well need again?—and I lost any sense of occasion I'd had.

On our way back I told The Journalist about the students' boss who'd no doubt be at the hotel by now. One of the things I admired about *my* mentor was his instant interest in a story, in getting to the bottom of things, after fifty years of the same kind of stuff. The Journalist was attentive and flatteringly interested. When we got to our room I left him to interview the student and stood myself against the wall.

It was an object lesson in reportorial or even police interviewing. With a few deft questions The Journalist discovered the student's antecedents, dissected them and asked why he was against Laloo when he should have been for him. The student was palpably nervous. I offered him a drink to steady his nerves (it was twelve noon). He declined, but I poured him a drink all the same—knowing how IMFL is drunk in India, it was a tumblerful of neat whisky. He reached for it and gulped it down. By now The Journalist was declaring loudly and scornfully, '*Yeh to* spy *hai, yeh to* informer *hai.*' Turning to me he said indignantly, '*Arre*, this man is a paid agent for Laloo, he is just creating misinformation.' With another glass of whisky in him the student sat happily nodding his head.

I left Madhepura perplexed by the subtleties of electoral politics in Bihar.

*

The Journalist and I broke our journey back to stop off at his brother-in-law's house north of the Ganga—we'd not taken the highway past M____ this time—while Garu hurried back to Patna to file his interview with Sharad Yadav. Agencies will take any copy they get—the important thing is that the story should be filed on time, not that it should be newsworthy. And the amount of agency news our 'leading' newspapers take . . . but we'll go into all that, or anyway I will, in the next chapter.

The old house was occupied by The Journalist's widowed sister and her sons. The sister was the local MLA, having inherited the Assembly seat from her husband; she was affable but did not talk much politics. The sons were hospitable as everyone is in Bihar; they left us alone in a room to talk. Next morning we caught a bus for Patna.

Road traffic to Patna from north of the Ganga has to cross an interminably long bridge. But this was the day before the elections, and all vehicles were halted at the northern end. There was nothing we could do about it. There weren't even buses waiting at the southern end as would have been the case in any city with normal entrepreneurial instincts.

As I've said, it was quite hot; and we had to walk two

kilometres across the bridge. I was really worried for my friend, who was elderly and overweight and distressed by the exercise. And even at the southern end, we would be twelve kilometres from Patna, with no buses there. There was a police chowki halfway along the bridge but the cops were uninterested. The disclosure of our journalistic status did not move them in the least. They were stationed there to keep traffic out, not to help the public, leave alone presswalas.

Once we were across I went down the embankment into the suburban slums and managed to find a cycle-rickshaw puller who was willing to drag us to town. His fee was exorbitant by Patna standards but laughable in any other state—fifty bucks. Sweating prodigiously, we settled ourselves in the seat, which canted to the left at a steep angle, so my friend took the right side. And thus we sat for two hours while the scrawny bit of humanity before us grunted and pushed and cursed us home. If you want to be really depressed try a two-hour ride in a Patna cycle-rickshaw. We talked for a while but the heat and strain were too intense and we just wanted to be inside The Journalist's house and outside a bottle of beer.

In Patna I found out why there had been no buses at the southern end of the Hajipur bridge. They had been impounded for 'election duty'. Gandhi Maidan on 16 February was half-filled with rows and rows of lorries and buses. There must have been a thousand of them.

This 'impounding' is of course a means of extortion; but as a lorry owner cannot get a receipt for a bribe, he may have to pay it several times over in different parts of Bihar, and it's cheaper to allow his vehicle to be seized. Owners of private vehicles are not let off either. Those with influence secure a permit of 'exemption'. Those who cannot are quite likely to have their cars taken away—sometimes by the police, when they are not 'seized' but 'requisitioned for election duty'—and put to uses often unofficial. The exemption comes with money and connections, not necessary work. Even ambulances run by non-government agencies are liable to seizure. The Sisters of Charity, who on principle refuse to pay bribes, at their Provincial House in Patna secreted their brand-new Mahindra Commander in a garage for two weeks. At M____ the Sisters could count on local influence, but they made no trips outside the area.

Influence too is an ephemeral thing, not there when you seek to grasp it. I was told at a Delhi cocktail party in February '98 that just two weeks earlier Laloo Prasad's family doctor had had his car seized by goondas whom he recognized as his most favoured client's hirelings. Confident that justice would be done, he went to 1 Anne Marg and poured out his troubles to Laloo. '*Achha, achha,*' Laloo is reported to have said, '*sab kuchh theek karva doonga* (I'll set everything right).' He called for the goondas named and asked them if they had seized the car. They said yes, grinning all the while. 'Very well,' said Laloo turning to the doctor. 'You give them five lakhs and take back your car.' The goondas roared. With the grave yawning before him the doctor abandoned his practice and fled Patna. I'm not entirely sure if this story is apocryphal, for by some strange fortuity a spice-trader in the small Kerala town we had moved to turned out to be the doctor's brother-in-law, and many months later he told us the same tale when he learned we had just come from Bihar. The doctor had settled in Bangalore, he said.

Naturally, there are few engined vehicles on Patna's streets at election time; travelling in a rickshaw is almost a pleasure because the streets are uncrowded and smoke-free.

In other respects, too, Patna is different from comparable Indian cities when its denizens are given the opportunity to exercise their franchise. For one thing, it's the only city or town I've ever been in where the liquor shops are open on election day. Laloo Prasad's formula to keep the citizens happy is not original—give them *panem et circenses*—and has probably been used to good effect by his predecessors on the *gaddi.* When I left Bihar the price of a 750 ml bottle of standard IMFL—none of your fancy dimpled bottles and aristocratic vintages—was Rs 125. In Delhi, Bombay and the South it varied from one and a half times to twice as much. Reductions in excise taxes do affect the state's revenue; however, there are compensations in public enthusiasm and the relative ease with which violence can be provoked. Bread is expensive in comparison, but there's always sattu; and the circuses come without charge.

(About violence—there's always violence in Patna and all over Bihar at election time, but I never saw any of it. I mentioned in the last chapter, when writing about my experiences on Bihar trains, that the gods who look after fools, madmen and drunkards had kept me safe; naturally I had no printed guarantee from them but I trusted to my luck and was all right. There were times when I took a rickshaw from The Journalist's house back to my hotel—some five or six kilometres—around midnight, and I felt a good deal safer than I did a week later on Rafi Marg in the heart of New Delhi. There even at eight in the evening I was constantly turning back to see if anyone was behind me, some horned and hoofed fiend or, more to the point, some dope fiend with a knife.)

Speaking for myself, finding the liquor shops open when we returned from Madhepura was no great hardship; but my civic sense rebelled. It was no hardship to The Journalist either. That afternoon when we'd got over our rickshaw ride he told me, 'Arre Vijay, I'm sick of that Bagpiper you've been buying, it's *faaltu* stuff. Go out and get some Smirnoff.' It cost only Rs 300 around the corner. I'd not tried the Indian make before, and it went down like water, which was what The Journalist pretended it was when his wife came upstairs to ask why we hadn't yet had lunch. She looked to me for confirmation, and I had to say, '*Kya main kahoonga ki Bhai sahib jhooth bol rahe hain?* (Would I ever say that he's telling a lie?)' She went away satisfied. She was a simple lady who could not suspect evil in others.

But The Journalist's progeny were more worldly-wise. Two of them, a son and a daughter, called up to ask me what the hell I was doing luring their father to drink and destruction. 'You're a reporter, why don't you go out and report?' snarled the daughter. I replied with some heat that it was unjust to accuse me of corrupting a man who was not only old enough to be, but whom I esteemed as my father. But The Journalist was still filing his copy daily; after a couple of days both son and daughter called up to apologize for their rudeness and everything blew over.

(Reading this draft, Kavery's just told me that *she* called The Journalist from Delhi—where she was going to concerts and plays while I was working my fingers to the bone in Bihar—and gave him an earful for not stopping *me.* He has old-world manners and wouldn't dream of contradicting a lady, so he apologized to her and didn't even tell me about her call. He is a gentleman . . . of course I bawled Kavery out for bawling someone else out when she should have bawled me out.)

Looking back, I suppose it was rather unthinking of me to get The Journalist into such a scene of steady drinking as he hadn't experienced for twenty years. He was hypertensive, too. But I never *lured* him, I was just doing what came naturally; and he was so young at heart that I was soon after reaching Patna calling him by his first name and telling him dirty stories, while he told me dirty stories about JP and P.V. Narasimha Rao and others, which cannot be printed here . . . He taught me more about the political-journalistic game than I ever again intend to use, and I guess I brought some ten days' relief into his life.

*

In Madhepura the once-full moon of Laloo Prasad's destiny had appeared to be on the wane. In my first report to Madras I'd written:

> As it appears, the anti [-Laloo] factor is likely to be stressed. Votes are only to be counted in a couple of days, but it is not premature to assert that the Rashtriya Janata Dal will not win more than a dozen seats, and Laloo's own face may well be muddied in Madhepura—where not only was a bogus candidate set up, but rigging was resorted to on no small scale to ensure Laloo's victory.

It turned out, of course, that the assertion was premature—it was eighteen months too early. It was not until results of elections to the Thirteenth Lok Sabha were declared in September 1999 that Laloo had his face muddied in Madhepura and his RJD was reduced to single-digit presence. But as a matter of historical record—and because it contains observations which are still valid—I reproduce my second despatch to *The Hindu,* which appeared on 15 March 1998, two weeks after the first.

Perhaps the 'what' in the headline should be replaced by 'who':

BIHAR VOTED, BUT WHAT COUNTED?

It is mildly amusing, and very instructive, to see intellectuals and news analysts who have violently attacked Laloo Prasad Yadav for two years suddenly hailing him as a hero of secularism because he restricted the BJP-Samata alliance to 29 seats out of 53 in Bihar (a repoll will be held in Patna on March 10).

The truth is that for all his talk about secular forces uniting against the communal danger, Laloo's real target was the Janata Dal, which he perceived as having betrayed him on two counts—first, the CBI's assiduous pursuit of a conviction in the fodder scam (though that was more U.N. Biswas's doing than the Union Government's), and second, Sharad Yadav's supplanting him as JD President (though that had more to do with Sharad's vaulting ambition).

This was why Laloo went all the way to Madhepura to take on Sharad Yadav. This correspondent was probably foolish to say he would lose, though I did temper my claim with a stipulation of fair play. A margin of 50,000 votes is not large in the Ganga plain. Yet Laloo Prasad is still the most powerful man in Bihar, and controls the state machinery in the person of his wife. When he throws his whole power behind a candidate, there is little to prevent the latter's election, unless his opponent is a heavyweight. This is what happened with the five Kesri *chamchas* who made it to the Lok Sabha, and all of whom are on good terms with Laloo.

But given the voters' mood, not even Laloo could ensure the elimination of both the JD and the BJP. His talk of secular forces combining ended with a destruction of all possible rival claimants to the leadership of such forces, which is not quite the same thing. The United Front of course helped Laloo materially by failing to live up to its name, perhaps more so in Bihar (and Uttar Pradesh) than anywhere else.

The fact is that the BJP-Samata total went up from 24 in

1996 to 29 this year (to my satisfaction as a forecaster and sorrow on certain other counts). Laloo has stemmed the tide in the same way that the Finance Ministry's hired economists announce smugly, 'The rate of *increase of inflation* has declined.'

With 17 MPs, as yet uncommitted, Laloo Prasad may have substantial clout in the Twelfth Lok Sabha, but with unusual restraint he is playing his cards close to his chest. He has practically ruled out any support to a BJP-led government, but Laloo is a politician for whom nothing is impossible . . . and if he does throw his weight behind the secular forces, he will exact as his price nothing less than a Cabinet seat. Laloo Prasad Yadav as Union Home Minister: the mind boggles . . . U.N. Biswas will be condemned to death, and the Grand Trunk Road will be thrown open to bullocks riding scooters from Patiala to Patna . . . But if Mulayam Singh Yadav did it, so can Laloo Prasad.

For Laloo Prasad Yadav succeeded, in these elections, in something which is accounted very important on his home turf: He maintained his *mardangi* (manhood, honour) [forgive this repetition]. Sharad Yadav was beaten and made to look like a weakling, and the JD was wiped out in Bihar (with the sole exception of Ram Vilas Paswan, who can be defeated in Hajipur only by an act of God, like a major railway accident). That probably means more to Laloo than combating communal forces.

The Samata's emergence as a party in its own right is interesting, but in the long run will be recorded as just another instance of George Fernandes's attempts at meaningful politics translating themselves into attempts at survival. Nitish Kumar, though, is someone to watch out for.

Another point news analysts sometimes miss is that, in Bihar, the BJP's watchword of stability counts for more than its opponents' branding of it as 'communal'. Communal divisions are not a major problem in most of

> Bihar. (Bhagalpur is of course one glaring exception.) This may be because Muslims in the state are, by and large, poor and landless, and so are the large numbers of (Dalit) Christians; it may also be that in the drastically altered political agenda in Bihar which dates from the Laloo Prasad revolution in 1990, the minorities have had to be treated well by all parties.
>
> It is caste-consciousness, and the consequent factionalization of communities, which is Bihar's bane. That, and how skilfully the politicians used it, were what determined the outcome of elections this year in practically every constituency in the state. (The media have much to answer for in the matter . . .) On the whole, the BJP-Samata's calculations succeeded, primarily because the secular forces were fighting each other.

It is difficult now to say if Laloo would have won in '98 without unofficial tactics. Rigging and its associated phantoms are so prevalent in the Ganga plain that only someone deep in the heart of a campaign can make an accurate estimate of the just or what-would-have-been-just margin. And since Laloo was still in power, though not so firmly, in '99, Sharad Yadav's moderate winning margin of about 30,000 must have meant something much more substantial. Sharad Yadav ended up looking a fool as usual; he had gone on a fast unto death to reinforce his demand for a repoll, and when it turned out he'd won he had almost as much egg on his face as when he had lost the previous year.

It's worth detailing some of the illegal tactics used to ensure victory. When I referred to them as 'phantoms' in the preceding paragraph it was with reason; *India Today* carried this brief from Sanjay Kumar Jha on 30 August last year:

BOGUS BOXES, FRAUD FRANCHISE

District Election Officers (DEOs) from seven of Bihar's constituencies have confirmed discovering bogus ballot boxes among those used in the previous election [1996]. Siwan (510) and Samastipur (440) accounted for most. Twenty boxes found in Siwan are in the eye of the storm. D.C. Yadav (JD) who lost the Saharsa seat to A.L. Yadav (RJD) in 1998 says some of these boxes were used to help Laloo Yadav defeat Sharad Yadav in neighbouring Madhepura. Parts of Madhepura [constituency] come within the Saharsa DEO's purview. Laloo had claimed 'djinns' in ballot boxes helped him win.

When I came back South at the end of February '98 and read in the papers that allegations of booth-capturing had been levelled against the CPI (M)-led Left Front in Kerala and the DMK in Tamil Nadu I laughed. The manipulation of elections, and election returns, is practised in Bihar on a scale unknown in the South. It is not necessarily more scientific; what is staggering about it is precisely its overtness.

Three months before the '98 elections I wrote in *The Hindu* that I had heard stories of rigging so horrific that I would not dare to put them in print even if I'd had a hundred witnesses to back me up. But the elections desensitized me; in March I could write in the same columns, with a light heart:

But in the last three months, so much circumstantial abuse of politicians and their methods has found its way into print that I cannot help concluding

- politicians do not read newspapers, or
- politicians have become so thick-skinned and cynical that

nothing in the media touches them, or

- there are subversions of democracy in practice which are so much more horrifying that politicians do not mind the stories which are instanced, or
- all of the above.

Now I'm pretty sure it's all of the above.

Some of the stories I heard were rather funny. This one is from the '96 elections. A district in central Bihar happened to have an honest District Magistrate (a rarity in those parts). On polling day a rumour reached him that such-and-such a polling station had been captured; that genuine voters were being turned away while the polling official sat inside with a couple of cronies and a couple of extra rubber stamps they had manufactured, stuffing the ballot boxes as fast as they could. The DM got into his white Ambassador (with the red light on top) and was driven thither. At the door to the polling station the CRPF constable on duty refused to let him enter. '*Main* DM *hoon*,' the DM said indignantly. '*To phir* ID card *dikhao*,' said the CRPF man.

Now District Magistrates belong to that class of infallibles who do not carry, or need to carry, proofs of their identity upon their person. But there was no help for it. The honest DM went back to his office in his white Ambassador, and when he returned with his ID card the polling official had gone home with a cramp in his elbow but otherwise happy and all the voting was done.

I heard an even more fantastic story about '98: that a convoy of vehicles laden with ballot boxes heading for the counting station was cunningly diverted and another convoy took its place, the ballots it bore being strictly ersatz . . . I didn't know it was possible to counterfeit ballot boxes, and neither (I hope) do most of us; but the *India Today* story shows it's possible. And done.

But '98 was not a very gripping election. Even the violence was at a low level, and fewer lives were lost in six weeks of campaigning and one week with elections at either end than died on a brutal night early the previous December at Lakshmanpur Bathe in Jehanabad district.

There was one gruesome murder in '96. Devendranath Dubey, Samajwadi Party MLA and candidate for the Motihari Lok Sabha seat in East Champaran (one of Bihar's most backward and violent districts; NGO workers there refer to the two Champarans as East and West Apaharan, or abduction) was ambushed and killed on 24 February, along with five 'supporters' who were travelling with him.

I was in Delhi then, and had to rely on the papers; only *The Statesman* had a detailed account, credited to 'eyewitnesses', though God knows who they were and why they were there. According to them, Dubey's car was overtaken on a lonely road and stopped by a few vans from which disembarked thirty-five or forty men in police and military uniforms, all armed with Kalashnikovs. More than 200 rounds were fired, and Dubey's body was 'lacerated' (what a word to use!) beyond recognition.

The obvious culprit was RJD MLA and then State Energy Minister (earlier Minister for Science and Technology, which might explain the sophistication of the operation) Braj Bihari Prasad, who had been at outs with Dubey for a long time and whose wife Rama Devi was the RJD candidate in Motihari. All that was straightforward enough, but the whole business was on a scale staggering even for Bihar. And I was also surprised that Dubey had been foolhardy enough to travel with so little protection.

Braj Bihari resigned from the state cabinet, but it didn't save him. About a year later he was shot dead in his own house; the TV networks, starved for gore, went to town with footage of the puddles of blood in the courtyard and the tearful family. Rama Devi (who had won the election) wept and tore her hair in the Lok Sabha and Laloo Prasad made an impassioned speech there denouncing his political rivals who had stained their hands for ever with innocent blood.

No one else is going to shed too many tears for these two murdered goons, or even for Rama Devi. Braj Bihari had a number of criminal cases against him, and Dubey was actually a proclaimed absconder, a Member of the Legislative Assembly wanted by the courts and the police while he was campaigning in full public view. But all too often it *is* the innocents who get killed.

*

(*Note*: The next six paragraphs were written before the Assembly elections of February 2000, and I leave them untouched; what follows offers after-the-event wisdom.)

As I am writing this there comes a news bulletin saying Prime Minister Atal Behari Vajpayee has announced projects worth Rs 26,000 crore for Bihar. He has already stuffed the Union Council of Ministers with Biharis in preparation for the Assembly elections. This is typical of the Centre's attitude to Bihar; feed them glory and rob them of their riches. Tragic, because those in New Delhi are the only people who can do something about Bihar.

The BJP Leader of the Opposition in the Assembly and Laloo's most consistent critic, Sushil Kumar Modi, ought by rights to become Chief Minister if the unwieldy BJP-Samata-Janata Dal (United) alliance wins; but he's a long-term player and appears to have indicated that he will step aside for Yashwant Sinha or Ram Vilas Paswan or Sharad Yadav or whoever else the Centre wants.

Modi is an interesting character. He was secretary of the Patna University Students Union when Laloo was its president, and knows his enemy well. He speaks sense most of the time but you have to read the newspapers in Bihar to figure that out: He's hardly ever mentioned in the national media.

But will Laloo Prasad be so easy to displace? Temporarily, perhaps; he is out of the Lok Sabha (thanks to his unbelievable foolhardiness in going back to Madhepura, loving not power less but honour more) and; since this government has a good chance of completing its five years, has no recourse but to the local stage. With the charges of corruption pending against him, and unfriendly governments in both New Delhi and Patna, he will find it difficult. Rabri Devi might go back to the kitchen, but her husband has only one place to go back to, and that is jail. But this is not the moment, or the place, to write his epitaph. He will be around for a long time.

I write this well before the Assembly elections, and I've no idea if the publishing schedule will let me get a few words in about them. No matter. The last Lok Sabha elections threw up a strange bunch of political jobbers uneasily sharing one bed. The Assembly elections are certain to do the same, whoever wins.

What can be safely said is that we can be sure the people will lose. And the elections will be violent, very violent. That is Laloo Prasad's unforgivable crime, that each time he embarks on one of his wild political adventures he puts not only his own fate to the touch but all Bihar to the torch as well.

*

I wish I'd taken bets on Laloo being returned to power after the Assembly elections. My instincts told me Laloo might not win, but he wouldn't be beaten; however, I was too much in awe of the newsmagazines and their high-powered analysts and opinion polls. Stupid of me. After so many years in the racket I should have known better: No 50,000-rupee-a-month deputy editor sitting on his backside in New Delhi and flying down to Patna for a two-day visit (when he stays at the Maurya and talks to all the wrong people, politicians and lobbyists and editors) is likely to know better than I do what is and is not possible in Bihar.

I was wrong about the violence, thankfully. But when I wrote the preceding passage I had no foreknowledge that the elections would be held in three phases, nor that there would be such a massive paramilitary presence.

The events leading up to Rabri Devi's installation as Chief Minister for the third time are too fresh in our minds to need recapitulation, or analysis: The TV channels and the newsmagazines have already done all that. It was no victory for secularism, as some claim. The election agenda as it has been through three elections since the announcement of the 1998 Lok Sabha polls was purely Laloo's performance and integrity, not the BJP's Hindutva connections. Nitish Kumar had a point when he said Laloo had lost the referendum. Communal harmony is not a big issue in Bihar.

Nitish Kumar, as I wrote to my paper two years ago, is someone to watch out for, but I cannot help feeling his future lies at the Centre. No one is going to be able to dominate Bihar politics as long as Laloo is around in his present incarnation, a blend of ruthless political brilliance and genuine socialism, the former overshadowing the latter as he fights for survival. He did not win the mandate, but he's simply too good at manipulation. Handling Sonia

Gandhi and the rest must have been child's play to him.

Sushil Kumar Modi. . . I'd like to see him as Chief Minister, he's the one guy there who might restore sanity to the state; but will he be given an opportunity even by his own party? There are too many has-beens who are bigger than him in Delhi's strabismal eye: Ram Vilas Paswan will never lose an election but his power base is too narrow and the BJP will strain at swallowing a Dalit as Chief Minister; Yashwant Sinha and Sharad Yadav have no popular base at all.

A point of interest to me in the reports of the election results and the subsequent skulduggery was the prominence enjoyed by Suraj Bhan Singh, who standing as an NDA-supported Independent defeated Dilip Singh of the RJD in my native constituency. (With all that coverage the identity of M____ is blown, but what the hell; it's also known to quiz freaks who James Bond's chief, 'M', really was.)

Suraj Bhan was one of the two gang leaders in our time—Sanjay Singh being the other—and he's come to Kavery's OPD attended by his bodyguards to be treated for a knee problem resulting from an old gunshot wound. He led the criminal element which supported Nitish Kumar, and every journal had a picture of him and his cohorts at the swearing-in. News to us, Suraj Bhan was reported to be the biggest underworld don in the UP-Bihar belt and king of M____. I wonder what's happened to Sanjay Singh. Suraj Bhan has also expressed his intention of making M____ a crime-free area. I laughed when I read that, but he's about the only person who can do it.

*

It feels funny-peculiar to be sitting in this hill haven on the Tamil Nadu-Kerala border some 2,000 km from the action as I write about it. It's like I've retired and am writing my memoirs.

I'll probably go back to Bihar some years from now and write about it, but never again as a native. And I'm sure my reportage will be tinged more with sorrow than with nostalgia: Because Laloo Prasad Yadav is going to be around for a good long time to come.

Killing the divine king

'What *is* the answer?' . . . [Silence] . . . 'In that case, what is the question?'

— Gertrude Stein's last words

In Bihar, our only window to the outside world was the Patna edition of *The Times of India*. I'd rejected *The Hindustan Times* on principle, since I don't go along with those in Delhi who subscribe to it for its weight and therefore value to *kabadiwalas*; we didn't have a TV, also on principle. We had a radio, of course, but we only used it for listening to news bulletins, old film songs and cricket commentaries. We got *Sportstar* and *Frontline* (again, on principle) whenever possible, i.e. whenever they arrived from Patna. Our news boy was a slight young chap who sang old Hindi film songs on his rounds in a very pleasant tenor. It was nice listening to him at seven in the morning and knowing the paper was about to be tucked in behind the bolt on the front door.

I have several times previously made animadversions to the Patna edition of *The Times of India*. I must say that though I have an animus against the *TOI* as a whole, the Patna edition had its own problems . . . A few years ago the *TOI Sunday Review* passed a policy decision not to review any book which had been published in India, and what do we book reviewers do? I've also been turned down twice when I asked for a job, long years ago, once at *The Independent* and once at *The Economic Times*, both times by Management when the editors (Anil Dharkar and T.N. Ninan respectively) were willing to tolerate me. I state these facts so you know where I stand. And each passing year so much more of the paper's editorial content becomes slush . . . With the *TOI* around, we don't need Rupert Murdoch.

The Patna *TOI* was then edited by a gentleman named Uttam Sengupta whom I know nothing about except that he had been shot at by a person or persons unknown in 1997, and two bullets had lodged themselves in the back of his Fiat. Perhaps that incident had affected his skills; no, that's mean. He was probably a competent editor, but the paper he edited was unabashedly given over to producing revenue rather than readability. At any rate, the Patna *TOI* was the most consistently uproarious newspaper I've ever read.

Typographical errors are common enough in any newspaper, and they're getting more frequent even in journals which set high standards for themselves, as I know to my dismay and discontent. But where do you see typos in the lead headline on the front page? Answer: In the Patna *TOI*. Stories on the front page were repeated inside, identical except as to format; stories which appeared one day frequently had a reincarnation the next; and most criminal of all, the comic strips were abandoned to sub-editorial anarchy. They were often jumbled so that they ran chronologically backward; and on one bright occasion, the same strip of *Garfield* ran for six consecutive days. I've often laughed at *Garfield*, but for different reasons; and I've never before had reason to curse it either.

The Bihar newspapers . . . I sometimes got to see the *Hindustan Times* and Hindi papers like *Jansatta* and *Navbharat Times* (which is, or used to be —I haven't read it for some years—the most consistently good northern newspaper). The Bihar newspapers mostly featured Bihar news, and if I hadn't read them I wouldn't be writing this book. It is from reading them that I made up my mind about state BJP chief Sushil Modi, and about various other persona and phenomena. Once *Dainik Hindustan* featured the gang warfare in M____, with a photograph of criminals appropriately masked and weaponed standing before a wall.

Perhaps it was a Good Thing we didn't have TV or access to the web, and we still don't. I could make up my own mind about what was happening around me, which is a luxury denied journalists and media consumers, which means practically everyone in these troubled times when above all they need to use their own judgement.

*

Writing this book has been relatively easy, for it has no plot and the characters came ready to use. If it's taken me two years that's only because writing is terribly hard work for me—not the actual writing, but the sitting down to it. There's lots I haven't expatiated on, or even mentioned: Christmas in the Hospital; the politics of multinational agencies; the affection Biharis have for their children; how I bought a *tola* of weed a *chillum*'s throw from the thana in M____ for forty bucks; how Kavery after one of our evening walks almost stepped on a ten-foot long, chocolate-brown snake on the doorstep of the doctors' quarters and ran back screaming into my arms; my meeting with Mohammed Kuddoos, who had organized N.T. Rama Rao's seminal *rath yatras* and been borrowed by Laloo Prasad for his election campaigns, and bore the title of 'Rath-in-Charge', and who told me things I can't write about though none disparaging Laloo . . .

But writing the book, I've been wondering why I am doing it, and who I am to do it. What is my angle? Bihar is being exploited in every possible way, not least by the media, and am I not, too, cashing in? If Bihar has a bad image, is that not the fault of the image-makers and image-breakers, and am I not one of them?

Laloo Prasad says Bihar has had a bad press: '*Presswalon ne badnaam kiya hai*.' That is not entirely the presswalas' fault. You can't expect them to pass up a massacre or a juicy bit like a state cabinet minister telling a delegation of intellectuals that corruption should be tolerated until it passes the sixty per cent mark. Has Laloo given the media anything good to report in the last ten years? There are no development stories because there has been no development, and Laloo himself has put that issue, in vivid journalistic parlance, 'on the backburner'. In campaigning for the Assembly elections, Laloo made no promises about 'development'. The plank he strutted on was the much more emotive one of 'empowerment'. Development was left to relatively straightforward politicians like Nitish Kumar.

Laloo Prasad is more directly at fault as well. His most relentless enemy after Sushil Modi, the Central Bureau of Investigation, has discovered that at least eight senior Bihar journalists are on Laloo's payroll. (This is off the record; I heard it from someone in Patna who ought to know, and mentioned it in an article in *The Hindu* two years ago. It's not the kind of item you'd find in the news columns, because presswalas like members of any other guild protect their own.) 'On the payroll' could mean anything from accepting a complimentary house or plot in a government-sanctioned and paid-for housing colony, to actually getting a bagful of cash.

And politicians manipulate the media as they

manipulate everything else. There are relatively few journals left with ideologies or principles, having which means they can be manipulated only through their ignorance. In the last chapter I described our meeting with a college politico in Madhepura who pretended to be anti-Laloo and wanted to talk to us presswalas. Why, if not to create doubt and get information? There are far subtler ways of doing it, and Laloo Prasad is a pastmaster at all of them; indeed, he probably invented some of the subtlest.

It's cheaper to buy endorsement than to do something positive that will win objective endorsement; it's cheaper to pay for development stories than do anything about development. (Though that's a bit too much, even for Laloo; even a reporter deep in his pocket would hesitate to file positive stories on development in Bihar. He can, however, be persuaded not to file too many negative stories about lack of development.)

Ideology can corrupt too. Way back in Arun Shourie's palmy days at *The Indian Express*, when he was laying into Rajiv Gandhi, who was the PM at that time, I did a feature article on the freedom of the press for a Delhi magazine, and my first stop was naturally the *Express*. A very articulate and intelligent journalist there, who went on to make a name for herself on TV, told me off the record, 'What freedom of the press? It's freedom of Arun Shourie. We're not supposed to write anything positive about development.'

If more newspaper readers were aware that this kind of fraud is practised on them it would be a Good Thing. The International Press Institute Report two years ago carried a survey of newspaper readers in cities such as Rome, Buenos Aires and Bangkok, who all expressed a healthy disbelief in the validity of press coverage, or suspicion of the motives behind it. I'd like to see a similar survey of Indian readers;

but I fear even the educated and urbanized—or is it particularly the educated and urbanized, who are rather less in touch with the facts which form the staple of press reportage—have little knowledge of the workings of the media. When Kavery's last novel was published many people we know took it for granted that she'd written the reviews herself, in journals as diverse as *Outlook, Business Standard* and *The Pioneer*. This was a case of attributing subjectivity to objective reports; but far more often what is read in the papers or heard on TV is taken as gospel.

This is dangerous. It was dangerous enough when journalists were ill-paid and could afford to be honest; it's deadly perilous now because too many people with wealth and therefore power have only the media as a pipeline to knowledge. Ten years ago when I was in Bombay a paragraph in the business journals saying the right things about a scrip or a product was worth one lakh; with the so-called stock market's so-called boom it's ten or twenty times that now. Idealistic features writers who in '89 sat up nights working on one phrase or one stanza were three years later fighting to get on to the business magazines and speaking with a light in their eyes of Harshad Mehta.

*

I don't distrust my own motives in this regard. But I am a practitioner of a trade, and I distrust the motives of the trade—which is a sorry predicament to find oneself in. As a features writer I could pretty much stay out of all the sordidness, in fact I didn't even have to hear anything about it if I didn't want to. But when I began to write features articles about Bihar I had willy-nilly to touch on political aspects, and when I was foolish enough to ask to be sent back to Bihar for the '98 elections there was no way I could close my eyes and ears to what was going on in the media.

What I found particularly outrageous was the way caste is written about. Our Founding Fathers enshrined caste in the Constitution with the noblest motives—in fact, 'enshrined' is the wrong word because it implies permanence, and reservations were to go as soon as both sides of the casteist equation had been balanced. But that didn't happen; we have all accepted with Indian stoicism and as a fact of life the ingenious knavishness with which our politicians have been playing ducks and drakes with our goodwill on the issue, and with their own heritage, ever since.

It seems the Mandal Commission's report did more than split our society right down the middle; it permitted a situation where explicitly casteist formulations were the most accurate portrayals of our society, or at least the easiest to do. Before 1990 they generally evoked some opposition, and they were ventured upon in print only in extreme need. Now you even find them in the headlines, and in the tabulations of pre- and post-election surveys by reputed agencies, and there is talk of introducing them into the decennial census.

Do we need it?

*

> Democracy is the theory that the common people know what they want, and deserve to get it good and hard.
>
> —Mencken

What is the function of journalism in India? In a so-called Free Society with a liberalized economy the style is to tell the truth and damn the consequences. But that is the ideal. Even in the USA—or especially in the USA—it doesn't work, because newspaper owners belong to a very exclusive club of rich and powerful people, and they wouldn't want to harm each other's interests.

Besides, globalization is the primrose path to monopoly, and the spate of media mergers in recent years points to a time in the foreseeable future when all the world's media will be owned or controlled by half a dozen individuals or corporate entities, just as the world's wealth already is. Even the uninformed would agree this is not a good idea.

It's already happened in Australia (a good test case, given its small population and high degree of affluence) and you don't need much research to discover the crimes and cover-ups that the political-media baron nexus has produced there—over East Timor and nuclear testing, for instance. Not much truth gets told about the rich and powerful, and the consequence of an electoral turnaround in a rich and powerful country is almost always the coming to office of a new set of people backed by the same old money and power.

In an economy like ours, feeling its way as helplessly as a mole in the sunlight of American attention and the Information Technology boom (ha ha) everyone's wanting to be telling the truth and damning the consequences. A harsh new style of media comment has evolved, exemplified by Tavleen Singh and Swapan Dasgupta in *India Today*. The news analysts are all Objective about the economy and the consequences of Clinton's visit; the gatherers of news are all Objective about casteist forces and the polarization of the polity. Everyone in Bihar is voting according to their caste, but the reporters and psephologists aren't—oh dear me, no.

I have never been a believer in objective reporting, probably because I discovered the New Journalism when I was just getting started in this racket. There is always going to be a veil of the reporter's personal opinion, however thin, between the event and the reader. Unless you are reporting on the Mayor cutting the ribbon at the dog show, or on the consecration of a new idol at the city's oldest temple . . . And you can scratch those two examples as well: The stringer sent to the dog show may have had her mother die of rabies, and the cub sent to the temple with instructions to bring back *prasad* for the chief reporter may happen to be an agnostic.

Accepting our subjectivity, then, are we members of the Indian press expected to function with the assumption that we have a social purpose—that we should bear caste in mind only as the members of the Constituent Assembly did, with the intention of extirpating it? The phrase 'social purpose', while high-sounding, is also rather plastic, and can be twisted to meet anyone's requirements; but on the whole I think we must be aware of the peculiar contradictions within our society, of its unique checks and balances—or imbalances; we must be aware of the great difference the tone of our reporting can make to our fellow citizens, to our fellow human beings; and being aware of all this we must so function that that awareness is seen to have mattered.

If this is not important to us, we might as well go into advertising.

*

What is the reality of electoral politics in most of India? Caste. Therefore, say the realists, the reality of electoral reporting must also be caste. Before elections, the chances of candidates in practically every constituency are discussed in these terms:

Rampur has 40 per cent Thakurs and 30 per cent Backwards, while Krishnapur has only 25 per cent Thakurs, 10 per cent Kayasths and 35 per cent Muslims, the rest being Backwards; therefore Brijranjan Prasad wants to switch to the Krishnapur ticket *unless* Syed Nijamuddin throws his hat in the ring which would divide the Muslim vote and so Brijranjan would be better advised to stick to Rampur where the presence of Aravind Sahay need not be taken seriously; if not . . .

On the campaign trail the first question visiting journalists ask in a constituency they are new to is about the caste break-up. And they are invariably accommodated by some informed native: the local news agency stringer, the local college lecturer, the panchayat boss. These people have the facts at their fingertips, because they are usually involved in local politics. (They also have an excellent opportunity of falsifying the facts, as the Begusarai stringer did to us in '98.) Two paragraphs of this stuff pads out the day's copy nicely, and it is also, regrettably, instant wisdom; because what eventually transpires in the election more often than not takes shape against this background.

Perhaps it's worse in the North; but it isn't very good in the South either. In southern Karnataka every report will state exactly what percentage of the population is Vokkaliga and what Lingayat. Even in Kerala and Tamil Nadu, where caste did not matter for many years but for different reasons, it is beginning to be mentioned. The Thevar-Dalit divide is assuming ugly proportions in Tamil Nadu, and has already thrown up three or four small parties which have begun to matter locally—always a bad sign; in Kerala ideology is increasingly taking second place to religion and caste.

From highest to lowest—no, that is wrong; we are a republic. From first to ordinary citizen, we are beginning again to be defined by an archaic and degenerate social structure based on nothing more than the circumstances of one's birth. When K.R. Narayanan was proposed as candidate for President in 1997, surely few public figures could have been found more worthy of the office. Yet practically every news medium found it necessary to stress his origins, and show how wise a *political* move his candidature was. (*Postscript*: This was written long before Narayanan's visit to France in April 2000.)

Before 1990, there were certain journalistic fig leaves in common use which we younger reporters used to laugh at. 'Members of a certain community' was one; it was abundantly clear from the context which community was in question. Now that I'm ten years older and have lived in Bihar I see the importance of fig leaves. Here is an extract from a report on the capsizing of two boats on the river Koel in Bihar, which appeared in the Patna edition of *The Times of India* on 19 August 1997:

> The tragedy also saw a Muslim passenger, Haider Ali, rescuing Hindu passengers. The DC, M.W.A. Anjum, has assured him a suitable reward. The Barwadih police officer-in-charge assured Ali a new set of clothes.

Would a Hindu or Sikh who had done as much been as 'suitably rewarded'? What would a Christian have got? And suppose Haider Ali had rescued Muslim passengers? Are we going to have reservations, according to caste and creed, in the Republic Day Bravery Awards and in the armed forces?

It looks like we are. Here is another newspaper report, from the UNI, dateline New Delhi, filed on 26 January this year:

> Mr K. Vadivel Raj has been conferred the 1999 Kabir Puraskar, for rescuing 11 persons of another community

during caste violence in September 1998 at Mattupatti village in Tamil Nadu.
The Kabir Puraskar is a national award instituted by the Government in April 1990, for recognising acts of physical and moral courage displayed by a member of one caste, community or ethnic group in saving the life and property of a member of another caste.
The award is given annually in the grades—grade-I, and grade-III [*sic*: presumably II] carrying a cash amount of Rs 1,00,000 and Rs 50,000 respectively.
Mr Vadivel Raj will be awarded Rs 1 lakh.

So his was grade-I courage. Indeed. Now we know. And it's an easy way to pick up money, for these awards are bound to proliferate; just step around next new moon night to the nearest colony inhabited by people belonging to another 'caste, community or ethnic group' and indulge your taste for arson; then rescue a few people and get yourself recommended by the local superintendent of police.

Where will it end? Is every possible division that can be made along these lines to become fact?

It needs a mathematician to handle this. Chaos theory . . . Mandelbrot sets . . . fractals . . . Even chaos has a symmetry to it; the deeper you go, the smaller your scale, much the same identity exists. So the division doesn't have to end until neighbour is estranged from neighbour and husband from wife. Why stop there? Until atom is estranged from atom, which is what the course of events set in train by Pokhran-II may very well lead to.

*

See, I too have transgressed. This book is full of identifications according to caste: Yadav, Bhumihar,

Musahar, Paswan, Kurmi, Dom, Brahmin, Rajput, Lala, Kayasth; and it has enough about Catholic, Protestant, Muslim and Hindu sinners in it as well. I have not been consistent; the effect I have attained is not in tune with my philosophy. That's another of the things about the book that's made me unhappy. I will not plead reality as an excuse. The disease is one we all, not only journalists, suffer from, and I confess I have no clue as to a remedy. Wiser and more experienced heads must be brought to bear on it. Perhaps the Press Council will find a cure, but in today's atmosphere I doubt it. There are so many kinds of corruption that none of us can pretend to be untainted. The American journalist Hunter Thompson was being only half-ironical when he wrote thirty years ago, 'I never knew a reporter who could even *say* the word "corrupt" without pissing in his pants from pure guilt.'

The first thing I'm unhappy about is of course the chapter entitled 'O ladies who have seen the light', and I've said so in that chapter. Though no longer an Establishment secularist, I loathe the revivalist forces (of whatever hue) that have brought us to where we stand in 2000. The pace of fragmentation of our society has been stepped up in the last decade by several factors, and the Mandal Report is only one of them. Politically, socially, culturally we are being divided and misruled.

So writing as I have about the Sisters of Charity in M____, though it is accurate as far as my knowledge and perceptions go, has also made me doubt myself. There is enough gratuitous anti-Christian shit hitting the fan without my taking a hammer to the flush tank. My point is that the hardline anti-fundamentalist stand of the secular Establishment is used by the Church for its own purposes; and the secularists will not acknowledge it.

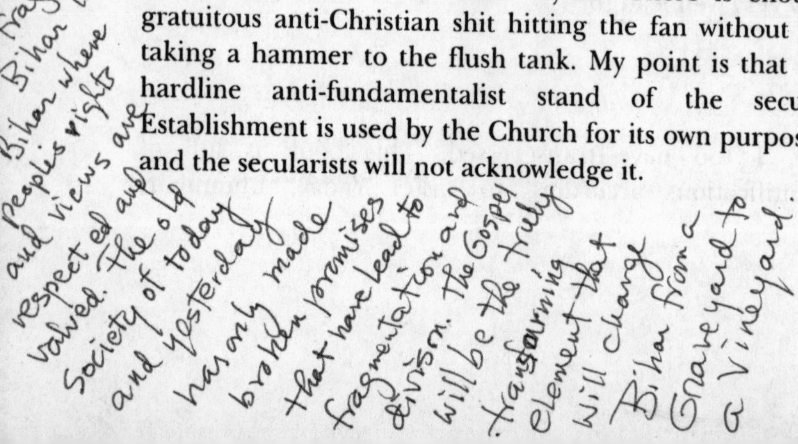

I'll probably lose a few friends with this passage, but what the hell . . . The secularists are just as fascist as the fundamentalists in their anti-Hindutva approach. They want to deny them the right to be heard.

> When democracy granted democratic methods to us in times of opposition, this was bound to happen in a democratic system. However, we National Socialists never asserted that we represented a democratic point of view, but we have declared openly that we used the democratic methods only in order to gain power and that, after assuming the power, we would deny to our adversaries without any consideration the means which were granted to us in times of our opposition.
>
> —Joseph Goebbels

Almost five years ago I was doing a story, quite in tune with the philosophy of the paper I worked for, on the Sangh Parivar's attitude to culture. Through a friend who is very much a member of the secular Establishment, I had obtained an interview with a liberal historian who gave me a lot of background; and that evening while speaking to my friend over the telephone I casually mentioned that next day I was to interview the chief of the Hindu Munnani, an organization somewhat to the right of Bal Thackeray.

'What!' he screamed at me, 'You're going to meet that ____Rama Gopalan? Why should you give him space?' and so on until I had to hang up on him. His indignation was great and sincere, and so was his bewilderment that I, writing for a paper whose platform is secularism, should want to feature in it a confessed revivalist.

My friend is a journalist himself; and this is another reason why I'm afraid for the profession. If we secularists are going to adopt the methods of the fundamentalists to oppose them—even to the point of denying them free speech—what distinguishes us from them? Can one who says the ends justify the means be a Gandhian? Or, as Thyagaraja sang in *Rama niyada*, does assuming female attire enable a man to know what it is to be a woman?

The secularists are borrowing a hardline stance that was borrowed by the revivalists from the regimented practices of European fascism. I have heard people say, to support their argument that Deepa Mehta should not shoot a film that shows Hindu practices in a bad light, 'Would Muslims allow her to make a film like that about Muslim widows?' But shouldn't Hindus evolve their own methods of tolerance—or intolerance, instead of aping militant Islam? 'Why should we?'

This is a strange and schizophrenic age, when liberals can be rightly accused of fascism. Another friend of mine, an extreme free-thinker, happened to be staying with us when one morning I breakfasted on sausages and bacon, which I'm partial to and occasionally indulge in. He began to jeer at me: 'How can you eat that muck, you don't even know where the pig's been and what it's eaten.' He breakfasts, lunches and dines exclusively off sprouts, dal, wheatgerm, fresh vegetables and water; but I don't jeer at his diet. I respect him for being able to stick to that stuff and even like it, so why shouldn't he tolerate me?

Where is the spirit of play, the *leela* that once characterized us, or which at least we once affected?

*

What has all this got to do with Bihar? Secularism is not much of a watchword there: Laloo Prasad reserves it for out-of-state use, to win over other parties opposed to the

BJP and Establishment secularists in the media. And he has a very high success rate with it; it is practically his last resort and at the same time his first line of offence.

I'm amazed at the ease with which Laloo wins over secularists. I have no doubt that Nitish Kumar—starting with a clean slate—or Sushil Kumar Modi, who has been in the thick of Bihar politics for twenty-five years without blotting his escutcheon, would not only bring development to the state but prove vastly more efficient administrators than Laloo. (One reason the state has gone to rot under Laloo is that he prefers home-grown promotees from the Bihar Administrative Service to young IAS officers for posts in the districts; they are easier to sway and closer to retirement.)

From what I've seen of Bihar, the problem there is not communalism but caste. Then how can 'intellectuals' pass over Laloo Prasad's dismal record as an administrator, his governance of a state almost exclusively by either using or disregarding the use of violent means, and a political career which in the last ten years consists solely of an unmatched brilliance in playing off caste factors, and hail him as the bulwark of secular and liberal ideas solely because he has time and again prevented the BJP and its allies from sweeping Bihar? If Laloo is a liberal I am Chandragupta Maurya.

*

The accursed power which stands on Privilege
(And goes with Women, and Champagne, and Bridge)
Broke—and Democracy resumed her reign:
(Which goes with Bridge, and Women and Champagne).

—Hilaire Belloc, 'On a Great Election'

This morning's news told me that Rabri Devi and Laloo Prasad have both surrendered before the CBI Special Judge in the assets-disproportionate-to-income case, and Laloo has been packed off, not for the first time, to Beur Jail; that the NDA leaders have begun a *dharna* to press for Rabri's resignation; and that twelve villagers have burned to death—how or why they don't know—in West Champaran district. Only the third item is unimportant.

Events are coming so thick and fast in Bihar that it's tough letting go of this book, and Penguin may have to send someone to drag it out of my clutches . . . No, the hell with it. I've been lugging it around for two years now, and I've had fun with it, and it's time to turn to more inspiring things. I long ago gave up believing that statesmen, world or national leaders, glow in the dark; and nothing will persuade me that any new entrant—however immaculate—into the Chief Minister's Office in Patna (or for that matter the Prime Minister's Office in South Block) will cause lilies to sprout from the carpet beneath his, or her, or its tread, as the Asoka tree is said to flower at the touch of a virgin's foot.

Even Misa being made Chief Minister tomorrow, as Sushil Modi predicted, will only wring a tired smile from me. I may also take an axe to the radio.

No one who *wants* to be President of the United States should be allowed to, said someone; I suspect it was Hunter Thompson again, but it could equally well have been Thomas Jefferson or Adlai Stevenson.

But Kavery, no assiduous student of political affairs, has a better idea. Recently reading *The Golden Bough,* she was much taken by the ancient practice of the killing of the divine king. In many parts of the world it was followed down to virtually modern times: Until late in the seventeenth century (Frazer writes) the Zamorin of Calicut, having reigned twelve years, cut his throat on a public scaffold. (In later years contenders to the throne had to run the gauntlet of his army to kill him.) In Sumatra the period varied according to the wishes of the citizens. So it was among the old Slavs; and whoever killed the king succeeded to throne and wives and power. The pre-Christian Swedish kings were killed after eight or nine years on the throne; the ancient Greek kings may have had their reigns limited to eight years. Among the Ijebu tribe of the Yoruba race in Nigeria, until the British seized the land, the period was three years; in ancient Babylon the ritual of dying appears to have been annual. So too in Hawaii. And Frazer mentions a tribe in ancient Congo where 'the rule obtains that the chief who assumes the cap of sovereignty is always killed on the night after his coronation.'

(Frazer's uniquely original contribution to the study of comparative mythologies, though it has in many respects been found unsound by later scholars, quotes too many different authorities, in this context, to be wholly inaccurate.)

I have no doubt the custom is connected to the ancient practice of sacrificing a slave, or an infant, or the most beautiful maiden, or the king's son, annually before the sowing or in some cases before the harvest, so that it might be plentiful. This practice was followed all over the ancient world, even in the isolated South American empires; and vestiges of the accompanying rituals can still be seen in many lands. (The ancient Canaanites and their descendants the Carthaginians employed crucifixion as the mode of sacrifice, and it was widespread in so-called pagan Europe. There are many traces of pagan rites in ancient Christianity too, and certainly there is a connection between Jesus's claim to kingship and his mode of death, as Robert Graves

has shown . . . but let's not get into that.)

You've long since got the point, of course. The king, or his surrogate, died for the good of the people, usually to ensure against famine but also 'that one good custom may not corrupt the world'. Let our politicians, who simper that they are only working for the people's good, also do the same. Let Prime Ministers and Chief Ministers, at the very least—perhaps cabinet ministers as well; I haven't worked it out fully—get a term of, say, six years, and then depart acclaimed by all. Spouse and children will have to share the same fate, naturally; it's so much easier to die for one's family than for one's country.

The Americans limit their Presidents, and in some states their governors, to eight years in office; but that's a lame compromise. Clinton at fifty-four can still do a lot of harm and not only to impressionable young women. Besides, in eight years a Prime Minister can amass enough money to make him look forward to retirement.

In this year of a constitutional review, this suggestion is worth considering. It will ensure that *no one who is not willing to die for the Indian people will stand for high office.*

*

> The St. Petersburg Paradox: In any game of equal chances, a lucky rich man will always beat a lucky poor man.
>
> —Jakob Bernoulli

Laloo Prasad Yadav, and all the other politicians, have been found guilty by public opinion . . . Maybe a referendum should establish a politician's guilt; it would avoid the long-drawn-out and invariably delayed judicial process; besides, in this age when psephologists are supposed to be performing statistical wonders, devising a representational sample should be easy, instead of a state- or nationwide poll . . . My, the ideas are really flowing today; it must be because that glare from the monitor's screen is the light at the end of the tunnel.

But is anyone at all innocent in Bihar? Mention that you are a Bihari or living there at any gathering in Bombay or Delhi or Madras and you have to start fielding pitying, even condescending glances. Usually it raises a laugh, if not at your expense then at Bihar's.

This is why so many people who are from Bihar hesitate to admit it in the wrong circles, which are the right circles if you know what I mean. A few months ago in Munnar I met a fashionable photographer who gave the impression he was from Delhi. It's all one to me; I was asking him about mutual acquaintances, photographers I haven't met in ten years. With a laugh, the journalist he was travelling with revealed that he was actually from Begusarai. I was excited: I saw it as a bond, and began to talk about M____, which is less than an hour away. But he wasn't interested. Later, when I told him I was working on this book, he raised his eyebrows and asked contemptuously, 'Will it sell even five copies?' His scorn was directed not at my writing skills, of which he'd seen no samples, but at the subject.

In the eyes of this set, and of an appreciable fraction of the Indian population, all Biharis are guilty of complicity in whatever Bihar is guilty of: guilty of being exploited by politicians and business interests; guilty of people not being allowed education or any chance to acquire material wealth if they are from the wrong caste; guilty of being liable to sudden and savage murder; guilty of being swayed by demagogues because there are no real leaders in any intellectual or professional sense, only the politicians.

But we're all guilty of all of that. We're all responsible for Bihar. Yet I say it not in shame but in hope and with a sense of belonging, not expecting the plaudits Kennedy got either: *Aakhir main bhi Bihari hoon. Hum sab Bihari hain.* And if that 'h' in 'Bihari' gets carelessly typeset as 'm' then dammit I'm not going to change it in the proofs. *Stet,* which to proofreaders and compositors means much the same as Amen.

*

Bihar has cast its spell on me, I know. It draws me back, not necessarily to write about it, even though there were things about our one and a half years there which have left scars that will last twenty. In Kerala if I heard a firecracker go off in the night I've started from sleep and looked across at Kavery, for an instant wondering if she'd be called to surgery. I will be wary when I see a stranger on a train lift his shirt to scratch his belly, for in Bihar the choice place for concealment of a pistol is in the waistband.

There are positive results too: I will think twice before I let anyone pick a fight with me, and I shall be twice as sceptical of politicians and their words. I have seen one Bihar MLA up close, and it was a gross sight. There was enough material to furnish two MLAs, and the face was seamed and lined with corruption. But he was, just then, my representative in the Assembly; and I felt like Dorian Grey.

According to Eliot, Webster 'saw the skull beneath the skin'. He would have found it easy to do in Bihar, for the MLA was an exception. Bihar's skull is very like the skin; for after all it is the fleshless face of deprivation and lack of privilege which is the face of Bihar: leather drawn tight over the cheekbones, staring eyes and a sheen to the skin that has nothing to do with eating well. The skull is the skin, the face is the skull. Skin is merely an excuse for being a voter, a flimsy barrier between life and death.

In the democracy we have designed for ourselves, political will is necessary to win battles against ignorance and tyranny. There is only so much that schools and NGOs can achieve. Bihar is in a condition which can be set right only from above. Given a leader and a will it can be India's showpiece in ten years.

Bihar as I have been portraying it since 1997, in conversation, in newspaper articles and in this book, is not an ideal place to live in, especially for one gently bred in the South. But Bihar is not only as I have described it: Or rather, as I have described it, it is a state of mind as well as of being. It lies all about us wherever we are. We create it, foster it, carry it about with us; and when, treated harshly by this creature we fashioned to betray, we condemn it, we have only ourselves to blame. Bihar justifies the attitude you carry to it: Bihar is in the eye of the beholder.

Epilogue

So there we were once again on Platform 1 of the railway station in M____, with suitcases and bags and shapeless bundles. We were not wholly downcast because once again we thought we were going to where we could make a difference; and we carried away fond memories. But we *had* hoped to stay five years at least . . .

We had decided to leave the Hospital mainly because the doctors, i.e. the medical experts, were not allowed a say in determining medical policy even within the existing framework of administration, which needed an overhaul anyway. Our warnings that a forty-year-old tradition could not survive if it remained static were ignored. We had enough ego not to want to stay where we were not allowed to make a difference . . . This is not important, for I have stayed away from matters medical throughout this book, and I won't go into details. I put it down simply that no one should think we were running away from the grimness of life in Bihar, or running away at all.

The Sisters were disappointed at Kavery's leaving, but so were we. The nurses were sorrowful. Our neighbour Dr Kishore tried to play both ends against the middle. Dr Arvind was openly indignant that Kavery could be let go of. Kishan was accepting; he was planning to leave himself and wanted us to send word of southern opportunities. He came every day with loads of what he called cartoons. This puzzled us at first; but cartoons were what all the locals called the cardboard boxes which had become so much a part of our lives: We had moved thrice in the last three years and were to do so twice more in the next eighteen months. Indeed so confident was I of my prowess at packing that I did not start sorting our books until five days before loading time. William Williamson, the Tamil X-ray technician from Jamshedpur, and Akhilesh helped with tying up the filled cartoons, but I let no one come between me and the books.

A southbound lorry was spoken for from Begusarai; when it arrived on the Campus the day before our departure it turned out to be manned by Tamils. A huge smile appeared on the driver's face when I came out of the doctors' quarters and gave him directions in Tamil on how to get his tail within the gate. There was a smile inside me too, for I missed the South. I missed it a lot but would never for that reason have left Bihar. Mardangi.

There were farewell parties and gifts. The Hospital administration held a function on the day of loading, so Kavery had to go alone while I toiled in filthy T-shirt and shorts, pouring sweat on that overcast January day, dismantling a home and leaving it a flat. The Sisters were generous as ever with their gifts: They gave us a complete set of bed linen. Ten days earlier, at Christmas—though they had known we were leaving—they had sent us a well-filled Christmas hamper and a melamine dinner set just as they had a year earlier.

The bachelors upstairs had given us a dinner the previous night. In Akhilesh's room, perhaps fifteen feet square, six of us crowded behind a table and sampled pulao, meat, dal, veg and kheer each separate dish of which had been cooked by Ranjit over a hotplate that evening. I think I felt, at leaving those bright young men, as Kavery did at leaving the nurses.

The nurses loaded us with gifts. There was a gift from all of them—again a set of bed linen—but so many of them came singly with individual gifts. A hot-case, a table-stand for pickles, a sari . . . one girl gave us a magnificent bedcover with gold embroidery on dark green. We're still to feel ourselves worthy of it. Kavery had half a mind to return it, for it must have cost hundreds and these girls were just about to go out into the world; but that would never have done.

Our saddest and loneliest parting was from Pushpa, who'd worked in our house, but I cannot write of that here.

The last evening, the doctors gave us a dinner in Dr Kishore's flat. There was a man with a video camera and the usual sidekick with the flash, so the occasion lost some of its pain for us. We played *antakshari* as was usual at all such gatherings (I don't know how I've missed mentioning that so far), the men in chairs along one side of the room and the ladies on the other, until dinner was ready. At the end the two of us had to stand behind a table and get photographed and make a speech—I said something stupid in Hindi, I was worn out from the day's loading—and Kishore made one and was photographed handing Kavery our farewell gift. It was all very ministerial if you know what I mean. But the gift, when unwrapped, turned out to be a dozen cassettes of ghazals and semi-classical songs and 'Best Of', so it more than made up for the video camera.

Early next morning I went to call a rickshaw. That is the scene I've described in the Prologue. But we weren't going to the station yet, we were bound for Kishan's house. His mother was as domineering as usual but sad, Kishan cheerful. The Bahu, Gopal's bride, came out with *pallu* over her head and chattered away to Kavery like a child. She touched our feet, we blessed her, *dirgha sumangali bhava.* I touched the feet of Kishan's parents. They gave us a silver bowl mounted in a red box. Kishan said we'd meet at the station, and we went out and found another rickshaw to take us back to the Hospital.

*

> I brought nothing with me into the world, and I go out carrying the fruits of my sins.
>
> —Aurangzeb

We had disembarked sixteen months earlier on a deserted railway platform at four in the morning to be greeted by a lone 'security'. We were leaving from a platform crowded with our friends in M____. I remembered Aurangzeb's words and thought how appropriately inapt they were; or how their aptness is to be measured only by each human's doings.

Almost everyone we knew was there: Sister Supriya, now happily having completed her term as administrator and leaving soon for a retreat in Allahabad; her erstwhile deputy and successor, Cassandra; Rose, Amelia, Beena, almost all the Sisters we had known well in the Hospital and convent. I had nothing at all against them then, only sorrow at parting.

Akhilesh was there, and Ranjit, and William; all the doctors; Kishan and Bipan. But the nurses were missing, except for a couple who were going home to Kerala. One of them later told us on the train that all the girls had wanted to come but their request had been turned down, and rightly, on grounds of hazard; the station is two kilometres from the campus. A Malayali gentleman on the train, who worked in Barauni, also told me that the administration had been answering well-wishers like him who asked why Kavery was leaving, 'Her husband needs a job.' That reawakened all my animus against the Sisters, or at least those who ran the Hospital. Bloody hell, I'd *left* a good job so Kavery could come and work in their godforsaken Hospital.

The train was due to leave Patna at two in the afternoon and arrive at M____ about four; four went by, and five and six, and it didn't come. The station master's office returned the identical answer each time the question was asked: The train was stuck halfway to M____ because the Deputy General Manager's train, which was before it, had had its cables cut. We pressed our friends to leave but they refused. It was freezing cold: Akhilesh said the *daytime* high in Patna had been 5°C.

At last the train was announced. It was past eight. Kishan 'organized' the luggage. There were embraces all round. All the Sisters hugged Kavery, and I—my animus was yet to be reawakened—hugged those I knew well, including Supriya (Kishan's eyes danced at the sight) and planted the obligatory air kisses. We got on, Kishan hustled us and our belongings through to our berths as he'd so often done before. Then, his eyes still dancing, he embraced me. 'See you in the South,' I told him.

The train picked up speed. I leaned out as far as I could and kept waving. Two of Kavery's particular friends among the Sisters, one almost sixty years old, ran behind the train waving their handkerchiefs, ran on almost until the sloping end of the platform, stopping just when I was reaching for the chain.

At last they were out of sight. We settled back drearily and got out our dinners: sandwiches from the Hospital kitchen and spicy Marwari food from Kishan's mother, enough of each for a week.

Two days later we reached our destination in Idukki district of Kerala. But that's another story.